THE INTERSECTION

Fisher Body Works.

Photo by Matt Ragen

Detroit Journalism
C O O P E R A T I V E

The Detroit Journalism Cooperative is a partnership of five nonprofit Detroit area media outlets reporting on the city's recovery from bankruptcy in an historic collaboration of journalistic resources — on-air, online and in the community.

The Cooperative includes The Center for Michigan's Bridge Magazine, Detroit Public Television (DPTV), Michigan Radio, WDET and New Michigan Media, a partnership of ethnic and minority newspapers.

Funded by the John S. and James L. Knight Foundation, The Ford Foundation, and the Corporation for Public Broadcasting, the DJC partners are reporting about and creating community engagement opportunities relevant to the city's bankruptcy, recovery and restructuring.

The Intersection

What Detroit has gained, and lost, 50 years after the uprisings of 1967

By Bridge Magazine
and The Detroit Journalism Collective

Design by Heather Lee Shaw

Front cover photo: Walter P. Reuther Library of Labor and Urban Affairs

Back cover photo by Bill McGraw

ISBN: 978-1-943995-26-4

Library of Congress Control Number: 2017904161

MISSION POINT PRESS

Published by Mission Point Press,
Traverse City, Michigan.

Printed in the United States of Amercia.

THE INTERSECTION

What Detroit has gained, and lost, 50 years after the uprisings of 1967

by Bridge Magazine and
The Detroit Journalism Cooperative

Members of the Detroit Fire Department brace themselves as they fight fires at two buildings on Michigan Avenue at Trumbull.

TABLE OF CONTENTS

ACKNOWLEDGMENTS

A birds-eye view of the area surrounding Warren and Grand River on Detroit's West Side as it is consumed by fires set during the civil unrest of 1967.

....

Walter P. Reuther Library of Labor and Urban Affairs

This book was produced with grant support from the John S. and James L. Knight Foundation.

The following writers, editors, producers and managers are among those who contributed to this book and to The Intersection project for the Detroit Journalism Cooperative: Bill McGraw, Chastity Pratt Dawsey, Mike Wilkinson, Nancy Derringer, A.J. Jones, Brian Widdis, Alyssa Schukar, John Bebow and David Zeman of Bridge Magazine; Lester Graham, Vince Duffy, Zoe Clark and Sarah Hulett of Michigan Radio; Sandra Svoboda, Joan Cherry Isabella, Michelle Srbinovich, Jake Neher, Gabrielle Settles, Melissa Mason, Laura Herberg, Stephen Henderson, Courtney Hurtt and Jerome Vaughn of WDET; Georgeann Herbert, Ed Moore, Scott McCartney, Cheryl Jones, Christy McDonald and Bill Kubota of DPTV; Hayg Oshagan, Osama Siblani, Arthur Horwitz, Jackie Headapohl, Keri Guten Cohen, Shari S. Cohen, Kim Clowes, Ali Harb, Robin Schwartz, Elias Gutierrez, Sergio Martinez-Beltrán, Tack Yong Kim and Keith Owens of New Michigan Media.

The Detroit Free Press, Detroit Historical Museum, Walter P. Reuther Library at Wayne State University, and Bentley Historical Library at the University of Michigan provided many of the photographs and records used or cited in this project.

FOREWORD

By Stephen Henderson

In 2007, on the 40th anniversary of Detroit's 1967 uprising, I had a conversation with then-Mayor Kwame Kilpatrick about what the riots meant to the lives of our children.

We concluded, perhaps wrongly, that there was no real effect: They were growing up in a Detroit that was not fundamentally shaped by 1967.

Kilpatrick and I were born the same year, 1970, when the city was still trying to figure out what happened in 1967 and set things back on a pace of recovery. The disturbances framed a lot of things for us as children. The strain between black and white, city and suburb, was made more urgent by 1967 and if you grew up here in the 1970s and 80s, you were always reminded of it.

The physical reminders of 1967 were sometimes garish; Kilpatrick told me about the bullet holes that remained in his grandfather's house in the Lasalle neighborhood. And the emptiness that began to creep over neighborhoods in the city during that time was a signal that life was moving away from Detroit, that the city was dying.

But our children were living in a city that had revived Campus Martius, the public square in the center of downtown. They lived in a city that was beginning to experience new investment and enthusiasm about the whole idea of Detroit.

And they were living in a city where the rise of black political power, largely in response to 1967, had created opportunities that had been unimaginable.

Now, as we approach the 50-year mark since the 1967 disturbance, my conversation with Kilpatrick seems odd, maybe even delusional. I think we both got caught in the snare of desire to cast the city's story forward, to propel it to away from a low point and toward something higher. I think like many Detroiters, we sought to beguile ourselves out of the disappointment and pain that might suggest we hadn't made as much progress as we'd have liked.

But reality is so much more sober, and so much starker.

There are so many ways that the factors that led to the uprising are still with us. There are so many reminders, both physical and metaphorical.

If there is good news, 50 years after the 1967 uprising, it is probably that we are all much more honest about the ways in which the problems of then still haunt us now. There's nowhere near as much gloss or self-kidding as we used to indulge.

This book, a collection of the coverage by the Detroit Journalism Cooperative during 2016, is a testament to that.

The deep poverty and isolation that traps so many is on more minds now, and was deeply explored through stories and discussions. The tattered remains of the city's school system, the victim of such cynical disinvestment, are detailed through vivid example and narrative. And the imbalances in the criminal justice system – the very ones that led police to the aggressive behavior that started the uprising – are still with us, documented so meticulously in these pages.

That doesn't make this volume a downer.

It's a diagnosis, an incisive assessment of where we were, where we are, and what the difference between those two places really looks like.

For those of us living here now, it's a look in the mirror – and a jarring one, a call to all the work that is unfinished, to the equality and justice that still elude us badly.

Fifty years after anger and frustration over police-community relations boiled over into a rebellion in Detroit, there are lots of people asking what we've learned, how we've changed.

In some ways, the simplest answer sits at the corner where it all started, 12th Street (now Rosa Parks Boulevard) and Clairmount Street, on the city's near west side.

Even in 1967, this was the heart of a pretty vibrant neighborhood, changing from white (and largely Jewish) to black, struggling with the tensions of that change but still very much intact.

Today, there just isn't much left. The businesses that lined 12th Street are mostly gone. Many of the houses left in the area have vacant lots for neighbors, others have burned out hulks. Nearby schools are closed. Opportunity has blown away like embers from a brush fire.

It's easy to stand at the corner where the disturbance began 50 years ago and conclude: we have fixed almost nothing, and we have learned even less.

But the work of this book shows what we do know, and what paths we need to follow to reshape that corner, this city, and ourselves.

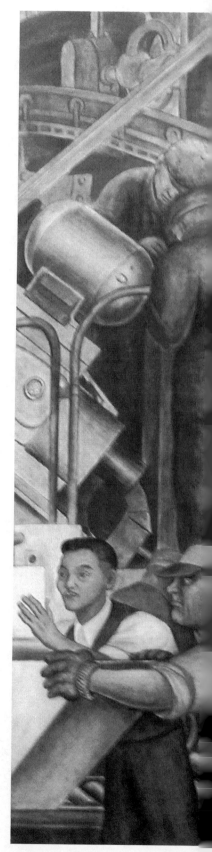

Detroit native Stephen Henderson is the Pulitzer Prize-winning editorial page editor at *The Detroit Free Press*. He is also morning host of Detroit Today on WDET, Detroit's public radio station.

This page: Photo by James R. Martin
Next page: National Guardsmen patrol the area around Linwood and Stanley on Detroit's West Side during the civil unrest of 1967.

Walter P. Reuther Library of Labor and Urban Affairs

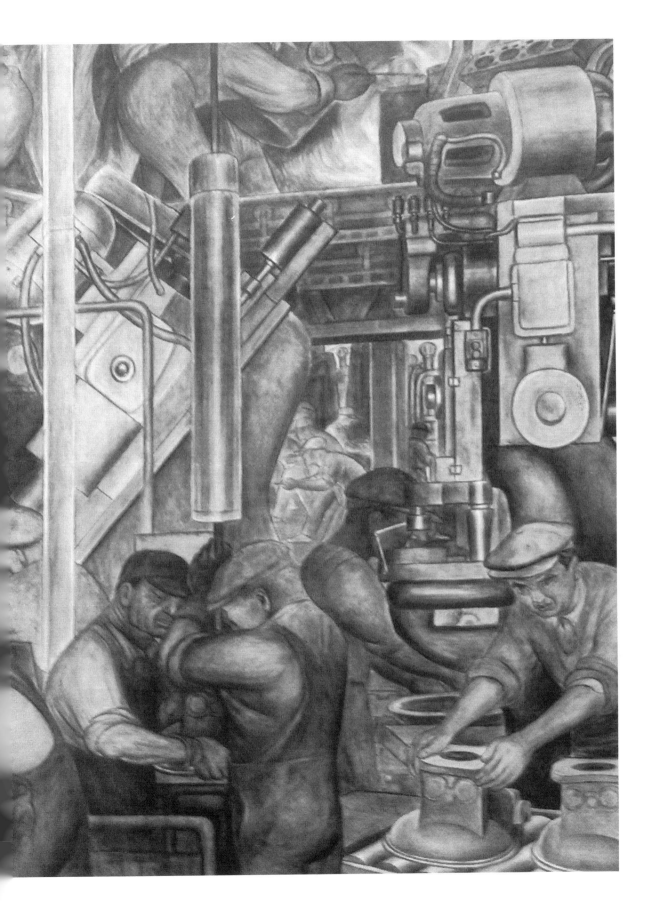

INTRODUCTION

THE INTERSECTION

INTRODUCTION

Even as smoke still drifted over thousands of charred homes and buildings after days of deadly insurrection and looting in Detroit, President Lyndon B. Johnson called upon experts to determine the root cause of racial disorders that had swept scores of U.S. cities in the summer of 1967.

Those experts, sitting on what came to be known as the Kerner Commission, reached this haunting conclusion: "Our nation is moving toward two societies, one black, one white — separate but unequal."

A police raid at 12th Street and Clairmount on Detroit's west side had ignited a firestorm of long-suppressed rage in the city's African-American community. Rage at a nearly all-white police force notorious for brutalizing and humiliating people of color; at a political structure that marginalized the voices of African-American residents; at schools and neighborhoods that kept integration at bay, and at a future with little prospect for black advancement. So it was that a confrontation at one Detroit intersection led the city to launch decades of efforts to mitigate the fallout: economic policies, political campaigns, crime initiatives and social movements, mixed with no shortage of heartache, all meant to reverse the tide of history.

In 2016, the five nonprofit members of the Detroit Journalism Cooperative (DJC) set out to explore whether the social and economic conditions that sparked the tragic events of 1967 have changed or improved in Detroit in the nearly 50 years since. In the wake of unrest and violence in Ferguson, Mo., Baltimore, Charleston, S.C., and other American cities, such questions are hardly academic. This book represents the culmination of our reporting in 2016, the year leading up to the 50th anniversary of what came to be known as the Detroit riot. It's also work that is not yet complete. The DJC will continue to document challenges in this ever-evolving city, and pursue solutions where they can be found, in the months and years ahead.

We begin with an exploration of power and whether ordinary residents, the vast majority of whom are African-American, have more of a voice in the city's destiny as Detroit attempts to rebuild from a shattering bankruptcy. In future chapters, we will tackle other conditions that helped ignite the violence of 1967 — damaging racial attitudes, questionable police tactics, poverty, segregation, etc. — and track what progress Detroit has made, or not, over a half-century of attempted reforms.

Our examination comes as Detroit's central business, Midtown and downtown areas enjoy a buzzy vibrancy following the city's much-publicized journey through bankruptcy. News media around the world are talking about Detroit's resurgence. Politicians in the city and the state are eager to hype revitalization efforts in some neighborhoods. "Today," declared Gov. Rick Snyder, Detroit is "America's comeback city."

But that's a woefully incomplete postscript to the story of Detroit. By some measures, black residents in Detroit's far-flung neighborhoods are in worse shape now than black residents were during the civil rights struggles in the 1960s.

Paul Lee, a Detroit historian, is among those who have concluded that economic conditions are not any better today for African Americans than they were in the '60s, and perhaps worse. "Our situation — that is, the situation of African-Americans in Detroit and throughout the country — is much more precarious than it's been perhaps in a century," he said.

This collection of reporting is our bid to document how much has been gained in the half-century since the violence of 1967, and what has been lost.

Twelfth St. through a telephoto lens a week before the rioting: busy and bustling

Twelfth St. today photographed near the same spot after days of rioting: barren and broken

BANNER headlines in two London newspapers shout news of rioting and violence in America. U.S. papers editorially have condemned the rioting and called for more controls to prevent future violence.

Papers Condemn Riots, Urge Cures

As armed violence echoes through Detroit, repercussions are being felt across the nation. Newspapers, many in cities where the memory of racial violence is fresh, have joined in condemning the lawlessness in Detroit while calling for eradication of the deep-rooted social ills that have made ghettos tinderboxes.

Chicago Tribune: "A mindless mania has taken over much of our urban civilization. Revolutionaries and our enemies rejoice, while decent Americans of all races and classes can only register sick disbelief, horror and revulsion.

"... If hops and shops are burned and destroyed, the exponents of Great Society panaceas offer the prescription that there should be more spending for housing, rent subsidies, anti-poverty handouts of all sorts."

Newark Star-Ledger: "Several striking parallels can be drawn from the tragic disturbances that erupted first in Newark and then in Detroit, a profile of government frustration in attempting to deal with fundamental social and economic problems that have eroded the moral fibre of mother urban centers."

New York Times: "This grave domestic crisis demands a level and a quality of mature leadership that have been shocking in their absences. President Johnson has offended most conspicuously in his moralizing response to the debacle in Detroit. And when he did act, Mr. Johnson issued a proclamation and a personal statement, both of which were clearly designed to place the entire political responsibility on Gov. Romney."

Miami Herald: "What took place was plain and simple criminality, totally divorced from the civil rights movement ... It was a bunch of bums and hoodlums who started the brawling."

San Francisco Chronicle: "Detroit's white and black leaders duly complain that

'a small number of hoodlums and hate-mongers, a completely lawless element' has now undone the work of years toward creating an integrated city devoid of racial antagonism. The events of the weekend attest that that difficult task had not yet been entirely completed."

Albany Times-Union: "What happened in Newark and now in Detroit is far from a simple protest reaction. Such riots are eruptions of utter lawlessness which cannot be condoned in any way. They have absolutely no social excuse."

Atlanta Constitution: "The past two and a half decades — those years of most intense Negro farm-to-city migration — are precisely the period in which the American economy has automated, and opportunities for the unskilled and unlettered have shrunk to vanishing. These difficulties add up to the most severe handicap of all: A lack of sense of community or neighborhood. From it spring rootlessness and hopelessness."

Chicago Sun-Times: "The flash fires of anarchy — which knows no boundaries of race or color — must be stamped out, even if it takes the full weight of military power to do so."

Pittsburgh Post-Gazette: "No matter how pointless or reprehensible the ghetto may be, it will not be cured by night-sticks and guns. The current wave of disorders is likely to end only when there is a radical change in the conditions which give rise to them — general upgrading of housing for Negroes, the provision of better education, the creation of more and better employment opportunities, insistance on fairer law enforcement for the black man."

Nashville Tennessean: "It takes massive means to stop a riot once it has begun. It likewise takes massive means to seek out the problems, find solutions, and then effectively eliminate the causes of violence and hatred."

Gawkers and Snipers Are Drawn To Twelfth St.'s Charred Ruins

Detroit's Twelfth and Philadelphia intersection was bustling with life a week ago—cars jammed the streets, stores did a lively business, people were everywhere.

Today Twelfth and Philadelphia is a skeleton of its former self—a defeated block, devastated by fire, stripped by looters, stained by violence

Cars filled with the curious now move slowly through the street, gawking at the ruins. Negroes pass through the charred remains of the once crowded and gaudy business district. A

few snipers hide in the shadows of frames of former stores.

Suddenly there is nowhere in the neighborhood to buy bread, to cash checks, to go to eat.

And there are policemen on the streets. And reporters and photographers. Children can't walk the streets alone.

The arson and looting on Twelfth has stopped. There is nothing left to burn, nothing left to rob. The present danger is from snipers, who cannot be seen and cannot be anticipated. The threat they

pose is as terrifying as the threat of destruction that hung over the citizens' heads during the days of looting and burning.

Twelfth is a ghost of a street. A pall of silence hangs over it. There is nothing left but ruins. The street is eerie, desperate, broken.

"I guess they'll rebuild it," said a woman who was burned out of her apartment above a Twelfth street store. "But that doesn't help much now. We've lost everything; I don't know what to do. And it's all so senseless, so senseless."

A WORKER on Linwood watches cleanup operations Wednesday after four days of civil disturbances. His helmet tells a story of its own.

A quick guide to the 1967 Detroit riot

By Bill McGraw / Bridge Magazine

DATES

SUNDAY, JULY 23 THROUGH THURSDAY, JULY 27

BY THE NUMBERS

DEATHS: 43 (10 whites and 33 African Americans, most at the hands of law enforcement)

INJURIES: 1,189

DAMAGE: The official total was put at between $287 million and $323 million, in 2016 dollars, but that did not include losses by businesses and individuals who had partial insurance or were uninsured. It also did not include business-interruption costs and financial losses to individuals and city government, lost wages and lost retail sales outside the riot area.

ARRESTS: 7,231

STORES LOOTED OR BURNED: 2,509, including 611 food markets; 537 cleaners; 285 liquor stores; and 240 drug stores. The vast majority of damaged buildings were never rebuilt.

HOMES: While the total is uncertain, Detroit was the only city in 1967 whose disorder caused significant damage to residential districts. Some 388 families were displaced.

FIRES: The Detroit Fire Department responded to 3,034 calls during the seven days of the riot week. A total of 690 buildings were destroyed or had to be demolished. Two firefighters died and 84 were seriously injured. A fire expert who studied Detroit's riot blazes concluded the "city had narrowly averted a firestorm" like those in Tokyo, Berlin other urban war zones during World War II. Dozens of suburban departments came to Detroit's aid.

LAW ENFORCEMENT: It took about 17,000 members of various organizations to quell the riot: Vietnam-hardened and integrated U.S. Army troops from the 82d and 101st Airborne units; Detroit Police; Michigan National Guard; and Michigan State Police. Observers generally praised the work of the well-trained army personnel and state police. Inexperienced and largely white National Guard troops received widespread criticism for their lack of discipline. There were significant reports of verbal and physical abuse by Detroit police. There were also nearly constant rumors of sniper fire which, when combined with the long work hours during the uprising, left many officers exhausted and on edge.

PERCENT DETROIT RESIDENTS WHO WERE BLACK: About 38 percent.

PERCENT OF DETROIT POLICE WHO WERE BLACK: Five percent (237 of 4,326 officers).

THE RIOT IN CONTEXT

A TUMULTUOUS SUMMER: Civil disorders of varying sizes broke out in 128 cities in 1967. Some cities had more than one riot; New York City had five. But Detroit's disorder was by far the biggest that summer in loss of life and property damage, and is considered one of the worst insurrections in American history.

A PROGRESSIVE MAYOR: Mayor Jerome Cavanagh was a liberal visionary. In the years before the riot, "he moved farther on racial issues than any other big city mayor," wrote historian Kevin Boyle. Cavanagh, who was white, also aggressively embraced President Lyndon Johnson's Great Society program, and Detroit became a so-called "Model City," receiving millions in federal funds to finance Cavanagh's ambitious Total Action Against Poverty program. But the city's economy deteriorated in the 1960s as it had in the 1950s. Jobs, and white residents, fled to the suburbs, and Cavanagh never was able to control the abuses and systematic denigrations of the African-American by the nearly all-white Detroit Police Department.

CHIEF CAUSES OF UNREST

POLICE BRUTALITY; UNEMPLOYMENT; SEGREGATED AND SUBSTANDARD HOUSING AND PUBLIC SCHOOLS; A SENSE OF POWERLESSNESS; LACK OF OPPORTUNITY; RACISM.

CHRONOLOGY

SUNDAY, JULY 23: The riot ignited when police raided a "blind pig" (an after-hours drinking and gambling club) at 12th Street and Clairmount — then a raucous commercial and nightlife district — at 3:30 a.m. Sunday. Looting and arson spread during the early morning and afternoon hours, as Detroit police officials employed a strategy of restraint, banning the use of tear gas and firearms and ordering street officers to passively contain the disturbance to the 12th Street area, where several thousand people had gathered, rather than take aggressive steps to make arrests. That initial strategy failed and was widely criticized. By 3 p.m. Sunday rioting spread west to Linwood Avenue, and the National Guard was mobilized.

Remarkably, officials Sunday morning convinced the local media to refrain from reporting about the growing disorder, though rumors circulated rapidly, and ominous plumes of black smoke arose over the near west side. Radio and TV reports started in mid-afternoon. By nightfall, rioting had spread east of Woodward. Mayor Jerome Cavanagh ordered the closing of all bars, theaters and gas stations. A 9 p.m. curfew was widely ignored.

MONDAY, JULY 24: The riot escalated on Monday, spreading along Grand River and Livernois. By daylight, sniper fire pinned down officers in precinct stations at Mack and Gratiot and St. Jean and Jefferson on the east side. By 4 p.m. 30 fires were burning out of control, as snipers and looters also harassed fire fighters. The chaos on the streets was matched by confusion among city leaders and law enforcement officials.

THE REST OF THE WEEK: After much haggling and vacillation among political leaders in Detroit, Lansing and Washington, battle-hardened, well-trained paratroopers were deployed Tuesday on the city's east side, which they quickly pacified, while the National Guard struggled on the west side. On Wednesday, in one of the uprising's most notorious episodes, three black teens were killed at point-blank range by police looking for snipers, while other young black men (and two white women) were roughed up at the seedy Algiers Motel. (Only one officer went to trial for the shootings; he was acquitted by an all-white jury).

On Thursday, Cavanagh called together city business, labor and political leaders to plan the rebuilding of the city. On Friday, President Johnson announced the formation of the Kerner Commission to study the causes of, and remedies for, more than 100 civil disturbances that year.

AFTERMATH

- Sparked the hiring of minorities among some Detroit businesses, especially by large companies.

- Led to the creation of the civil rights organizations New Detroit Inc. and Focus: HOPE.

- Accelerated the flight of the white middle class (along with jobs) to the suburbs, a trend that actually began in the early 1950s.

- Prompted passage by the state legislature of the Michigan Fair Housing Act, to combat residential segregation.

- Started a trend of high-crime rates — especially homicide — and arson fires that continued for decades.

- Ignited deep paranoia among white Detroiters and suburbanites as rumors spread for more than a year about the possibility of another riot.

- Led to a "Riot Renaissance" architectural style of cement-block windows, barbed wire, security guards and led city institutions and entertainment venues to provide "secure, well-lighted parking."

- Led to the election of Coleman Young as Detroit's first black mayor in 1973.

- Gave rise to Detroit's image internationally as a volatile urban war zone, an image the city is still trying to shed.

THE RIOT IN POPULAR CULTURE

SONGS WITH A RIOT THEME:

"The Motor City is Burning," by Detroit-based blues legend John Lee Hooker; it was later covered by the MC5, which changed some of the lyrics, substituting, for instance, "Gestapo" for "police."

"Black Day in July," by Gordon Lightfoot.

"Det.riot '67," by Moodymann (Kenny Dixon Jr.), a Detroit-based techno/house musician.

David Bowie's "Panic in Detroit" is sometimes described as inspired by the events of 1967, but it is also said to be based on his friend Iggy Pop's recollection of the city's revolutionary era during the late 1960s.

BOOKS:

"Violence in the Model City: The Cavanagh Administration, Race Relations, and the Detroit Riot of 1967," by Sidney Fine. The 648-page tome by the late University of Michigan historian remains the definitive account of the riot.

"The Algiers Motel Incident," by John Hersey. The famous chronicler of Hiroshima after the atom bomb examined the execution-style deaths of three young black men during the riot in a motel at Virginia Park and Woodward.

"Whose Detroit?: Politics, Labor, and Race in a Modern American City," by Heather Ann Thompson. Thompson sorts through the riot's aftermath, including white flight, radical labor activism, conservative white homeowners, radical white activists and the election of Mayor Coleman Young.

"The Origins of the Urban Crisis: Race and Inequality in Postwar Detroit," by Thomas J. Sugrue. Published 20 years ago, "Origins" became famous for its multi-faceted description of Detroit's decline and its obliteration of the idea that the riot was largely responsible for the city's 21st-Century woes.

"The Anatomy of a Riot: A Detroit Judge's Report," by James H. Lincoln.

"The Detroit Riot of 1967," by Hubert G. Locke.

"them," Joyce Carol Oates' 1969 novel, contains important scenes that take place during the riot.

"Middlesex," Jeffrey Eugenides's 2002 novel, also uses the riot as a backdrop.

SOURCES

"Violence in the Model City: The Cavanagh Administration, Race Relations, and the Detroit Riot of 1967," by Sidney Fine; Detroit Free Press, Detroit News; The Detroit Almanac, "After the Rainbow Sign: Jerome Cavanagh and 1960s Detroit," by Kevin Boyle.; Report of the National Advisory Commission on Civil Disorders;" Seven Fires: The Urban Infernos That Reshaped America," by Peter Charles Hoffer.

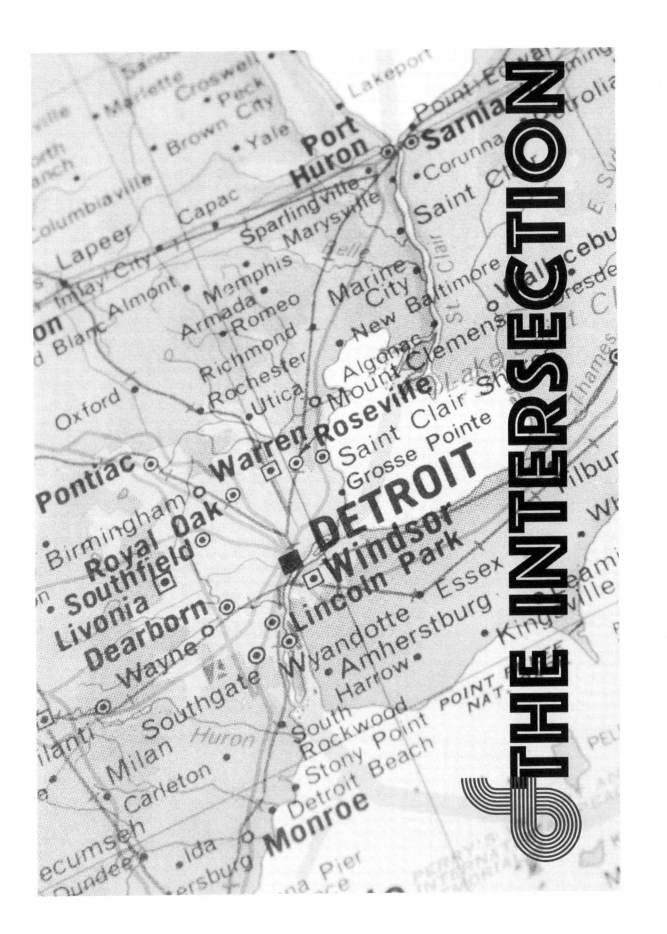

CHAPTER 1
POWER

Rev. Charles Williams II, president of the National Action Network Michigan Chapter, had tough words for Mayor Mike Duggan at a Saturday rally at Historic King Solomon Church in Detroit.

Bridge photo by Brian Widdis

"The ghetto symbolizes the dilemma: a widening gap between human needs and public resources and a growing cynicism regarding the commitment of community institutions and leadership to meet those needs." — Kerner Commission

In an African-American city, black clout wanes

By Bill McGraw | Bridge Magazine

DETROIT — Stately, stout Charles Williams II takes the microphone in an old church auditorium on Detroit's west side and convenes the Saturday rally with a familiar war cry.

"NO JUSTICE!" Rev. Williams shouts, stopping conversations and focusing attention on the front of a smallish room.

"NO PEACE!" yell back some 65 people.

The rally is a weekly meeting of the Detroit chapter of the National Action Network, the nationwide civil rights organization founded by the Rev. Al Sharpton in 1991. Williams heads the local chapter, in addition to serving as pastor of Historic King Solomon Missionary Baptist Church, a renowned house of worship that now needs repairs, located a few blocks from the Motown Museum on the city's west side.

There are several items on the agenda, and Williams touches on issues that have driven the group into Detroit's streets in the recent past: home foreclosures; water shutoffs; Michigan's emergency manager law; the city's bankruptcy and cutbacks to pensioners; violence; Flint's water crisis; and Detroit Mayor Mike Duggan.

While Duggan has a positive image among many Detroiters, suburbanites and the local media as a commanding Mr. Fixit who is shoring up the city as it recovers from bankruptcy, the view at King Solomon on this Saturday morning is considerably more skeptical.

Williams, 35, who sometimes calls Duggan "Livonia Mike" — a sarcastic reference to the white mayor's longtime suburban home before he moved into Detroit to run for mayor — tells the crowd Duggan has invited him to his office for a meeting, but he's having second thoughts about attending.

Switching into preaching cadence, Williams says, "We have to make sure we hold them folks accountable," as the audience cheers. "So I may not do no backroom meeting. I may have to tell him to come here, in the front row. That might be the better way to deal with him, and to make sure he has an opportunity to hear what people are saying.

Rev. Charles Williams II, center left, ushers U.S. Rep. John Conyers through the crowd at the National Action Network Michigan Chapter's Dream Keepers Brunch and Award Ceremony in January at the Detroit Athletic Club, one of many venues in the city that were not welcoming to blacks in 1967.

....

Bridge photo by Brian Widdis

"Because what happens is, you've got folks who go around insulating him. And you've got black folks who go around insulating him."

To laughter and hoots from the crowd, Williams pretends he is the mayor, talking to his acolytes:

"Do they like me?"

Playing Duggan's admirer, Williams answer himself: "Yeah, Everybody likes you. You're the best mayor ever."

Turning serious, Williams says, "We will have him here. We will address him. And we will address him straight up. We're not going to play no games. This is not a moment for playing games."

Power to the people

This is indeed a fraught moment for Detroit. The city's short-term financial recovery, newly lit streetlights and restaurants that serve celery root agnolotti in a short rib ragù have attracted a burst of positive international attention. Locally, Detroit has become so cool in some quarters that suburbanites who repeat the once-familiar boast that they haven't ventured downtown in years come across as tone-deaf dinosaurs.

But to many black residents, the resurgence around downtown, while welcome, has done little to lift the despair that permeates desolate corners of their sprawling city. In their view, the rehabbed condos, rising hockey arena and farm-to-table dining establishments in the Woodward Avenue corridor cater to the pleasure of the young, mostly white professionals who have returned to live, work or party downtown.

African Americans may now control who's elected mayor or to city council in this predominantly black city. But nearly 50 years after racial despair led to deadly insurrection and rioting, a view persists that white political and business interests (in Lansing, the state capital, and across Detroit's more affluent suburbs) continue to steer the city's course.

It is against this backdrop — and the national "Black Lives Matter" protests — that Williams's group and other activist organizations, most of which have formed in the past few years, have stormed city streets with a militancy and drama that recall the days immediately following the events of 1967, even if their gains are harder to gauge.

Back then, the city brimmed with aggressively radical organizations of blacks and whites such as the West Central Organization (focusing on urban renewal and school desegregation): State of Emergency Committee and Ad Hoc Committee (police); League of Black Revolutionary Workers and Dodge Revolutionary Union Movement (labor); Shrine of the Black Madonna (black nationalism); Parents and Students for Community Control (schools) and Marxist, Trotskyist and Maoist groups.

As one economist later told the Kerner Commission, convened by President Lyndon B. Johnson to examine the cause of racial uprisings across dozens of U.S. cities in 1967, "black power" groups had come to conclude that despite the gains of the civil rights movement, blacks had "not experienced tangible benefits in a significant way." Real change could only come about when blacks united as a political force.

That meant "organizing a black political party or controlling the political machinery within the ghetto without the guidance or support of white politicians," Kerner noted, on the belief that "only a well-organized and cohesive bloc of Negro voters could provide for the needs of the black masses."

Heather Ann Thompson, a history professor at the University of Michigan who grew up in Detroit, recalled in her 2001 book, "Whose Detroit?", that radicals, conservatives and liberals slugged it out for their vision of the city, and "Detroit became a war zone" following 1967.

Detroit police were a particular target for '60s-era radicals. Black Detroiters had long viewed the overwhelmingly white DPD as an army of occupation. By the early 1970s, under Mayor Roman Gribbs, the hated police force unleashed an undercover decoy squad called STRESS — Stop the Robberies, Enjoy Safe Streets — that in its first nine months of operation killed 10 suspects, nine of them black. Led by Marxist attorney Kenneth Cockrel Sr., Detroiters organized marches, rallies and media campaigns to get rid of the unit.

One of the results of those marches and proselytizing was the election of Coleman Young as Detroit's first black mayor in 1974, a landmark in the city's halting progress on racial issues.

Yet today, activists still struggle with many of the same issues — neighborhood revitalization, education, poverty, racism and jobs. They are demanding social and economic justice for neighborhoods eviscerated by 60 years of white flight, business disinvestment, crime, drugs and government indifference.

The Shrine of the Black Madonna in Detroit promoted black nationalism and was one of many groups active in trying to foster political change after 1967.

....

Photo from Wikimedia, via Creative Commons

7

Detroit Mayor Roman Gribbs, who served from 1970-74, oversaw the police department when it created an undercover unit known as STRESS, which was widely despised by the black community.

But while many concerns, hauntingly, remain the same, the context has changed: Black Detroiters made up more than 40 percent of the city's population after the events of 1967, but had little presence or say in city government. A large part of the dissension then revolved around getting a seat at the table.

Today, blacks are routinely elected to leadership positions, while filling nearly every level of city government. The irony is that, through a variety of factors from Detroit's shrinking population to what residents perceive as the state legislature's barely disguised antipathy toward the city, Detroit's political leaders don't carry nearly the clout they wielded in 1967.

And so a new generation of community activists is trying to fill that void.

One group, New Era Detroit, a highly disciplined, black-nationalist organization, blockaded a Detroit gas station in November 2015 whose employee, the group said, harassed a young African-American boy.

That Christmas Day, New Era members stood in military formation in front of the police headquarters in neighboring Dearborn, to protest the shooting of an unarmed, mentally ill black man by a white Dearborn police officer who had chased the man across the border into Detroit (Prosecutors eventually decided not to charge the officer; a lawsuit against the department remains pending). Their red, black and green Pan-African flag flapped in the wind. New Era later returned to Dearborn to call for a boycott of the Fairlane Town Center mall and gathered at city hall, standing in well-organized ranks, fists sometimes thrust in the air, rapidly and loudly chanting a slogan made popular by the Black Panthers: "ALL POWER TO THE PEOPLE!"

It was, in many ways, the same potent demand for black power that activists painted on buildings and streets during and after 1967. Black power became a reality in Detroit in many ways in the years that followed, as a cadre of young, idealistic African Americans — and a number of white lawyers and activists — changed the jury-selection process in Detroit's criminal court to include more black jurors; confronted the brutality of the Detroit police, and, most importantly, elected Coleman Young.

Young's election demonstrated — for the first time — what black Detroiters were capable of achieving once they were given the reins of government. At a time of extreme racial polarization, Young recognized his election was made possible by the white evacuation that eventually gave Detroit the most unusual demographics of any large American city — by 2000, more than 8-in-10 residents were African American.

White Detroiters, Young observed, "were getting the hell out, more than happy to turn over their troubles to a black sucker like me."

As Young noted in his 1994 autobiography, "White people not only lost control of Detroit, but find it, as a rule, racially foreign and consequently frightening."

Coleman Young, Mayor of Detroit.

Young's assessment was fueled by often caustic rhetoric and Detroit bashing from suburban residents and leaders, personified in the obstructionism and criticism of L. Brooks Patterson, the longtime Oakland County Executive, the county north of Detroit. "I don't give a damn about Detroit," he was once famously quoted as saying.

A changing landscape

Today, the long-hardened boundaries between city and suburbs — long symbolized by 8 Mile Road — are slowly blurring. In some ways the city is becoming suburbanized, and the suburbs are becoming urbanized. That can be seen as a mostly positive development in breaking down regional segregation, but one that's also had the effect of diluting the influence of city leaders.

In one remarkable reversal, white people are beginning to move into the city, even as African Americans who can afford to continue to move out, according to U.S. Census data, though Detroit remains overwhelmingly black.

9

Detroit's suburbs, even such one-time bastions of segregation as Dearborn to the west and the Grosse Pointes to the east, are increasingly diverse, which has lowered the temperature of anti-Detroit rhetoric. Even so, some observers note a scarcity of African Americans in Detroit's burgeoning shopping and entertainment spots, which in turn has ignited a sometimes contentious debate over why that is so, or even if it is true.

No one in Coleman Young's day would have predicted that, in the early 21st Century, suburbia would produce Detroit's two most recent mayors: Duggan, who is white, and Dave Bing, who is black. Both moved into Detroit after decades on the outside for the sole purpose of running for office. At the same time, many of Duggan's top appointees live outside the city, which would have been unheard of — and against a now-defunct residency ordinance — 25 years ago.

More recently, regionalization initiatives have diminished the mayor's power, driven largely by the city's financial crisis. After decades of bickering, a drive to regionalize services and institutions once controlled by Detroit has become a fait accompli in some important ways: The operations of the Cobo convention center, the zoo, museums, city water department and Eastern Market are now run by authorities and nonprofits with boards made up of Detroiters and suburbanites. The state has run the island park of Belle Isle for more than a year. And millages passed by suburban residents in Wayne, Oakland and Macomb counties in the past decade help support the Detroit Institute of Arts and Detroit Zoo.

Mayor Young often referred to many of these landmarks as Detroit's "jewels," which he vowed never to relinquish, though the city still owns them all.

Despite the gradual improvement of Detroit's image and city-suburban relationship, one fact hasn't changed since 1967: Too many black Detroiters remain impoverished, unskilled, badly educated and alienated from the improvements in the city's core. By several statistical measurements, conditions for black Detroiters have not improved in the nearly 50 years since the riot.

"It's gotten worse," argues Joe T. Darden, a Michigan State University geography professor who has studied Detroit for years. "Change has been in the opposite direction, not in the direction it should have been."

Two crises, the Flint water emergency and the financial and physical deterioration of Detroit and its schools, have trained a national spotlight on state government's indifference toward poor, black city residents, according to activists like Rev. Williams.

Williams notes that corporate interests downtown, led by Quicken Loans founder Dan Gilbert and Little Caesars Pizza owner Mike Ilitch, who also owns the Detroit Tigers, Red Wings and the Fox Theatre, appear to be thriving, with companies controlled by both men gobbling buildings and real estate in downtown and Midtown.

Riot or rebellion? The debate over what to call the 1967 disorder continues

By Bill McGraw | Bridge Magazine

Was it a riot or a rebellion?

Or both?

Nearly five decades after the last fire was extinguished, the discussion continues over what to call the events in Detroit during July 1967.

The word "riot" – often spoken or written in the plural, as "the Detroit riots" – remains the most commonly used noun to describe the five days of unrest that left 43 dead, more than 1,000 injured and hundreds of buildings in flames. But "rebellion" surfaces frequently, especially among African Americans and others who discern a political nature in the disorder.

Joe T. Darden and Richard W. Thomas, professors at Michigan State University, write in their 2013 book, "Detroit: Race Riots, Racial Conflicts, and Efforts to Bridge the Racial Divide," that the process of redefining the riot began shortly after it ended, with black militants who began calling the riot a rebellion of African Americans fighting against police brutality and discrimination in housing, jobs and education.

"The 1967 riot, or rebellion, as many blacks preferred to call it, was the result of decades of white institutionalized racism," they write. "Few whites were willing or able to connect the historical and social causes to their tragic consequences. Most blacks had no trouble doing so."

In a recent interview, Darden said understanding why many people consider 1967 a "rebellion" is important to racial healing. "There's a need to educate the white population on this whole matter," he said.

In a similar vein, Jack Schneider, an education professor at the College of the Holy Cross in Massachusetts, contends that whether violence is framed for the public as a riot (bad) or rebellion (admirable) has often turned on the color of the actors. Writing in the Huffington Post in 2014 on unrest in Ferguson.:

"If whites are involved, uprisings tend to be framed as rebellions. Flip through the index of any social studies text, and you'll find several of them: Bacon's Rebellion, Shays's Rebellion, Dorr's Rebellion. The list goes on.

"When blacks are involved, however, an uprising isn't a rebellion; it's a riot. Harlem, Watts, Chicago. Or, more recently, Ferguson.

"The point here is not that a riot and a rebellion are one and the same. They aren't. A rebellion is inherently meaningful. It connotes resistance to authority or control. A riot, by contrast, disturbs an otherwise peaceful society – it is an expression of power and energy rather than of simmering resentment and honest anger. After a riot, everyone goes home and sobers up."

The 1967 Detroit disturbance is sometimes called a "race riot," but experts say that's inaccurate so far as it suggests fighting between the races.

There was almost no fighting among black and white residents in 1967. In fact, the first fatality in 1967 was a man with a Polish surname who was shot while looting a grocery store by the Arab-American owner.

By contrast, 1943 clashes in Detroit saw whites and blacks fighting each other in vicious hand-to-hand combat, and 34 people dying over two days. No one disputes that was a race riot.

Yet the clear dynamic in 1967 was black Detroiters rising up against police, firefighters, National Guard troops and merchants, the vast majority of them white. (Federal paratroopers in Detroit were integrated, but they arrived late in the disturbance and quickly pacified their sector of the city.)

Sidney Fine, the late University of Michigan history professor, noted that 56 percent of black Detroiters polled several months after the uprising chose to characterize the violence of 1967 as a "rebellion" or "revolution." Fine, however, leaned toward calling the clashes a riot.

"Those involved in the disturbance in Detroit can hardly be described as having been engaged in 'organized armed resistance to an established government,' as rebellion is commonly defined," Fine wrote in "Violence in the Motor City."

The Kerner Commission, which investigated Detroit's riot and other disturbances across the country in the 1960s, avoided the riot/rebellion question. It referred to the disturbances as "civil disorders" that were racial in character, but not interracial. §

The Rev. David Alexander Bullock leading a protest outside Dearborn police headquarters three days after a white Dearborn police officer shot and killed an unarmed black Detroiter he had chased across the border into Detroit.

....

Bridge photo by Bill McGraw

Williams acknowledges that corporations must flourish in a healthy economy. But he said the gap between haves and have-nots in Detroit appears to be widening, and outside greater downtown "there are plenty of people who are still not being able to enjoy the boost or boom that the city of Detroit is supposedly in."

"I think many Detroiters are feeling this," he said. "It can't be so one-sided."

In some ways, criticism of Duggan — who has served just over two years as mayor — reflects the decades-old imbalance between downtown and neighborhoods and the even older inequity between white and black wealth in the United States. Duggan has made neighborhood improvement the main focus from the first day of his campaign, and his administration has shown results in turning on street lights, demolishing abandoned structures, cleaning up city parks and making it easier to purchase and pay taxes on houses.

Darden, the MSU professor, acknowledges the mayor's accomplishments, but notes there has been far less business investment in neighborhoods outside downtown and, despite the presence of many African-American business people and professionals, almost no black Detroiter with vast wealth who is making a major mark on the city.

That imbalance is on vivid display as suburban billionaires Gilbert and Ilitch, who are white, remake downtown with investments and projects that are widely praised, and in the case of the new Red Wings' hockey arena, partially supported by the public.

"Detroit is not controlled by African Americans. Never has been, and it's still not," Darden said. "The white population controls the city. They own it, pretty much. Blacks don't own it. They're there, but they don't own the place."

Bing, the former mayor, doesn't disagree, saying there was a growing frustration in the African-American community with a lack of black involvement in Detroit's comeback.

"As much as we say or think we are being inclusive, the reality is we are not," Bing told a policy conference in early 2015. "Detroit's not far from Ferguson, Baltimore or Chicago. Maybe just an incident away."

Still, it's not entirely clear how many black residents share that view. Certainly, for many Detroiters the future is not as bleak as it was before the city entered bankruptcy in 2013. A 2016 poll by the Detroit Free Press found roughly 7-in-10 residents saying they were optimistic about the city's future. Even on combustible issues like whether the state should continue to have oversight of the city's fiscal affairs, there is no consensus among residents.

The Rev. David Alexander Bullock, who leads the three-year-old social justice organization Change Agent Consortium, said he sees a large divide between African Americans who are economically comfortable and those who are poor. In his view, more comfortable black Detroiters and suburbanites are generally unmotivated to go to bat for struggling African-American residents, who in turn are too busy fighting for survival to mobilize politically.

"There are really three groups of blacks," said Bullock, pastor of Greater St. Matthew Baptist Church in Highland Park, and a star of the Oxygen network's "Preachers of Detroit" reality show.

"There are elite blacks; the formerly middle class blacks who are barely middle class, and their children and grandchildren; and the blacks that nobody wants — the mentally ill, the people who are constantly going in and out of prison, the folks that can't read.

"There's about 150,000 of those in Detroit. Nobody wants them. You could build a boat. Somebody would pay to get those folks on that boat."

Many well-off blacks have adopted "a politics of accommodation," Bullock said, because they feel they've made it. Regionalizing Detroit's cultural institutions and services may not be in the interest of Detroit residents, he said, but not enough people who had the power to complain did so.

"If you had a stronger protest movement in Detroit many of those things would not have happened," Bullock said.

Of course, not all residents necessarily object to the changes reshaping their city. Indeed, many Detroiters share the view that Belle Isle, Eastern Market, the museums and Cobo are better financed and in better shape today than when they were controlled exclusively by the cash-strapped city.

In the Free Press poll, published after city bankruptcy ended, more than half of city residents said conditions had improved. They gave high marks to Duggan and Police Chief James Craig, a media-genic executive under whom some crime has dropped and police emergency response times appear to have improved (though 43 percent said they would leave Detroit if they could afford to).

Sheila Cockrel, a business consultant and Wayne State University instructor who is a former member of the Detroit City Council, said it's important to remember that Detroit continues to own the "jewels" that are now under a more regionalized control. She argues the arrangements make sense for the city — still struggling financially despite emerging from bankruptcy — and its residents.

"You really don't have the tax base in Detroit" to properly maintain those institutions, Cockrel said. "You don't have the resources. So you come up with strategies. You're getting other people to pay for something that you own. How isn't that a true exercise of true power? Of economic power?"

Power on the wane

If Coleman Young's election marked the apex of black political power, the years following his death have corresponded with a decline in the authority and power granted to Detroit mayors.

Young entered office vowing to reform police and give black Detroiters a voice in city government that they never had before. And he delivered.

Young dismantled the despised police STRESS unit and established affirmative action programs in the DPD and other city departments. To establish community-based policing, Young opened mini-stations in dozens of neighborhoods, and saw that city contracts were spread out to black businesspeople, who largely had been shut out before a black man became the boss at city hall.

While Young could be abrasive and profane, and he alienated whites by bringing up the problem of racism in metro Detroit, he was an integrationist who had a diverse team of appointees and generally preached the necessity of racial unity.

Even as he called for harmony, Young also communicated the idea of black pride to Detroiters. During election campaigns, he sometimes spoke in a coded racial language about how "we" have fought to maintain the city in the face of outside oppression and how "they" (that is, suburban whites) want to control the city and steal the "jewels." He defended even legitimate criticism of the police department as attacks on affirmative action. He cracked down on city workers, especially white cops and firefighters, who violated the city's residency requirement.

Young decided not to run for a sixth term in 1993 after 20 years in office. He died in 1997, and some argue that an era of strong black political power died with him.

That same year, the state legislature abolished Recorder's Court, Detroit's criminal court since 1824, and ordered its judges and staff merged with the court system of surrounding Wayne County, which was mostly white. In 1998, management of the Detroit Institute of Arts was spun off to the Founders Society, the longtime nonprofit associated with the museum.

In 1999, acting on pleas of mainly white cops and firefighters, the state legislature ended Detroit's decades-long rule that required city workers to live in the city, a move that accelerated flight to the sub-urbs and, with it, the loss of desperately needed tax revenue. Detroit's other institutions were reorganized in the ensuing years.

Other decisions coming from Lansing also rankled, from steep cuts in state aid to, most notably, the state's decision to appoint an emergency manager for Detroit before the city sought federal bank-ruptcy protection.

A new era

Times have changed since the civil rights battles of the 1960s and 70s, and so have the activists seeking to change Detroit.

With thick-rimmed glasses, a studious appearance and well-tai-lored suits, Rev. Williams blends in with the crowd at the Detroit Athletic Club, where he is a member. Once a fussy citadel of WASP-ish privilege, the DAC, like virtually all institutions in Detroit, was whites-only until the 1970s. The DAC admitted its first black member in 1979 - Robert P. Young Jr., now chief justice of the Mich-igan Supreme Court.

Rev. Williams was born the next year in Henry Ford Hospital in Detroit, but his family moved four years later to Birmingham, Ala-bama, where his father, a postal worker, had been transferred. Wil-liams said the seeds of his activism were sown as he grew up reading about the civil rights movement, and a personal experience when he was 12 while shopping with his mother in an Alabama fabric store.

"There were two white ladies, and I was standing next to my mother," he recalled. "The one white lady sees me and whispered to the other lady, 'Watch your purse.'

"Right in front of me! I saw that. And I felt that feeling. For the first time in my life, really, and after that I became hyper-sensitive to it and I see it all the time."

Williams returned to Michigan for college at Eastern Michi-gan University, where he started working with Sharpton's National Action Network around the issue of affirmative action in education. He later worked in labor and community organizations before decid-ing to become a minister.

His church, Historic King Solomon Baptist Church on 14th Street, was the site of speeches by both the Rev. Martin Luther King, Jr. and Malcolm X.

"There are really three groups of blacks. There are elite blacks; the formerly middle class blacks who are barely middle class, and their children and grandchildren; and the blacks that nobody wants — the mentally ill, the people who are constantly going in and out of prison, the folks that can't read. There's about 150,000 of those in Detroit. Nobody wants them. You could build a boat. Somebody would pay to get those folks on that boat."

— Rev. David Alexander Bullock, pastor of Greater St. Matthew Baptist Church in Highland Park

Williams contends that a lot of the issues in Detroit are explained as race issues, but they are actually more about class. But the racial angle prevents needy people of both races from working together.

"My mission is not necessarily to be a race leader or a race baiter or a race this or a race that. The mission is to make sure everybody has a chance to be taken care of. And that everybody gets access and opportunity."

It's why Williams used Mayor Duggan as a foil during his Saturday rally, and attacks wealthy white business people who received tax breaks, public financing and discounts on their water bills, even as impoverished black residents have had their drinking water turned off.

"How many black businessmen and women do you know out here that have the opportunity to buy property, assemble real estate?" Williams asked that morning. "They ain't getting no deal on their taxes."

The crowd urged him on: "That's right!"

"I ain't doing no play time," the reverend said to the mayor who wasn't there.

"'Do you think I'm doing a good job?'

"NO!" the crowd answered.

"If you want to talk to me," the reverend said, "then you're going to hear what you don't want to hear."

Lester Graham of Michigan Radio contributed to this report

16

This bridge connects Belle Isle with the City of Detroit

Photo by Carl Ballou

Dr. Abdul El-Sayed, director of Detroit's
Department of Public Health
....

Fayrouz Saad
....

Arab Americans looking to raise presence as Detroit recovers

By Ali Harb | The Arab American News

DETROIT — Arab-American business owners pride themselves on having stayed in Detroit when others left during the city's decline, so they want to be a part of its future as it recovers. But the Arab influence in Detroit is already expanding beyond small stores.

Mayor Mike Duggan appointed three Arab Americans to lead the city departments of Public Health, Immigrant Affairs and Constituent Services. These city officials say they are there to serve the entire community and help soothe some of the tensions among ethnic groups.

African Americans make up more than 80 percent of the city's population. In 1967, disenfranchised black residents engaged in violent protests against inequality and unfair representation. The '67 riot changed the city drastically. The unrest eventually empowered African Americans in city government, but also contributed to the exodus of white residents.

After the 2014 bankruptcy case ended, Detroit began another chapter, where Arab-American groups say they are looking to be partners in that change. But as their presence grows, advocates and officials are urging small business owners to reform their sometimes fraught relationship with black Detroiters.

"NOTHING TO DO WITH POWER"

Dr. Abdul El-Sayed, director of Detroit's Department of Public Health, said he feels a responsibility to fight racial and economic inequality in his field and finds the city a ripe environment for such advocacy. But sometimes, he is asked about his place of origin, and if his family owns a gas station.

"As an Arab American, there's always a question about 'Where are you from?' For me the answer to that question is 'I'm from Detroit,'" he said. "This is home."

El-Sayed, 31, oversees all aspects of public health in the city. That includes inspecting restaurants, protecting against the spread of disease and providing healthcare services, such as immunization. He said he felt elation and fear when he was offered the job. He was residing in New York City but left for the position in Detroit.

"It has nothing to do with money, prestige or power; it has everything to do with the opportunity to fulfill a responsibility," he said. "It's a responsibility I took on the day I decided I wanted to be a doctor, and the day I decided that I cared about helping folks have their best possible life."

But he knew it was not going to be an easy job. The Duggan Administration says it wants to see across the sprawling city, especially in the neighborhoods. "One of the great things about public health is that we are in a position to really make sure that as Detroit grows and improves, it gets better for everybody," El-Sayed said.

EASTERN MARKET TO CITY HALL

Officials and activists say immigrants can play a major role in repopulating and reviving Detroit.

Fayrouz Saad is the daughter of Lebanese immigrants. Her father has owned a business in Eastern Market for four decades. As the Director of Immigrant Affairs, Saad helps promote the integration of newcomers across Detroit. Saad said existing immigrant communities have done a great job establishing themselves and contributing to the city.

"But I think there's always room to do better," Saad said. "That's why it's important to have an office like this to build those relationships."

Despite anti-immigrant rhetoric at the national level and in some surrounding communities, Saad said the city's welcoming attitude toward residents and leadership help ease the assimilation of new Detroiters. She said her office aims to establish and promote ties between different groups to increase cooperation.

RESPONSIBILITY TO SERVE

El-Sayed, of the health department, said he is proud of his Egyptian heritage, but considers it a great honor to work alongside African Americans, who he said have suffered the most from the nation's "egregious inequality."

"I'm a human first and foremost, and an American second," he said. "And fundamentally, as humans and Americans, we have a responsibility to equity. That's the responsibility I serve every day."

El-Sayed criticized some Arab-American business owners in the city, saying the owners of some liquor stores and gas stations don't treat black customers properly.

"A number of folks don't treat the community with respect and dignity," he said. "Part of my being here is to say, 'There are many of us. There's not one group of Arab Americans. Not all of us own liquor stores that are contributing to the social ills of the neighborhood.'"

He said as local Arabs push against racism that targets them, they need to address bigotry in their own communities. "If we believe all people are equal, then we treat all people equally," El-Sayed said. "We should not extract from communities."

He urged small business owners to be involved in Detroit's neighborhoods beyond making a profit.

"Sometimes it's easy for us to retreat outside of Detroit, come in, sit behind a bullet proof glass, treat people poorly, sell them products that harm them, and then say: 'I am just a businessman,'" he said. "It is not that simple. We are a part of a community. We have an opportunity to sew ourselves into the fabric of that community."

An environment rife with injustice harms everyone, he said.

"The question is how do you address the climate of discrimination, and what is our role in the climate of discrimination," El-Sayed said. "The moment you point the finger and you're like, 'I am the victim here,' you have three others pointing back at you."

Former State Rep. Rashida Tlaib, who represented Southwest Detroit, echoed El-Sayed's comments. She said most African Americans' first encounter with Arab Americans is at a cash register, so when the relationship is not positive, it reflects badly on all Arab Americans. Tlaib, a Palestinian American born and raised in Detroit, added that she has store clerks who insult customers in Arabic.

"That's something that we haven't been able to deal with," she said. "We can tell people that not all Arab Americans are like that, but at the end of the day those are the experiences that a lot of my neighbors who are African American are having."

She urged businesses to give staff sensitivity training about the African-American community, in the same way that Arab Americans ask for cultural training for law enforcement on their community. Having more Arab Americans in local government can help mend some of this friction.

"Being in the room to make decisions, of course, is good," she said. §

The Kerner Commission, and why its recommendations were ignored

By Lester Graham | Michigan Radio

Nathaniel R. Jones was Assistant General Counsel for the Commission

The summer of 1967 saw dozens of uprisings in cities across the nation.

Detroit's was the worst, with 43 people killed, most of them black.

Thousands of National Guard troops and thousands more police were already on the streets. The mayor and governor wanted more help. President Lyndon Johnson sent in five thousand U.S. soldiers.

"I take this action with the greatest regret," the president said, "and only because of the clear, the unmistakable, and the undisputed evidence that Governor Romney of Michigan and the local officials in Detroit have been unable to bring the situation under control."

Before the fires in Detroit were out, Johnson spoke to the nation again. He was appointing an 11-member National Advisory Commission on Civil Disorders. It was chaired by Illinois Gov. Otto Kerner and became known as the Kerner Commission.

"The Commission will investigate the origins of the recent disorders in our cities. It will make recommendations — to me, to the Congress, to the state Governors, and to the mayors — for measures to prevent or contain such disasters in the future," Johnson announced.

The president wanted to know why the uprisings happened. Within seven months the Kerner Commission had an answer.

Nathaniel R. Jones was assistant general counsel for the commission.

"One of the conclusions of the Kerner Report was that white racism was at work, was the cause of the upsets and the uprisings that we had. In fact, the report stated that white society created it, perpetuates it, and sustains it," Jones said.

In other words, white racism, white attitudes were the underlying reasons for racial unrest in the cities. It's a finding that many white politicians and news media vehemently resisted.

Before 1967, Detroit had been viewed as a model of positive race relations. Many black people were getting jobs in Detroit that simply were not available to people of color in much of the rest of the country.

Overlooked was the fact that Detroit African-Americans often were given the hardest and dirtiest jobs, often were passed up for promotions, and generally made less money. Housing was inferior. Unemployment among people of color was higher. Relationships with police were strained.

The commission also blamed the violent outbreaks on federal and state governments ignoring the plight of black residents. It blamed mainstream media for ignoring the problems and consistently presenting only the white point of view.

"The commission said in its report that there was a combination of complex social, psychological problems, poverty all tangled up which create this feeling on the part of people that they can't trust authority. And that was true as a lead-in to what happened in the '60s and it's true now," Jones said.

The report's most quoted conclusion read, "Our nation is moving toward two societies, one black, one white — separate and unequal."

The Kerner Report was published in paperback. It became a best seller.

But President Johnson barely acknowledged it. According to Joe T. Darden, a professor at Michigan State University and co-author of a book on the 1967 riot, the Kerner Report challenged whites' attitudes about blacks and caused the president to worry that its findings of white-enforced, institutional racism would damage the Democrats' chance to keep the White House in 1968.

"The report put the responsibility for all of this stuff on white society and white institutions. That, I think, was a surprise to some white Americans and I think that was part of the reason he was very careful not to upset the large segment of white society. That was why I think it happened like that."

Another factor in President Johnson's silence on the Kerner Report was his own ego. He felt the report ignored the accomplishments of his Great Society programs.

In a 1969 interview for the LBJ Library Commission Chair, Otto Kerner said the panel declined to praise Johnson's work to, for instance, reduce poverty, because that would have given the report a political flavor that commission members were steadfast to avoid.

Kerner said, however, that Johnson privately told him he was working quietly to implement Kerner Report recommendations.

"He said, 'You know, we've been trying to do these things that you've recommended in the report, and as you know Congress is not very acceptable to the things that I proposed. But I want you to know that I have the members of the cabinet and the White House staff people still trying to have accepted those things I've already recommended,'" Kerner said.

But that's not what Johnson told one of his political buddies.

A secretly taped phone call between President Johnson and Chicago Mayor Richard J. Daley reveals Johnson had problems with the report.

President Johnson's former Attorney General, Robert F. Kennedy, was running for president. He pushed the Kerner Report's recommendations. But Johnson felt the commission's vice chair, New York City Mayor John Lindsay, had pushed the commission too far.

"And Bobby just gave me hell today for not carrying out the Kerner Commission study," the president said on the recorded phone conversation. "Well, I didn't realize when I appointed Kerner that this son-of-a-bitch from New York, Lindsey, would take charge. He did take charge and he recommended I hire two-and-a-half million people on federal payroll. And I just, I've not wanted to reflect on Kerner and criticize the commission. At the same time, I couldn't embrace it because I've got a budget" – a budget that had already doubled with the U.S. escalation of the war in Vietnam.

While Johnson saw it as impractical, nearly five decades later, the Kerner report is considered by historians today as one of the most insightful documents on race relations and remedies for discrimination ever published by the government.

MSU Professor Joe T. Darden says the cost of ignoring the Kerner Report has meant further decades of less opportunity for African-Americans.

"That would have eliminated this separation we have: central city/suburb, white suburb/black central city, white affluent/black poverty. That would have prevented that. They didn't take that alternative, what the Kerner Commission really wanted society to do," Darden said. §

Former police station
at 4150 Grand River, Detroit.

Photo by Aivoges

CHAPTER 2
POLICE

Detroit Police Chief James Craig, shown here during a press conference, says he deliberately courts the media to put a public face on what his police force is doing in the community.

Bridge photo by Brian Widdis

"To many Negroes police have come to symbolize white power, white racism and white repression. And the fact is that many police do reflect and express these white attitudes. The atmosphere of hostility and cynicism is reinforced by a widespread perception among Negroes of the existence of police brutality and corruption. And of a "double standard" of justice and protection — one for Negroes and one for whites."
— Kerner Commission

In a city with long memories of racial torment, Detroit's police chief seeks to turn a corner

By Bill McGraw | Bridge Magazine

The Black Lives Matter movement was peaking in spring 2015 when protesters took to the streets of Baltimore over the death of a black man in police custody. On the same day, an angry crowd gathered on Evergreen Road on Detroit's west side.

The situation on Evergreen quickly grew tense. An agent from U.S. Immigration and Customs Enforcement on a task force with Detroit police had shot and killed a 20-year-old black Detroiter, Terrance Kellom, a parole absconder wanted for armed robbery.

"Huge crowd. We were surrounded," Assistant Chief Steven Dolunt recalled in late March. "They were calling for the chief. I called him. I said, 'You need to get here right away. Now.'"

The chief of police is James Craig, The crowd knew him because in nearly three years as chief of the Detroit Police Department, he has become such a familiar figure on city streets and media outlets that some called him "Hollywood." Despite the moniker, Craig's style is low-key and controlled, more Woodward Avenue than Sunset Strip, but he said he doesn't mind the nickname. His visibility is part of a deliberate strategy to more effectively communicate with Detroiters.

On that afternoon, Craig walked into the crowd and simply talked to people in a calm voice. Some made references to the previous deaths of black men across the nation, but Craig assured them detectives would conduct a fair investigation, and promised to meet the community in a public forum within 48 hours, which he did.

CHAPTER 2 POLICE

Three years into his job as Detroit's police chief, James Craig said the department is turning a corner in gaining trust among city residents.

....

Bridge photo by Brian Widdis

"Any time a parent loses their child, it's a tragedy," Craig told reporters and bystanders that day. "I'm committed that the investigation will be thorough, and I will have a conversation with the prosecutor's office."

That day, Craig revealed that Kellom was wanted on a felony warrant and had brandished a hammer at the agent, an African American whom Craig said was retreating during the confrontation. Craig also met with Kellom's family members. Kellom's father had an outstanding warrant for a non-violent fraud accusation, but Craig said officers would let him grieve and deal with that matter later.

By nightfall, Baltimore was burning.

Detroit was calm.

Turning a corner

The chief's deft defusing of emotions on Evergreen that April afternoon may have saved Detroit from joining a growing list of cities torn apart over police clashes with the black community. Detroit has its own painful history of mistrust between cops and African Americans, most notably the 1967 raid on a 12th Street blind pig that ignited one of the worst civil disorders in U.S. history, an uprising largely fueled by decades of blatant abuse of black Detroiters by an overwhelmingly white police force. In 2016, the city emerged from 13 years of oversight by the U.S. Justice Department over questionable shootings of suspects, unconstitutional investigative techniques and mistreatment of prisoners.

Was the crowd's reaction a sign of growing trust between police and Detroit's majority African-American community?

Craig, 59, contends the department is turning a corner. He cites a variety of statistics as well as improvements the department made under federal supervision. And he says the afternoon on Evergreen illustrates the transparency and public engagement that he has attempted to employ since July 2013. That's when Craig assumed the unforgiving position of chief in a city has had one of the nation's highest crime rates for decades, running a department that is short of manpower and lacking the resources to adequately attack crime.

The situation on Evergreen "had the makings of a problem," Craig recalled. "But we have relationships with people in the community. I made promises that I kept."

Some critics attacked Craig for quickly disclosing Kellom's record and a description of his hammer attack. Craig said he did not make the revelations lightly.

"We have a responsibility to our community to say as much as we can about what's going on because the media will go out and find someone in the neighborhood, and they will give an account," he said. "It probably won't be the right one, but it will be the only account that's out there."

Sometimes the facts in such incidents, as initially put out by officials in Detroit and elsewhere, have turned out to be inaccurate, as the original police narrative on the shooting of Laquan McDonald in Chicago notably showed. But in the Kellom case, Craig's early account held up. In August, Wayne County Prosecutor Kym Worthy announced there would be no charges against the federal agent, saying he had acted in lawful self-defense.

Craig is the 17th person to run the Detroit Police Department since the 1967 civil unrest. Almost all of his predecessors were insiders, products of the culture they were tasked with reforming once they reached the top job.

"We have a responsibility to our community to say as much as we can about what's going on because the media will go out and find someone in the neighborhood, and they will give an account," he said. "It probably won't be the right one, but it will be the only account that's out there."

Craig was the seventh chief in the previous seven years, a chaotic period that included the political corruption scandal of Mayor Kwame Kilpatrick followed by municipal bankruptcy and two police chiefs who left the job after their sexual relationships with the same female underling came to light.

Craig was an unusual find: an insider and an outsider with broad experience. He is a Detroiter who began his career as a Detroit cop in 1977 but left more than 2 years later after being laid off. He went west, spending 28 years rising through the Los Angeles Police Department before running the forces of Portland, Maine and Cincinnati.

When Craig returned to Detroit 34 years later, he found a financially devastated city, the Justice Department poking around and, he said, rampant pessimism among police and residents.

"I said, 'This is interesting. The police department has low morale. The community has low morale. Some of it intersected. Police stations that were closed. Police officers felt disconnected. The community felt disconnected. Response times above one hour — that's even if the call is handled. A lot of things just didn't work.'"

Craig also found crime. More crime per capita than he encountered in Los Angeles, Portland and Cincinnati. More crime than virtually any big city in America. In 2014, for example, Los Angeles, with three million more people than Detroit, had 39 fewer homicides.

In the nearly 50 years since the police raid on the blind pig, much has changed in Detroit. Mayors and police chiefs have come and gone. "No Crime Days," crackdowns on crack, rape summits and the DPD's feared STRESS unit have come and gone. One thing remains - crime, fueled by the city's increasing job loss and poverty. The 1967 riot - or rebellion, as many people call it - coincided with a spike in murder, arson and other serious criminal offenses. And the violence of that era, while reduced, continues today, plaguing residents, bedeviling city leaders, tarnishing Detroit's reputation and giving the city a severe look of razor wire, barred windows and acrylic glass shields.

Celebrating gun owners

At the time of that volatile street scene on Evergreen, 23,495 people had been slain in Detroit since 1967 - roughly the population of Romulus. But the city's annual number of homicides peaked at 714 in 1974, when the Motor City became known internationally as the Murder City. That number has dropped to the 300 level in the recent past, along with the reduction in the number of Detroit residents.

Under Craig, homicides and much other crime are down. But Detroit's ratio of homicides to population remains almost 10 times the national aver-

age, and its violent crime rate is more than five times the national average, according to Forbes Magazine, which in October 2015 ranked Detroit as the most dangerous city in the United States.

The chief speaks of crime in a composed manner, with authority but without drama. He is smaller in person than he seems on TV, and slender, with delicate hands. Despite his calm demeanor, he has not shied away from views that can be difficult for residents to hear.

He has said that Detroiters as a community has become desensitized to crime, too willing to accept high levels of violence as part of life, instead of fighting back. Contrary to the policies of many big-city chiefs and mayors, Craig advocates a well-armed citizenry, even once appearing on the cover of the National Rifle Association's monthly magazine, America's 1st Freedom, next to his own words, "We're not advocating violence, we're advocates for not being victims."

He has called gunmen who fired into a crowd "urban terrorists," but has also displayed empathy with the conditions that spawn lawlessness in Detroit, the nation's poorest big city. In a report on Detroit for Yahoo! News, Katie Couric asked Craig, "What is the link, in your view, between poverty, a sub-par education system, unemployment and crime?"

He answered: "Direct."

Detroit Police Chief James Craig laughs as he finishes the department's National Walking Day fitness event. The police union chief says Craig has lifted morale among officers by listening to the concerns of rank-and-file cops.

Bridge photo by Brian Widdis

Facing page: Three men brandishing firearms guard an unidentified market against further looting during the civil unrest of 1967.

Walter P. Reuther Library of Labor and Urban Affairs

New Bethel Incident marked a low in Detroit's relations with police

Kim Clowes | Michigan Korean Weekly

Detroit Recorder's Court Judge George Crockett, Jr., enraged the city's police department following a police shootout with a black nationalist group in 1969 in which an officer was killed. Crockett objected to the arrests of more than 100 African Americans who were at New Bethel Baptist Church when the confrontation turned violent, releasing most of them from police custody.

....

Nearly 50 years after the civil unrest of 1967, the New Bethel Incident stands among the historic low points for the relationship between the Detroit Police Department and the city's African-American community. The incident occurred on March 29th, 1969, nearly two years after the 1967 civil unrest.

The investigation of a black separatist meeting at New Bethel Baptist Church by two white police officers ended with Patrolman Michael Czapski dead and his partner Richard Worobec wounded. Squad cars from four precincts soon arrived and stormed the church, leading to mass arrests of the more than 100 people inside.

Within hours, Detroit Recorder's Court Judge George Crockett, Jr., an African American, entered the police commissioner's office with a court order demanding that those arrested but not charged be released. Crockett was concerned that police had conducted an illegal dragnet arrest of black residents, instead of concentrating on those who were truly homicide suspects. Within 24 hours, all but two of the prisoners were free. The release of the prisoners led to a hurricane of criticism directed at the judge's actions and fueled an increasingly polarized racial divide in the city. White cops picketed the home station of the two officers, protesting the handling of the case. Their picket signs, with messages like "Crockett Justice? Release Killers. Prosecute Prosecutors. Give License to kill policemen," reflected the sentiment of the city's police force.

Even as some city leaders stood by the judge, many in the political establishment weighed in critically, with Gov. William Milliken expressing his "extreme concern" regarding the judicial handling of the case and encouraging an investigation into Crockett's actions. Detroit Mayor Jerome Cavanaugh described Crockett's decision as "highly unusual (and) to some degree questionable."

In Lansing, the white-majority state Senate adopted a resolution asking the Judicial Tenure Commission, which probes judicial misconduct, to investigate Crockett's actions, a move that state senator and future Detroit mayor Coleman Young described as a "Senate lynching session." Civil rights groups joined Young in expressing their opposition to the legislature's response, with the local chapter of the NAACP commending the judge for his "courageous action in helping to secure the release of many members of the black community who were arrested in connection with the New Bethel incident."

On June 16, 1970, a majority-black jury voted to acquit the two men accused of shooting the two officers outside of New Bethel church. In hindsight, Crockett's ruling is considered by his supporters to have allowed the city to avoid another major uprising following the trauma of 1967. §

Craig's overall approach as Detroit's police chief has won him many admirers. In a scientific poll of city residents published in the Detroit Free Press, Craig had an approval rating of 75 percent, an unusually high number for a public figure in a demanding job. Mayor Mike Duggan, whose approval rating was 60 percent, extended Craig's contract for two years.

Even the head of the Detroit Police Officers Association has positive things to say about Craig. The union is often at odds with whoever is chief and mayor. But DPOA President Mark Diaz said while there is a range of opinions about Craig among DPOA members, the chief has been receptive to rank-and-file needs.

"Our officers recognize that the chief has an open ear," Diaz said. "He'll show up at a roll call to hear about things on the street. That was unheard of in the past. He actually goes to them to hear what their concerns are. That's never happened in my 22 years as a police officer."

Dolunt, the assistant chief, a 30-year veteran, said: "There's no scandals with this chief. Chiefs in the past we've had scandals. Chiefs in the past who didn't have a clue, but they were political puppets. Some chiefs really thought they had it together and didn't.

"He's willing to accept it when he's done something wrong. Always looks for input. Big on social media. He's really in the 21st Century."

Phillis Judkins, an organizer of the citizen patrol in the North End neighborhood south of Highland Park, also praised Craig's M.O.

"He shows up — that's what I like about him," she said. "He goes out and sees what's going on. I appreciate that."

Assistant Chief Steven Dolunt

Changing the culture

Driving down Vermont Street, a few blocks south of the Motown Museum on Detroit's west side, Neighborhood Police Officer Dale Dorsey spots a large pile of broken furniture and trash bags in front of a house. He stops his car and knocks on the door of the home next door.

"I'm Officer Dorsey of the Third Precinct," he tells the man who answers. "I'm wondering about this trash over here. That looks like a dump site."

The man explains that the neighbor had died, and people have been inside, working on the house. Dorsey asks what time they are usually arrive, and thanks the man.

"If we don't address the small problems fast, they turn into big problems," Dorsey says as he walks back to his scout car.

Dorsey's rank, neighborhood police officer, is new. It was created by Craig to better connect police to community, almost like suburban cops in the middle of Detroit.

31

Detroit Police Chief
CHRONOLOGY

Ray Girardin 1963-1968

Johannes Spreen 1968-1970

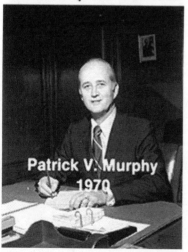

There are four NPOs in each of the city's 12 precincts. They don't answer radio runs, like other street officers, but are expected to be proactive, visiting businesses, introducing themselves to residents and giving out their phone numbers. Dorsey's photo, cell number and email address are displayed online, and Craig has been known to drop in on businesses and ask if the owner knows the local NPO.

"My phone rings seven days week," Dorsey said. "I get texts seven days a week."

Dorsey even teaches a daily law enforcement class to 16 high school students at University Preparatory Academy, a charter school in Midtown.

Neighborhood police officers are one of several changes Craig has brought to the department.

He instituted the ranks of captain, corporal and detective, and started the practice of placing bars on officers' uniform sleeves to denote every five years of service. "The officers love it," Dolunt said.

Craig quickly ended the "virtual precinct" program in which some stations were closed at night, and took front-line cops off the 12-hour shifts that many despised. He established a liaison to the LGBT community. He has revived CompStat meetings, in which department executives flyspeck crime patterns, quiz precinct captains about how they are responding and examine use-of-force statistics, even questioning superiors when their force numbers seem low. He also created partnerships with some of Detroit's protest leaders.

After hearing officers raise questions about possible discrimination in hiring and promotions, Craig established a Committee on Race and Equality to come up with solutions. (In a city that is about 80 percent black, the department is 62 percent African American; 33 percent white and five percent Hispanic, Asian and Native American; women make up 25 percent of the force.)

"I have to give him credit," said Officer John Bennett, co-leader of the committee and the officer behind a website that was highly critical of Jerry Oliver when he served as chief a decade ago in the early Kilpatrick years. "We have some problems in the department as it relates to race. It was his idea" to explore the issues.

When he returned to Detroit as chief, Craig said he talked first to the lowest-ranking members of the department and found they were afraid of being disciplined because of the Justice Department supervision and they were disillusioned because they were losing pay and benefits during the city's bankruptcy.

"My interpretation of that is that many of the POs didn't feel supported," Craig said. "There was no leadership in many ways. That's why they said, 'We want new bosses.'

"The first thing they told me was, 'Fire everybody above the rank of inspector. Get rid of them all. They're worthless.'

"I did that. Everybody has been changed out."

DETROIT POLICE DEPARTMENT
PROJECT GREEN LIGHT DETROIT
CITY OF DETROIT

Project Green Light providing 'safe haven' to city residents

Kim Clowes | Michigan Korean Weekly

Project Green Light is a partnership between local businesses, the City of Detroit and community groups. Following implementation of the Quicken Loans-sponsored Blue Light public safety surveillance system installed in Detroit's downtown and midtown neighborhoods, Detroit Police Chief James Craig said he was intrigued by Homeland Security's recognition of the program as a "best-practice" initiative.

"I started thinking about it. What does the blue light represent? Safe havens. A place that people can go if they need assistance. A location of safety. I thought that if we could identify some gas stations that were clean, that were safe, that were welcoming locations for safety, then why not elicit support and work closely with those businesses in the neighborhoods."

Under the program, Craig said, "private business owners who have said that they want to participate make the financial investment of between $5,000 and $6,000. They connect their high-definition cameras into our real-time crime center." If there is a robbery, a business participating in the program calls 911. The police monitoring center checks video at the location, and is then able to send descriptions of the suspects out in real time to responding police units.

Looking to the future, Craig said he sees opportunities to expand the program.

"As we evolve, as we tap into other video cameras across the city, there's something I'm calling virtual patrol," he said. "Let's say there are criminal activities occurring on a major thoroughfare where we know there are cameras. We know that there have been a rash of robberies (between) let's say, 7 and 10 on Thursdays and Fridays. Virtual patrol is nothing more than going to that location, scanning the area and looking for criminal activity based on descriptions which we've gotten. If during this virtual patrol our staff is monitoring some cameras at the location and they see some activity, or someone matching a description, they can then notify uniformed officers to go there and initiate an investigative stop for what they've seen."

Craig said he and Mayor Mike Duggan each see the benefits of technology to improve response times to crime.

"As the mayor and I started to talk about some of the initiatives we had going, one of the things that he knew I was passionate about was a real-time crime center, Craig said. "That's when the birth of the true private-public partnership began."

Among the few hundred Asian-owned businesses in Detroit, there is interest in the Green Light model.

Jung Joon Lim, who runs a beauty supply store on Fenkell Avenue, said he welcomes the project. "I am expanding my store and am ready to try the new monitoring system," he said. "The cost seems reasonable and the good thing is that the police are monitoring my store."

Chris Chae, the owner of Kimbrough Cleaners on Van Dyke, said that without crime control, Detroit cannot be attractive to business owners. "I appreciate to see that the police are doing something positive to protect our businesses and customers," he said. §

John Nichols 1970-1973

Stanley Knox 1991 - 1994

Charles Wilson 2001

Philip Tannian 1973-1974

Isaiah McKinnon 1994 - 1998

Jerry Oliver 2002 - 2003

William Hart 1976 - 1991

Benny Napoleon 1998 - 2001

Ella Cummings 2003 - 2008

As part of a strategy to confront the widespread sense among residents that criminals had free reign in Detroit, Craig began staging massive raids with hundreds of officers on neighborhoods troubled by crime or even, in one case, a notorious apartment building on E. Jefferson that is a short walk from the mayor's residence in the Manoogian Mansion. The media was invited to cover the raids, which make for vivid TV.

Some critics questioned the raids' impact, writing that few of the arrests result in prosecutions and concluding that the operations are largely for show.

Craig defends the operations, saying that residents are finally receiving what they want — police in their neighborhoods.

The raids signal, he said: "The police are here to serve you. To the criminals, we're not messing around."

Craig's most recent innovation is Project Green Light, a partnership with gas stations, party stores and fast-food restaurants that have installed high-definition cameras to stream live video to the department's Real Time Crime Center, where they are monitored. The cameras and their feeds are designed to act as a deterrent and, if they capture a crime, evidence. Craig said 25 percent of violent crime in Detroit takes place within 500 yards of a gas station, which serves in some neighborhoods as a corner store.

In one highly publicized incident, cameras caught a wild scene at a west-side station in which a woman wearing a short, fringed skirt and red boots pulled a gun out of her underwear and began firing into a car. The video was so clear viewers could see cartridges ejecting from her weapon. Police arrested the woman within two hours. The video went viral, and departments across the country are calling to ask about Detroit's high-definition crime-fighting tool.

Despite improvements, the department continues to face a serious shortage of manpower, which affects police response times, which remain a major citizen complaint. The total force has shrunk to about 2,200 — from 6,500 in the early 1970s — of which some 1,560 are police officers who patrol the streets and raid dope houses. Two or three serious incidents in one precinct can tie up enough personnel to strain resources and lengthen response, which appear to have improved in the past three years through streamlining dispatch processes and putting more cops in patrol jobs.

"Our manpower is (at) a critical level right now," said Diaz, the union president. "Our officers go from run to run, and they have to work doubles" — two successive shifts — "just to compensate for our lack of manpower on the street."

The department is trying to start a new academy class for recruits every month, but the attrition doesn't let up because up to 200 officers at all ranks leave every year, nearly half of them going to other departments.

James Barren 2008 - 2009

Warren Evans 2009 - 2010

Ralph Godbee 2010 - 2012

Chester Logan 2012 - 2013

James Craig May 2013 -

Detroit officers' pay starts at $36,000, and they earn around $53,000 after five years. Local and national agencies seek out Detroit cops because they are well trained and battled-hardened, and the salary can be $15,000 or more a year higher in suburban departments, where workload is generally lighter and less dangerous. In 1968, by contrast, Detroit police pay ranked third in the nation, behind only Los Angeles and Chicago.

"Our biggest challenge is retention," said Craig.

'Just sit there and be black'

Craig said he never had a bad experience with police as a child, but heard stories from his father about the DPD in the 1960s — and earlier — when the force was notorious for its mistreatment of the black community.

For three quarters of 20th Century, black Detroiters complained both of police brutality and the lack of police protection, as University of Michigan historian Sidney Fine noted in his book on the 1967 riot, "Violence in the Model City." Mistreatment ranged from racial slurs to fatal force. Many older black Detroiters have wrenching stories of harassment, such as from the so-called Big Four units — three plainclothes officers with a uniformed driver that cruised the city in hulking Buicks and Chryslers with a box of long guns in the trunk.

"My job was to teach the police they didn't have the constitutional right to beat up Negroes on arrest," said the late George Edwards, a former mayoral candidate and state Supreme Court Justice, whom Mayor Jerome Cavanagh appointed to run the department in 1962.

Before the riot, the local branch of the NAACP reported black residents were subjected to unreasonable and illegal arrests; indiscriminate searching on public streets, disrespectful language and violent reactions by the police to protests about the treatment.

Ray Girardin, who ran the department before, during and after the riot, once said cops believed the way to treat blacks was "to hit them on the side of the head."

In numerous polls and interviews at the time, black Detroiters cited police brutality as the number one cause of the 1967 disorder.

Why Do Police "Shoot to Kill"?

WDET

Why is it that sometimes police officers use lethal force and other times they don't? How do they determine when?"asked listener David Ewick of Southfield.

Law enforcement agencies are facing public scrutiny over recent police shootings, pushed further into the national spotlight by the "Black Lives Matter" movement. As part of our CuriosiD series, Ewick posed the question about how police are trained to use their guns.

To get to the bottom of David's question, WDET reporter Jake Neher visited the Oakland Police Academy in Auburn Hills where recruits were in the middle of shooting drills.

Everett Gard, an instructor and range master at the police academy and a 20-year veteran of the force in Pontiac, says not much has changed in recent decades when it comes to how officers are trained to use their guns. "With the recent events, we don't train any different," says Gard. "Because we've always been trained with, 'OK. You have to have a threat there.'"

Under case law set by the U.S. Supreme Court, police officers can use lethal force when they reasonably perceive their lives or others' lives are in danger. Law enforcement officials WDET spoke with say there's no science to determining whether there's a threat and that every situation is different.

"They're never trained to shoot to kill. But you intend to stop that action," says Oakland Police Academy Director Richard Tillman, who spent three decades with the Detroit Police Department. "Because of your training, you're taught to shoot center-mass and so forth. Death is likely to occur, but that isn't your intention.

You just want them to stop either charging you with a knife or stop firing that weapon at you."

So why can't police aim at the suspect's legs, or shoot the guns out of their hands?

Tillman says you don't want to aim for arms, legs, or other parts of the body that are smaller and likely to move around in these situations. If you miss the person, you don't know where that bullet is going to end up – which creates a greater danger for other people nearby. And shooting someone around the sternum area is most likely to incapacitate someone.

To evaluate the answers provided by the law enforcement community, WDET spoke with Carl Taylor, a Michigan State University professor who's studied police shootings. Taylor also has family members in law enforcement. He says he's not buying the idea that police don't intend to kill when they fire their guns.

"In all of my research, they have been taught to shoot to stop the challenge – and that is 'shoot-to-kill' in street terms," explains Taylor. "That's simply what it is. They have to."

Listener David Ewick says he's not surprised by any of those answers to his CuriosiD question. He says he had a hunch that's what we would find out. But he says it doesn't put the issue to bed.

"I did not believe that there was a simple answer," said Ewick. "And to me that was kind of why I wanted to present the question, because I do think that it is something that needs to be an ongoing conversation."

You can find more stories like this by visiting wdet.org/curious. There you can also let us know what you're curious about in Detroit and across the region. §

Only about five percent of the force was black in 1967, when African Americans made up nearly 40 percent of Detroit's population. The number of black officers increased gradually over the next several years, but Coleman Young, elected Detroit's first African American mayor in 1973, instituted an affirmative action program that began integrating the department at a rapid rate, to the consternation of many white veterans.

Craig was part of Young's initiative. In 1977, when he was a 19-year-old rookie, his first partner was a white cop with about 20 years of service.

"He just simply said to me, 'You're not going to drive this vehicle. You're not going to touch the radio. And don't talk to me. Just sit there and be black.'"

Craig said he decided to join the LAPD when he was laid off in Detroit because it was a storied force in a global city that he had seen positively portrayed on such television shows as "Adam 12" and "Dragnet." He received numerous promotions under legendary chiefs Bernard Parks and William Bratton, and said he learned the importance of using the media in police work, which was second nature to police executives there, surrounded by TV, film studios and, yes, Hollywood. He said while the LAPD was a sophisticated organization, Detroit by the 1980s was far ahead in community policing and hiring of minorities.

While Craig was in California, crime flourished in Detroit, but the growing number of black officers, as well as women, made an impression on the increasingly black city. A 1987 poll showed only 20 percent of black Detroiters thought police treated blacks worse than whites. Twenty years earlier, that figure was 82 percent.

Mayor Young, who had been roughed up by white cops while growing up before World War II — he once said police of that era "used to shoot black kids for fun" — took great pride in the integrated force, calling it the nation's "foremost example of a civil rights department."

But something went wrong along the way.

In 1992 alone, former Police Chief William Hart, convicted of embezzling $2.34 million in taxpayers' money while he led the department, was sentenced to a maximum 10 years in federal prison.

And the death of an unarmed black motorist, Malice Green, after an encounter with two white cops, Larry Nevers and Walter Budzyn, created a furor that lasted for months, coming not long after Los Angeles cops were acquitted in the videotaped beating of an uncooperative but unarmed black motorist, Rodney King.

In 2000, after Young had left office and died, another blow to the DPD's reputation: The Free Press revealed that Detroit Police lead the nation's largest cities in per capita fatal shootings of civilians — a rate 2 ½ times higher than that of New York City. The paper also found the department was failing to conduct thorough investigations or hold officers accountable.

In 2003, the city entered into agreements - known as consent decrees - with the U.S. Justice Department that imposed a number of requirements on the DPD, including how it reports such incidents, the manner in which the department holds pretrial detainees and how it conducts investigations.

After 13 years of scrutiny, which cost taxpayers about $50 million to pay for the federal oversight and reform, the city was finally released from federal oversight in early 2016. The department had made significant progress: It has halved the amount it paid out in civil lawsuits, cut civilian complaints and increased the rate at which its detectives solve homicide cases from 47 percent in 1998 to 70 percent in 2014.

The DPD also reduced holding-cell deaths from 19 between 1994-2000 to one between 2008 and 2014, and dropped fatal shootings from 47 between 1995-2000 to 18 from 2009-20014.

Ken Reed, spokesman for the Detroit Coalition Against Police Brutality, a citizens' group, said the DPD in some ways appears to operating differently than a decade ago.

"Detroit has made some strides, but I think the jury is still out," he said.

"I think the chief's head is in the right place," Reed continued. With Craig's age and experience, "he could have very easily rode off into the sunset. To come back here takes a lot of guts."

Bishop Edgar Vann Jr., a member of the Board of Police Commissioners, which has broad super-

An unseen Detroit Police Officer prepares to arrest four African American men, Detroit, Michigan. In the foreground, a National Guardsman trains his rifle on the suspects.
....
Photo by Tony Spina, Walter P. Reuther Library of Labor and Urban Affairs

Police officers accompany National Guardsmen as they disembark from their transport vehicle onto Linwood Avenue, Detroit, Michigan. In the background one can see burning businesses and a police blockade.
....
Photo by Tony Spina, Walter P. Reuther Library of Labor and Urban Affairs

Marchers on Grand River Avenue as they walk between Appleton and Riverview streets on a recent Friday evening peace march.

....

Bridge photo by Bill McGraw

visory power over the department, said Craig has changed the department's culture so it won't backslide into its old ways even after he is gone. He praised Craig for holding people accountable and restructuring the department.

"Any city can be a powder keg," Vann said. "But we've been able to avoid that with good community relations. This is another thing that the chief has done a great job with. At a very critical time nationally, he's been able to build even more bridges with the community."

Requiem for a 3-year-old

On a bright, chilly evening in early April 2016, about 75 people show up at the House of Help Church, located inside an old elementary school on Clarita in northwest Detroit. They plan to walk through the neighborhood in a peace march that on this night will honor Anaiya Montgomery, a 3-year-old girl who was killed five days earlier, on Easter Sunday, when a gunman burst into her nearby home and began firing. Anaiya died of multiple gunshot wounds; two adults were wounded.

Before starting out, the marchers gather inside a small auditorium to pray and listen to pep talks from organizers. Around the back are more than a dozen members of the Detroit Police Gang Intelligence Unit, led by Sgt. Edward Brannock. The cops — mostly young men and women who are black, white and brown - wear casual clothes, but their guns and handcuffs are in plain view, and they look like they mean business.

Brannock is invited to address the crowd, which occupies about half of the seats.

"We are here for you," he tells them. "There is a 3-year-old girl in the city of Detroit who has been killed. Every seat in this auditorium should be filled."

The crowd applauds.

Walking behind a banner declaring "Ceasefire Detroit," a non-violence program, the marchers stop periodically on Appleton and Riverview streets to pray with residents who emerge from their homes, curious why a chanting crowd is passing by. The cops follow in cars and on foot, and their presence is appreciated.

"The police are doing their job. You can't do nothing but appreciate that," said Polarius Crawford, 21. Asked how the police treat young people in Detroit, Crawford said: "It depends on what you're doing."

On Riverview, one of the organizers, the Rev. Cory Chavis, spotted a woman watching from behind her glass door and called out to her. "Would you pray with us, baby?"

Kim Day, 59, joined the crowd. Afterward, Day told of two recent close calls with criminals. Her 22-year-old nephew escaped a gunman who had demanded his cell phone, and she emerged unscathed from an encounter with a would-be stick-up artist, who ended up walking away.

"I gave the young man an option to leave me alone," Day said sardonically. She patted her hip as she told of the incident, assuming she was carrying her gun, but it turned out to be inside the house. "I thought I had it on," she said.

Chavis said he has met Chief Craig, and believes he is doing an excellent job.

"The chief doesn't patrol the streets, though,"

Chavis added. "Law enforcement can't be everywhere at the same time. The community must get involved."

Back at 1301 Third Street, Detroit's gleaming new public safety headquarters that replaced the mold-infested structure at 1300 Beaubien, Craig was attending a weekly meeting of the police board. The mood was upbeat as they announced that the federal supervision of the police department had officially ended.

Still, a couple of crime categories had inched up, a red flag in a data-driven organization.

During public comment, one of Craig's fans stood up and praised the chief for his light-hearted appearance on a TV show that morning, promoting physical fitness.

"Nice and loose," said the man. "I've never seen him so loose. He should get a license to be a comedian."

Craig, looking weary, laughed.

"I've always wanted to be a comedian," he said. "But as chief of the Detroit police, I don't often have the opportunity to tell a joke."

Chief Craig: In his own words

Keith A. Owens | The Michigan Chronicle

Detroit Police Chief James Craig explains his frank, sometimes controversial views on crime fighting in the Motor City, beginning with his belief that a well-armed citizenry will make the city safer:

ON THE BENEFITS OF AN ARMED CITIZENRY

"Some people were saying 'Oh my God, you're telling everybody in Detroit to arm up.' That's not true. That's not even logical or responsible."

Rather, Craig said he is simply noting the positive effect that "law-abiding, responsible, well-trained law abiding citizens can have on crime."

According to Craig, "research shows that criminals are more afraid of armed citizens than they are of the police. . . . So if that's a fact, if we believe the research, then do we believe that can have an effect on reducing violent crime?

"Over the last three years, we have seen a reduction of street crimes. Yes, great police work. But it's also no secret that there are a number of law-abiding citizens in Detroit who have obtained a concealed pistol license. I believe that has played a role in some way in reducing the incidents of robbery."

ON POLICE/COMMUNITY RELATIONS IN DETROIT

"I would say that police community relations today, certainly here in the city of Detroit given what is going on across this nation, we are certainly a model. We are a constitutional police department, which is reflective in the Department of Justice's decision to release us from [U.S. Justice Department] oversight. But when you look at and compare us to other cities that are struggling with their relationships in many areas of the minority community, we're certainly seeing an improvement."

ON OFFICER MORALE, RECRUITMENT EFFORTS AND THE CHALLENGE OF RETENTION

"When you look at attrition you have to ask why. One of the first, most notable reasons, it's no secret that pre-bankruptcy our police officers had 10 percent of their pay taken, which, when you compare us to the market, our police officers are some of the lowest paid in this country. But yet doing probably the most challenging job of any police department in this country.

"There was a revolving door of police chiefs. I mean, in 10 short years we went through maybe eight police chiefs. That certainly created a tremendous instability in leadership. The City of Detroit Police Department was under a consent decree for 13 years, the

Chief Craig

second-longest-running consent judgment in this country, only exceeded by Oakland, California. Clearly the revolving door of police chiefs had an impact."

"We're a more fully functional police department today than we were 2.5 years ago, and we have fewer police officers. We have faster response times, we have a clearance rate (of solving crimes) that hovers around the national average, 65 percent. We are making key arrests on some of the most violent crimes."

ON WHETHER DETROIT OFFICERS SHOULD RESIDE IN DETROIT

"While I understand why most in the city would want a Detroit police officer to live in their neighborhood, let me just say that after having spent 28 years in LA, probably 75 percent [of police] or even higher lived outside the city of LA. So the only thing you can hope for is that leadership, the police chief and his executive team, holds a police officer accountable to do the right job, the kind of job that the people of Detroit expect.

"Living in the city – and I know this angers some -- really doesn't make a difference. Now what we have done to compensate for that, one of the things we have done as part of our neighborhood policing program is those police officers who reside in the city of Detroit, we're in the process of giving them marked, take-home scout cars. One, because they're neighborhood police officers. Two, they live in the city. The response has been very favorable."

"The police are the people and the people are the police." §

Long-time Officer, Educator Reflects on 1967, Policing Career

Jake Neher | WDET

Richard Tillman was working in the auto industry in 1953 when a friend, newly hired at the Detroit Police Department, told him about what the work was like. Tillman thought it sounded interesting and applied.

Now in his 7th decade of law enforcement, Tillman's career began as a patrolman back when Detroit had nearly 2 million residents. He worked through the 1967 riots and retired from the department in the 1980s. Since then, Tillman has run the Oakland Police Academy where he oversees the training of dozens of cadets each year.

He spoke with WDET's Jake Neher as part of the station's "CuriousiD" segment, answering a listener's question about how officers are taught to make use-of-force decisions in an era of intense debate over police conduct in minority communities.

Tillman says criticism of some controversial police shootings of civilians is justified. "I've seen situations on television, shootings that have just embarrassed me, that were so wrong," he said. Here's some of his conversation with Neher:

JAKE NEHER: I understand that you were in Detroit in 1967. What was your experience with the riots?

RICHARD TILLMAN: I remember it very well. The city was totally burning during the day. I'm in police headquarters, the second floor, that's where I was stationed. I'd look out the window in the afternoon and I'd see smoke all over. It was on fire. We figured it was beyond our control, local police. Thank god President Johnson was on television and said — we were all watching it — and he said 'I have reluctantly ordered the 101sts Airborne Division into assist.' So when they arrived after several days of rioting, within a couple of days it was put down.

> "Thank god President Johnson was on television and said — we were all watching it — 'I have reluctantly ordered the 101sts Airborne Division into assist.'"

Police officers with a curfew violator on Jefferson near Belle Isle Bridge. A knife was found on one of the two men arrested.

Walter P. Reuther Library of Labor and Urban Affairs

43

National Guardsmen are pinned down by sniper fire at the McGraw police station in Detroit's 6th precinct.

Walter P. Reuther Library of Labor and Urban Affairs

JN: As a police office on the ground, how did it make you feel when you heard the president make that declaration?

RT: Those of us standing around the television watching it cheered because police agencies aren't set up to handle huge insurrections like that. You need help from the outside. A lot of people don't understand that, but that's the reason that today there are consortiums so agencies band together now to put these kinds of things down. It was really interesting driving around in a scout car after the curfew was on. Absolutely no cars at all on the road except police cars. It was strange. You never had to stop for a red light or a stop sign. So it was really interesting.

JN: Can you give me a couple of specific examples of what you remember of how your training played into that situation and maybe some of the biggest challenges to that?

RT: I was a patrolman back then, at the lowest level of the department. I'm basically told what to do all the time. My assignment was the transportation division, so we would transport people to different locations, particularly popular people, important people that came into Detroit and they needed a ride from one location. So that's what I did. Then I was taken out, I had to drive a medical examiner out to the scene of a lot of deaths, and he had to try to identify bodies, and for me that was a great experience just to watch how they did it.

JN: In some ways, was it a difficult experience or did you view it like you said more of an education kind of moment?

RT: It was real educational. It wasn't difficult. It was very educational to see how they operated. ... This is what you're talking about. The riots. '67. This is where they sent me. But those are the riots.

At this point during the interview, Tillman opened an envelope of 11 x 14 photos.

JN: Help us visualize, especially listeners who can't see. What are some of the things that strike you about these photos?

RT: The number of people. The fact that police were so outnumbered that they couldn't go down and police these areas. You see them standing back, observing. You see police officers here guarding firemen who are putting out a fire. They had to guard them otherwise their lives were in jeopardy. Firemen were shot at during that period (of) time. To see the military vehicles in these photographs, which you see a military vehicle back here and here. That meant a lot to these police officers who were looking for cover. So yeah, I do remember the riots of '67. I was there and I went down to this particular area here. What happened in this particular area is looters were in one of these stores which was a liquor store. They were looting the liquor store and it was on fire at the time. The floor gave away and a few of them fell into the basement. They lost their lives. So they brought these people up who were also burned very badly I brought them medical examiner out to help identify these people who were in the basement. That's what this is here.

JN: Can you talk from personal experience about what were, how was the interaction between police and the community before the riots and after the riots.

RT: I never had any problem with the police and the community. I thought we were doing well. At the time I was in what they called the Accident Prevention Bureau. We would ride up and down neighborhood streets. Back then kids would call out and say "Hey Police" and so forth. We got along quite well, and it was hard to understand why all this happened. §

Arab-American cops leaving Dearborn police force

By Ali Harb | Arab American News

DEARBORN — Middle Easterners in Dearborn call the city the capital of Arab America. That is evidenced by the demographics of the neighborhood's Arabic signs on storefronts, and an abundance of Middle Eastern businesses.

The city's culture and appearance have shifted over the past 30 years, but the police department still looks like that of a typical Midwestern city.

In 2014, The Arab American News reported that only seven of 184 Dearborn police officers were Arab American — less than 4 percent. Arab Americans are 42 percent of the city's population, according to U.S. Census estimates. Since then, Chief Ronald Haddad — who is Arab American — has tried to recruit people from the community.

However, the efforts appear to be falling short. At least four newly recruited Arab-American officers have left the department over the past year and a half.

Two of them cited racist attitudes in the department as the reason for their departures.

"They treat you with disrespect and insult in front your colleagues," one of the former Dearborn officers told The Arab American News.

The Dearborn Police Department has not returned repeated requests by The Arab American News for comment.

The newspaper also made Mary Laundroche, director of Dearborn's department of public information, aware of the former officer's allegations. Landrouche said she would work on arranging a meeting with the police chief to answer our questions. The newspaper extended the deadline for the story by four days to allow Landrouche to communicate with the chief.

We also inquired about the number of police officers who have quit the department over the past two years. The city directed The Arab American News to file a Freedom of Information Act Request, which the city's legal department had not responded to by the time this article was published.

There is a consensus among civil rights activists that police forces should reflect the communities in which they serve. In 1967, the Kerner Commission recommended hiring and promoting more African-American police officers to help soothe the relationship between law enforcement and the community. The commission's report was in response to racial unrest that unfolded across the country, including in Detroit, Dearborn's neighbor to the east.

Back then, Dearborn was ruled by Mayor Orville Hubbard, a man who openly wanted to keep African Americans out of the city. Dearborn advocates say the city has come a long way from those segregationist days. And so has Detroit. But while the Detroit police force has been diversified over the past 50 years, the growing Arab residential base in Dearborn still remains to be reflected in the police force.

> "I felt like fifth-class citizen," he said. "I felt like I did not belong."

45

After Dearborn officers fatally shot two black Detroiters within 35 days in December of 2015 and January 2016, there was renewed criticism of police conduct and attitudes directed toward the city.

"HOSTILE ENVIRONMENT"

One of the Arab officers who left Dearborn police last year was hired by Dearborn Heights. When he quit, a city official told The Arab American News that the officer left for better pay and benefits. But the other three officers resigned with no publicly stated reason — two of them within a month of each other in 2016.

One of the four officers who left said he faced daily harassment and discrimination by his colleagues and superiors at the Dearborn Police Department.

He said he heard and overheard anti-Arab sentiments, including, "We need this Arab guy out of here."

The officer, who spoke on the condition of anonymity because of concern about possible professional repercussions, said he almost got in a fight with a training officer over the disrespectful treatment he said he received.

The mistreatment ranged from slurs to aggressive scolding to deliberate alienation, according to the officer. He said fellow officers would not return greetings; they would whisper and laugh when he approached.

Asked if the rough treatment could have been a part of the training process, the former Dearborn policeman said white recruits were treated with more respect.

"How come when it's a white guy speaking to a white guy it's not like that," he asked.

He shared incidents where he said white officers were held to different standards but did not want the details published because they could lead to identifying him.

"I felt like fifth-class citizen," he said. "I felt like I did not belong."

The former Dearborn cop said he initially put up with the alleged abuse until it reached an intolerable point. "I'm not a sensitive person," he said. "But I couldn't deal with this hostile environment for the next 25 years of my life."

While declining to comment on behalf of the other officers who quit, the source said there is a pattern of bias.

"Four officers don't just leave a department like Dearborn out of nowhere," he said.

The officer said he has no intention of returning to Dearborn Police.

"I just want them to treat the next Arab recruit differently than how they have treated us," he said.

He said he did not submit a formal complaint or inform the chief of his grievances because he thought the problem was not fixable given the culture at the department.

He added that he joined the department with the goal of serving and giving back to the community.

"The sad part is that I actually wanted that to work," he said.

Another Arab-American and former Dearborn officer, who also requested anonymity because of potential consequences to future employment, had similar complaints.

He said he was insulted by his training officer, treated more harshly than others and even mocked. He said that when he voiced his grievances to the chief, Haddad asked him to speak to a lieutenant who the officer said dismissed his concerns.

"Basically they gave me no choice but to leave," he said.

This second officer added that he knew the challenges of working in law enforcement, but he said, "There's a difference between having thick skin and being disrespected every day."

He said rued his time at the Dearborn Police Department, and fears that his resignation may be a hurdle for future employment.

WHO CAN SERVE THE COMMUNITY

Fatina Abdrabboh, the Michigan director of the American-Arab Anti-Discrimination Committee (ADC), said allegations of racism in the police department should be taken seriously.

Abdrabboh cited Title VII of the Civil Rights Act of 1964, the Age Discrimination in Employment Act of 1967 and the Americans with Disabilities Act of 1990, saying that bullying, swearing, shouting, silent treatment and making up rules only for certain employees can amount to discrimination.

"ADC-Michigan sends the clear message to the city of Dearborn that we maintain a zero tolerance policy on any allegations of workplace discrimination," she said. "The pattern that has been presented to us raises serious issues and we call on the city of Dearborn to respond appropriately and swiftly."

She said, if true, the alleged discrimination would be stripping citizens of the right to serve their community.

Dawud Walid, the executive director of the Council on American Islamic Relations in Michigan, said the Dearborn Police Department has a problem with ethnic prejudice that runs deep.

Referring to Mayor Hubbard's legacy, Walid said there was a time when African Americans could not drive west of Wyoming Avenue across city lines between Dearborn and Detroit without being pulled over.

"In one of Malcolm X's last speeches in Michigan, he said Dearborn is Mississippi," Walid said. "Meaning the type of profiling African Americans faced from Dearborn police, as well as the positions, from its notorious Mayor Hubbard, were no different from what took place in the South."

Walid said police racism in Dearborn has eroded significantly but not totally.

"There's no question that it's not as bad in terms of people not being able to drive down Michigan or Warren Avenue, but nonetheless people of color continue to have complaints about the Dearborn Police Department," the CAIR director said.

He added that the department has a bigger issue than lack of reflection of the community's demographics.

"There is an institutional problem there," he said. "It's not something that can be changed by trying to hire a few officers. It is embedded in the culture of decades of anti-minority sentiments. That culture just doesn't go away by having an Arab American police chief, either. We know that to be a case from major departments that have black police chiefs, yet continue to have crises and complaint reports of police brutality against African Americans."

Walid added that "putting a few faces of color" does not change the structural bias.

He urged current and former Dearborn officers who have faced discrimination to contact civil rights organizations and make their grievances known.

A screengrab from a video showing Dearborn officers subduing Ali Baydoun, a mentally ill man who was riding his bike in the early morning hours of Dec. 7, 2013.

47

POLICE AND THE COMMUNITY

The officer who quit and complained about hostility of his former fellow Dearborn cops said that he did not see the racial attitudes on display within the department reflected in the streets. Cops were not biased against civilians, he said.

When the department was facing protests over the two fatal civilian shootings earlier this year, many prominent Arab Americans came to the defense of the police. Some Arab American social media users changed their profile photos to the Dearborn Police badge. Others put blue ribbons in front of their homes.

However, the relationship has not always been smooth.

In 2011, a young Arab American said police slammed him to the glass window of a coffee shop and forcibly arrested him after he had a verbal altercation with an employee there. In 2014, police executed a search warrant in the wrong home, terrifying an Arab American family of four in an ordeal that lasted 30 minutes. Chief Haddad personally apologized to the family. Weeks after that incident, The Arab American News obtained a video of Dearborn officers tackling Ali Baydoun, a mentally challenged man, who was riding his bike home from work in the early morning hours of Dec. 7, 2013.

Police said they tried to arrest Baydoun after he failed to tell them what he was doing in the neighborhood, adding that there had been larcenies by bike-riding suspects in the area.

Baydoun's lawyer argued that the police used excessive force and should not have stopped him from the beginning.

Early in 2016, the Dearborn Police implemented a policy that allows Muslim women who wear an hijab to keep their head-scarves on after they are arrested. But last year, a woman who was taken into custody over an unpaid parking ticket sued the department, saying that officers asked her to take off her hijab while booking her. The woman dropped the lawsuit after learning about the change in the department's hijab policy.

Walid, of CAIR, said he is sure that many residents have had positive interactions with individual officers, but the problem is institutional.

"Just as there are many people in the community who like the Dearborn police department, there are many others who have verbalized concerns about the department," he said. "My warning to people in the community who think the Dearborn police are 100 percent great is that they should not negate other people's experiences just because they have not experienced them personally."

CITY RESPONSE

Dearborn City Council member Mike Sareini said it is hard to verify if claims about racism within the department are true, "but the pattern doesn't look good because they keep losing these guys."

"It does make you question, hey, what's going on?" Sareini added.

Sareini, whose mother was the first Arab American to be elected to the council, said he spoke to the officers who quit. He cited the recruit who went on to work in Dearborn Heights, saying his departure was understandable.

Sareini has helped expand a police internship program, which allows Dearborn high school graduates, who include a high ratio of Arab Americans, to work at the police department while attending Henry Ford College. He said the point of the initiative is to pave the way for Dearborn residents to join the force, and to allow potential recruits to see if this is the job for them.

"The chief is trying," Sareini said. "Is he not picking the right guys, or is it a hostile environment?"

Sareini suggested conducting comprehensive exit interviews to detail the reason for recruits' departure.

He encouraged Arab Americans to apply for the department and consider being an officer a career in public service.

Sareini said the police force should look more like the community.

"But they have to be qualified," he said. "If you ask me, I would not choose and Arab American —even though he may represent the community— over a guy who is more qualified." §

Jewish leaders recall racial tensions in Detroit

By Jackie Headapohl | Jewish News

Civil rights attorney Bill Goodman.

Racial tensions in Detroit, from police mistreatment and economic disparity to discriminatory housing practices, had been smoldering long before the spark that ignited the riots in Detroit on July 23, 1967, when Detroit police raided a blind pig at 12th Street and Clairmount, in what long before was a temporary home of Congregation Shaarey Zedek.

Some members of the Jewish community were actively involved in civil rights and justice issues during the years before and after the 1967 riot, also known as the "Great Rebellion." Four of those leaders sat down with The Jewish News to discuss their memories.

BEFORE THE RIOT

Violence was nothing new on 12th Street, once home to the notorious Purple Gang, a ruthless group of Jewish gangsters who thrived on the illicit alcohol trade that flourished in Detroit during Prohibition. In the heart of the Jewish community, the street once boasted shop after shop of Jewish-owned businesses.

The racial makeup of the street began to gradually change from the 1950s on. As housing restrictions began to ease, middle-class black families began to move in from the east side. For a few years, there was a peaceful coexistence among black and Jewish neighbors.

49

"I was coming back from a trip to see my daughter at summer camp. As the plane flew into Metro you could see this smoke rising. When I drove downtown to work, I remember passing a street with soldiers."

— Judge Avern Cohn

"You could hear the sound of the tanks going down Gratiot. You could hear machine guns firing. It was horrible. I didn't have a gun, but I got a shotgun and kept it by the bed. One of my daughters has never forgotten it — that there was a gun in the house that night."

— Bruce Miller

However, with urban renewal, Black Bottom, the home to many poor African Americans in Detroit and once home to the Jewish community, was razed. Those blacks now followed the Jews over to 12th Street, which had begun to deteriorate in the years before the riot. The area had the highest crime rate in the city.

Retired U.S. Sen. Carl Levin describes the constant tension between police and the local African-American community. Levin had left his position as general counsel for the Michigan Civil Rights Commission the year before the uprisings to help create the Detroit Defender's Office, where he became appellate defender, handling the appeals of indigent people convicted of crimes.

"You had a nearly all-white police force, and the housing situation was segregated in fact if not in law," Levin says. "Neighborhoods were strongly segregated. It was a fact of life just as the tension between the black community and police was a fact of life."

The riot began a few doors away from where Levin used to practice law on 12th Street and Clairmount. Though shocked by the extent of the damage and the deaths, Levin said he can't say the riot was a total surprise "because the racial tensions that had always been significant had not been resolved. I'm not sure they've been resolved to this day."

POLICE BRUTALITY

In 1967, Detroit's police force was 93 percent white. "As the black population increased, the percentage of black police did not," said U.S. District Judge Avern Cohn, who served on the Michigan Civil Rights Commission and the Police Commission in the years following the riot. "There were a lot of programs that singled out African Americans. Police harshness built up resentment. Police seemed like an army of occupation and, on a hot summer night at the corner of 12th and Clairmount, it just erupted."

Jewish attorney Bruce Miller was active in civil rights issues long before the 1967 riot as part of the Detroit branch of the NAACP, where he later became general counsel. He became involved in two areas: discrimination in local labor unions and police brutality. He successfully garnered the first state censure against a Detroit police officer for brutality and went on to create a Citizens Review Board for the Detroit Police Department.

He understands the anger black Detroiters felt during the times leading up to the riot. "There certainly was a lot of tension. It was a case where there appeared to be no redress for any wrongs," he says.

A MINOR BREAKTHROUGH

Miller describes the case of police brutality against prostitute Barbara Jackson, which happened years before the riots. "She had picked up a married Canadian guy at the Purple Onion on Beaubien," he says. "She took him across the street to a whorehouse where she was waiting for a bedroom to come free."

While she was waiting, a police officer knocked on the door. "No one had called for him. He was probably there to pick up his white envelope," Miller says. "When he came through the door, the Canadian guy panicked and started yelling how Jackson had enticed him. Jackson was lippy and the police grabbed her and arrested her."

Miller continues, "As she was getting out of the car in the garage near the precinct, one of the officers grabbed her by the hair to pull her out. All he got was a wig and that infuriated him. As he was bringing her inside the police station, he mashed her face — literally ground her face — against the brick wall. She was a mess."

Miller decided to do something dramatic. He took Ms. Jackson downtown and parked her on Mayor Jerome Cavanagh's doorstep "so the mayor would know firsthand what police brutality looked like." The move got plenty of media coverage. "The mayor never forgave me," Miller says.

Miller also filed a complaint with the Civil Rights Commission. It took years, but Miller eventually succeeded in getting the police officer who brutalized Jackson censored.

"They got a black mark on their record, and that was it," Miller says. "That doesn't sound like much but that was the first time, to our knowledge, that a police officer had ever been reprimanded for that kind of conduct. It was a breakthrough."

DISCRIMINATORY POLICE DEPARTMENT

Renowned civil rights attorney Bill Goodman was visiting his parents the day the civil disturbance started.

As a young lawyer, he had joined his father, Ernest Goodman's, law firm, Goodman, Eden Millender and Bedrosian, which was the first racially integrated law firm in the United States and concentrated on constitutional and civil rights issues. He had also spent some time in the South, working on civil rights cases at a small firm in Virginia. When he returned to Detroit, he handled police misconduct and abuse cases.

Goodman said that as he drove home from his parents' house in Southwest Detroit, he could see all sorts of people streaming out of storefronts carrying things and people being arrested.

"The riot, or as I prefer to call it, the uprising or rebellion because it really was that, was the result of police oppression of the African-American community. It was clear to know that was what it arose from: an all-white police force policing a large and growing African American community and doing so in a way that was blatantly discriminatory.

"Young kids were being detained. Cops were picking up everybody based on skin color and nothing else. They were shooting people," he continues. "I ended up representing a kid named Albert Wilson who was shot in the back and paralyzed because he was in a store — at worst, he was looting the store, but you don't shoot someone for that. He was shot by an unknown Detroit cop who just left him on the ground to die."

REPRESENTING THOSE ARRESTED

"They arrested scores of people and locked them up in a detention center and in tents on Belle Isle, charging them with misdemeanors," Cohn says.

Goodman said people were held at Belle Isle for days and then brought on buses to Recorder's Court. "These were people who had been guilty of nothing more than a curfew violation — somebody who had happened to be out late at night," he says.

Goodman joined with his colleagues and friends in the National Lawyers Guild and gathered in Recorder's Court. "We just waited for names to be called and for people to be brought up in front of judges and volunteered to represent people."

"Negro snipers turned 140 square blocks north of West Grand Blvd. into a bloody battlefield for three hours last night, temporarily routing police and national guardsmen . . . Tanks thundered through the streets and heavy machine guns clattered . . . The scene was incredible. It was as though the Viet Cong had infiltrated the riot-blackened streets."

— Detroit News Archives

"The month before, a 27-year-old black army vet who lived four blocks from ground zero of the riots was killed by a group of young white men when he tried to protect his pregnant wife from their sexual advances. The police refused to arrest the gang. The incident was kept out of the major newspapers until the city's black newspaper made it a banner headline."

— According to "Hurt, Baby Hurt," a book written by an African-American participant in the violence

When they were overwhelmed by the sheer numbers of people, they assigned clients to other lawyers as well.

"My firm was asked to provide volunteer lawyers," Cohn says, "so I spent a full day in court representing the rioters."

The rioters he represented all pled guilty to vandalism and most were sentenced to probation. "Everybody had sympathy for the rioters," Cohn said. "We realized the anger that was there and the social dislocation that occurred."

AFTER THE RIOTS

Cohn took a seat on the newly formed police commission after the riot, where he supported a program of quotas for the police department.

"For every white, hire a black, for every female, hire a male," he says. "I resigned from the American Jewish Committee because they were opposed to quotas. But I believe that if you didn't have a police department that reflected the makeup of the community, it would be looked upon as an army of occupation."

Levin said he turned to politics to make a difference on justice issues. He was elected in 1969 to the Detroit City Council and took office in 1970.

"A number of people had urged me to run as someone who could get support from both the black and white communities, also because of my work in poverty law, they thought I could be part of the healing of Detroit," Levin says. "Being Jewish was a big plus when I ran for City Council."

He came in third out of nine city council members. Four years later, he became president of the Detroit City Council. During his tenure, which included the election of Coleman Young as the city's first black mayor, hiring factors in the Detroit Police Department changed significantly, creating a work force that more closely resembled the city's population.

He had very strong support from the Jewish community. "There have always been very strong connections between the Jewish and black communities," he said. "I think there still is a strong connection. The Jewish community has always strongly supported civil rights."

JEWISH COMMUNITY RESPONSE

Before the riots, the Jewish and black communities' relationship was largely in the purview of the Jewish Community Council (now the JCRC), Cohn recalled. "As a result of the riots, concern about the relationship among blacks and Jews as well as the general population became the responsibility of the Jewish Federation itself," Cohn said. "A special committee was appointed by Federation's board of governors. Alan E. Schwartz was chairman of that committee, and I was a member. We tried to set up a dialogue.

"The African American community complained there were no black doctors on the staff at Sinai Hospital. They talked about employment. Black physicians got their staff positions quickly," Cohn continues. "We looked at ways to enhance the betterment of the underprivileged, mainly the black community."

The day after riots started, a group of Protestant, Catholic and Jewish leaders met to establish the Interfaith Emergency Council. Shortly after, civic leaders formed New

Detroit, a private citizen's council focused on urban renewal. Max Fisher was the only Jewish person tapped to join the committee. Within months, Jewish leaders Stanley Winkelman, Mel Ravitz and Norman Drachler also joined.

More than half the Jewish businesses in the Seven Mile-Livernois area and 12th Street neighborhood fled the city, including Stanley Lipson who owned Sam Lipson's Variety Store on 12th Street, which was looted and burned. Ironically, Lipson had long attempted to form a biracial merchants' association.

COULD IT HAPPEN AGAIN?

In the wake of more recent civil uprisings in places like Ferguson, Mo., and Baltimore, largely sparked by African Americans who died in interactions with police, one has to wonder if another riot could happen in Detroit.

Not likely, according to Levin. "The city is on an upswing," he said of Detroit. "There is positive momentum and such incredible good will in the city, a feeling that we have a real turnaround. Young people are moving into the city who've overcome racial and other divisions that existed in our society."

Not that Levin thinks everything is rosy. "I don't want to suggest that there are not problems. There are. We still have huge black unemployment in the city, especially with black youth. There's still a problem with criminal justice in the black community, as it relates to marijuana arrests and incarceration."

Miller doesn't think the problems Detroit faces today are a function of racism. "I think you have a very depressed community within parts of the city that are really not part of the community anymore. They are not anchored to society or any social norms," Miller says. "The cops have the difficult job of maintaining order in the community, and they don't have respect for these people, but that's not essentially racist."

Cohn agrees. "I doubt seriously that this could happen again. If it did, it wouldn't be because of black-white relationships but rather a frustrated underprivileged class. But everyone is so much more alert now." §

Three year old Thomas Allen stands in the ruins of his home after it was burned down during the civil unrest of 1967.

Walter P. Reuther Library of Labor and Urban Affairs

CHAPTER 3
POVERTY

Photo by Ronald Manera

"Segregation and poverty have created in the racial ghetto a destructive environment totally unknown to most white Americans … Yet if the deepening cycle of poverty and dependence on welfare can be broken, if the children of the poor can be given the opportunity to scale the wall that now separates them from the rest of society, the return on this investment will be great indeed." — Kerner Commission

Detroiters in poverty face nearly insurmountable obstacles

By Lester Graham | Michigan Radio

Politicians and media reports indicate Detroit is in the middle of an economic resurgence. That's true for the central business districts. That's not the case for many residents in the poorest neighborhoods.

"Some people just don't have the hope. And, especially living in an environment like this, it's kind of hard. It's kind of hard. It's very stressful," said one Detroit resident, Alita Burton.

Many residents are trapped in poverty because they cannot get past obstacles such as getting a decent education, employment training, or reliable transportation to solid jobs.

A government survey recently showed 57 percent of Detroit children live in poverty and 39 percent of all households are impoverished. But some neighborhoods are worse than others.

The most impoverished census tract in the city is in the Chandler Park area on the city's east side. While Detroit's downtown has been booming, this section of town has seen increased poverty. Recent data posted by Detroitography show that since 2000 the area has seen one of the largest increases in racially concentrated poverty. Loveland Technology data show that of the 292 homes and lots in the area, only 23 are privately owned. The rest are held by the city, the county, the land bank, or the federal government.

Alita Burton lives in a federally subsidized housing project there called Parkside. She says getting a job in Detroit is difficult.

"A majority of all the jobs are taken by individuals that stay in different cities, which knocks you out of the competition," Burton explained.

She's got a part-time job, which she said is the best she's been able to find as of yet to support her and her 9-year-old son.

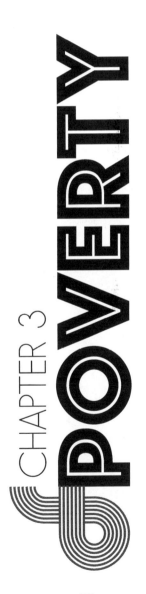

CHAPTER 3 POVERTY

Zachary Rowe heads up Friends of Parkside. He says even though there's a strip mall right across the street, the residents have a difficult time getting a job in any of the stores.

Transportation an obstacle to getting a job

She's among the more fortunate in her neighborhood. Twenty-six percent of Detroit households do not own a car. Burton does.

"Barely. The car is raggedy. I just be praying to keep it rolling, keep it going," she said.

But even with a car, the cost of auto insurance is another big obstacle.

The cost for Detroit residents is somewhere between $2,000 and $5,000 dollars a year. That's about double that of the surrounding suburbs.

It's a major problem for a lot of people living in Detroit.

At a Chandler Park Neighbors and Partners Association meeting, Walter Brown said one of his adult daughters is living with him. He explained she'd been in and out of jobs because of the cost of owning a car.

"She can't afford the insurance. And I think that's what comes down on a lot of young people with being able to find a job if they don't have the transportation method to get there."

City buses are often not much of a solution. Even with improvements in the bus service, many employers won't hire people who depend on public transportation because they don't consider it to be reliable.

That means for many people options for work are limited to nearby retail stores. Brown says that's not enough.

"I mean, these little jobs at the restaurants and little party stores, (for) a single mom it's very difficult for her to make a living off of that and raise the kids."

58

Bias among public housing residents

For people who live in Parkside public housing there's another obstacle.

Zachary Rowe heads up Friends of Parkside. He says even though there's a strip mall right across the street, the residents have a difficult time getting a job in any of the stores.

"One has to do with sort of the stigma or the perception of people that live in Parkside as local business view them. You would think it would be an advantage or a benefit to say you live in Parkside because you don't have those transportation issues. But in some cases it's actually a negative just because of how the residents are perceived."

Rowe says his group looked at the economic impact of the spending power of the residents. While many shopped at nearby stores and restaurants, very few were able to get a job at the establishments.

A boycott was considered at one time, but shopping elsewhere was more than an inconvenience for many of the residents. Because of transportation issues, it was nearly impossible. There wasn't enough support to make a boycott successful.

Jobs downtown

Since downtown is booming, you might think these residents would be headed there for work. Keven Boyle is an author and history professor at Northwestern University. He grew up on the east side of Detroit. He says there are few opportunities for Detroit residents in downtown.

"Because what the downtown is doing is it's creating jobs that poor people aren't going to get. It's creating high tech jobs in a city in — at least by one estimate that I've seen — says 47 percent of the adults in the city of Detroit are functionally illiterate. Now, that's not going to translate into high tech jobs downtown."

A construction company owner who lives near Chandler Park says he hires young Detroit workers, but he finds some of them can barely read or solve math problems on the job.

Zachary Rowe with Friends of Parkside says he's sometimes experienced the same problem with kids who went to both Detroit Public Schools and charter schools, including summer workers aged 14 to 24 who "have trouble doing basic math problems."

But one researcher says downtown's recent prosperity could still mean jobs for people who don't have high tech skills.

"As more people work in downtown Detroit, they're going to need a lot of services: lunch time and, you know, there's going to be security services. There is some amount of jobs that don't require an advanced education that will be generated by more employment in Detroit," said Reynolds Farley, a research professor emeritus at the University of Michigan.

Searching for hope

Boyle, at Northwestern, said it's good that Detroit's downtown areas are doing better, but until all of Detroit can share in the newfound prosperity, too many are being left behind.

"And, that's what you're seeing inside the city of Detroit today. You're seeing, to a really dramatic extent, an economic revival in the city of the Detroit that is not completely white, but is white dominated and a dramatic level of poverty and inequality for large numbers of African-Americans who live in the city."

Boyle says Detroit must find solutions for transportation, work skills training, and the other obstacles to residents in the neighborhood. Until they're able to get good paying jobs, Boyle says there's very little to celebrate. §

A man begs for money from a patron leaving one of Midtown's critically acclaimed restaurants, where a roasted mushroom salad is $14.

Bridge photo by Bill McGraw

Poverty and joblessness, fuel for '67 riot, even worse today

By Bill McGraw / Bridge Magazine

While Detroit has seen positive changes in the police department and the inclusion of African Americans in civic life since 1967, the decline of manufacturing and flight of people over the past five decades have contributed to significantly higher levels of unemployment and impoverished residents in the city. Reynolds Farley, a retired University of Michigan sociologist, notes that in 1950, Detroit had the nation's "most prosperous black population."

But the city's black community is now one of the nation's poorest, with much of the blame placed on decades of job loss, especially in auto and government jobs, and the migration of middle-class white and African Americans to the suburbs, where jobs are more plentiful. Below, some jarring numbers showing how far black Detroiters have economically regressed since the troubles of 1967.

PERCENT OF OWNER-OCCUPIED HOUSEHOLDS

1970
White 66%
Black 51%

2014
White 53.2%
Black 45%

Homes in the more upscale Rosedale Park-Grandmont neighborhood on the city's west side

Bridge photo by Bill McGraw

In 1967, housing conditions for black Detroiters were far worse than for whites. But home ownership for black Detroiters in the late 1960s and early 1970s was higher than for any black community in the United States, even though 120,000 black Detroiters still lived in slum conditions during the riot era.

Five decades later, as Detroit grew even poorer, the percentage of residents owning homes has dropped, especially among whites. The foreclosure crisis of the past decade hit both white and black Detroiters hard, and cost taxpayers millions. The Detroit News reported last year that there have been 65,000 mortgage foreclosures in the city since 2005. Of those, 36,400 homes (56 percent) were blighted or abandoned, with some 13,000 slated for demolition, at a cost of $195 million.

MEDIAN INCOME: AFRICAN AMERICANS LOSE GROUND

1970
White $5,889
Black $4,354

Black income as a percentage
of white: 74%

Detroit's loss of prosperity is reflected in the abandonment of its once-busy thoroughfares. Above: East 7 Mile Road.

Bridge photo by Bill McGraw

Just after the riot, when black Detroiters' income was three-quarters of white income, the black community in Detroit was one of the most prosperous in the nation. Today, though, black income in Detroit has slipped to a little more than half of white income, as African American elsewhere have made gains. According to the Pew Research Center, since the 1960s, household-income growth for African-Americans has outpaced that of whites. Median adjusted household income for blacks is now 59.2% that of whites, up slightly from 55.3% in 1967 (though in dollar terms the gap has widened).

PEOPLE IN POVERTY: TWICE THE PERCENTAGE AS 1967

1970
White 12.4%
Black 20%

2014
White 39.7%
Black 41%

Man sleeping on sidewalk in the mid-1960s.

Courtesy of Walter P. Reuther Library

By 1967, poverty was the focus of "wars" at both the federal and local levels. President Lyndon Johnson convinced Congress to pass extensive anti-poverty legislation in 1964 and 1965. Even before the federal government stepped in, Detroit Mayor Jerry Cavanagh, who took office in 1962, became one of the first big-city bosses to enact programs to help poor residents, including medical and dental services, job banks and work training. After the riot, though, critics raised questions about the effectiveness of Cavanagh's anti-poverty efforts.

Aggressive government action to help the poor faded over the decades, and Detroit continued to lose jobs at a steady rate. For many years, Detroit has been one of the nation's poorest big cities. By 2016, the city had received international attention for its large number of home foreclosures and water shutoffs, and a study this year published in The Journal of the American Medical Association showed life expectancies for Detroiters — 77.7 years — ranked among the shortest for residents of U.S. cities.

Unemployment overall
1967: 6.2%
2016 (April): 9.1%

Long lines for unemployment checks in Detroit in the 1980s.
....
Courtesy of Walter P. Reuther Library

Sources: U.S. Bureau of Labor Statistics; U.S. Census; "Violence in the Model City," by Sidney Fine; "Divided Detroit," Reynolds Farley, Sheldon Danziger and Harry J. Holzer; *New York Times; Detroit Free Press.*
....

UNEMPLOYMENT: FAR HIGHER TODAY

The flight of industry from Detroit began after World War II, and the city lost 165,000 jobs between 1955 and 1963. But for a few years before 1967 the local economy boomed, and Mayor Jerome Cavanagh's manpower programs helped keep the unemployment rate low. Joblessness, though, was growing again by the time of the civil disturbance in 1967. The city's 6.2 unemployment rate then was the highest it had been in five years, according to historian Sidney Fine. Unemployment in the riot areas was about twice the overall city rate, and among youths ages 18 to 24 the rate was estimated to be between 25 and 30 percent. In academic studies of the disturbance, experts found a strong correlation between self-identified rioters and unemployment, especially for rioters who had been out of work for a long time.

By 2016, five more decades of deindustrialization had taken its toll, especially on black Detroiters. High-tech jobs have grown, but there has been no major job creation for the low-educated. In April of 2016, city unemployment stood at 9.1 percent, far higher than 1967, but a dramatic improvement for the decade. In 2009, city unemployment exceeded 25 percent and just two years ago stood at 16.3 percent. But the black/white disparity remains. In 2014, the most recent year available for racial comparisons, 4.9 percent of white men in Detroit were unemployed, compared with 14.4 of black men. White women unemployment was at 5.3 percent, black women at 11.9 percent. §

The 1967 riot through the eyes of business owners: Who fled, who stayed and why?

By Robin Schwartz | Jewish News

Vivid memories remain in the hearts and minds of Jewish business owners nearly 50 years after the 1967 Detroit riot — from the jarring sound of broken glass, to the sight of flames and smoke rising over the city, heavily armed military members swooping in, and the fear that ultimately drove tens of thousands of white Detroiters to relocate to the suburbs.

The five days of disorder, destruction and violence that brought commerce to a standstill from July 23-27 left 2,509 stores looted, burned or in ruins. The majority of damaged businesses were grocery stores, 611 in all, along with hundreds of cleaners and laundromats, clothing stores, department stores and furriers, liquor stores, bars and lounges, drugstores, furniture stores and other businesses.

Before the riot, Jews owned 78 stores or 15 percent of the businesses in the 12th Street area alone. By Day Five of the uprising, only 39 Jewish businesses remained.

"A lot of people believed that black-owned stores were spared because a lot of black store owners wrote 'Soul Brother' on their doors, but that really isn't true. Stores were looted indiscriminately," says author Danielle McGuire, an associate professor of history at Wayne State University. McGuire is working on a book about the infamous slaying of three black teenagers by police at the Algiers Motel during the riot.

"People [who rioted] really saw all store owners as exploitative, with high prices, high interest rates and a pattern of treating certain customers with disrespect," McGuire said.

Some businesses remained intact simply because workers took up arms to protect the properties. Bruce Colton of Bloomfield Hills remembers that all too well.

"Six months before the riot, my dad bought a case of shotguns," he said. "I asked him, 'Why are you doing this?' and he said, 'Times are not looking so good and someday we may need them.' Boy, was he right!"

Colton's father, Sol, and grandfather, Isaac Liebson, founded Domestic Linen Supply in 1926. The company had one plant at 3800 18th St. in Detroit; they laundered and supplied uniforms, towels, aprons and linens to Detroit businesses. In 1967, Domestic Linen Supply employed about 100 people, half of whom lived in nearby neighborhoods.

"When the riot started, we picked up some key employees and went down to the facility and set up with the shotguns to protect the property," Colton says. "They were burning down buildings all around us. There was no law and order."

Colton says his family gave workers "war pay," which amounted to triple their normal wages, so they would sit up on the roof with shotguns. Some stayed overnight. A building across the street, which the company used for storage, burned to the ground. But, the main plant remained unscathed.

"There were a lot of people who wanted to save the business so they would have a job," Colton says. "You'd fire off a shotgun blast or two and people went someplace else."

Bruce Colton of Bloomfield Hills, his family started Domestic Linen Supply in 1926. Its headquarters is in Farmington Hills; a processing facility remains in Detroit.

Lester Shindler, 89, of Farmington Hills owned Parker Brothers Shoes and Menswear at 12th Street and Clairmount, next door to the "blind pig" Detroit Police raided, touching off the riot.

David Broner of West Bloomfield recalls his family's business, Broner Glove Company, was not damaged, he believes, because it was next to three schools. The building was sold to a church that wanted to expand. Broner Hat and Glove is now based in Auburn Hills.

....

Douglas Bloom of Birmingham recalls the business of his uncle, Imerman Industries, was guarded by paratroopers because they had a government contract to make bomb fuse adaptors. The company chose to remain in Detroit, moving operations to another of its buildings at Mack and Connor.

....

When the smoke cleared, a number of the company's customers were shut down. But business and deliveries slowly started up again. Domestic Linen Supply received some insurance money for their burned storage building but opted not to rebuild; instead, they turned the land into a parking lot. Colton watched as a steady stream of residents and businesses moved out of the city, but his company stayed. They still have the Detroit location to this day.

"We had a lot invested in that facility, all of our machinery," he says. "It would have cost a fortune to move it."

Now called Domestic Uniform Rental, the multi-generational family business continues to grow and thrive. Today, their headquarters are in Farmington Hills; they own eight processing facilities, including the Detroit plant, and have customers in 14 states.

NEAR GROUND ZERO

Parker Brothers Shoes and Menswear was near ground zero — at 12th Street and Clairmount Avenue — in the building right next to the unlicensed, after-hours bar (known as a "blind pig") raided by police, touching off the riot. Lester Shindler, 89, of Farmington Hills, owned the store. His father-in-law, Julius Parker, had opened it decades earlier.

"We sold men's, women's and children's shoes, men's clothing, shirts and pants, suits, and we had a shoe repair," he recalls. "Leather shoes, made in America, were $7.99, Levis were $2.99, and work shirts were 99 cents."

On the night of the riot, as buildings burned all around them, Parker Brothers was one of the only stores to remain standing. But, the solid brick structure with three ground-level storefronts and three second-floor apartments sustained plenty of damage.

"Four days later, we came back and the whole store was completely destroyed," Shindler says. "The windows were all broken. The display cases were smashed. They looted us and we lost everything."

Determined to remain in business, Parker Brothers reopened with the help of nine employees. But, the shop could not afford the high cost of insurance. Shindler sold clothing and shoes from the corner of the burned-out block for about a year until 1968, when the Rev. Martin Luther King, Jr. was assassinated. Police told him that afternoon, "You'd better leave." He did. And that was the last time he saw the store intact.

"By the time I got home, Guardian Alarm called," he recalls. "They said, 'They hit your store. Don't come back.'"

Shindler never returned. He donated the building to the city for a recreation center (he would drive by years later only to find it had been demolished) and bought Brody's Camp Supplies and Custom Printing in 1969. His loyal workers were left without jobs. He remained in touch with several families and attended the funerals of two former employees, but the lack of an adequate bus system to transport people from the city to the suburbs and back prevented them from moving with him. The same was true for many businesses.

"Most [of our employees] didn't have transportation," Shindler says. "One came and worked for me for a little while, but it just didn't work out."

Brody's moved from Oak Park to West Bloomfield in the late 1970s. Today, it remains a popular business on Orchard Lake Road, owned and operated by the Shindler family.

HEADING FOR THE "HILLS"

David Broner of West Bloomfield said his family's business, Broner Glove Company, was spared because of its proximity to three schools across the street. The business, founded in 1933 by his grandfather, Harry, and father, Barney, was located at 7501 Linwood St. During the riot, he could see military personnel and equipment stationed on the nearby school football fields.

"They were patrolling the streets because of the unrest. They had the National Guard with all kinds of Jeeps and equipment," he says. "Our building didn't have a scratch — but, when we went back to where our customers were, a lot of them were completely destroyed."

At the time, Broner had two sons, ages 2 and 4. He remembers the fear and uncertainty that kept many people home from work.

"My wife didn't want me to go to work — we really didn't know what was going on," he said. "There was a curfew and people were afraid to go out. It was an unsafe time; people were scared and they didn't know what to do — were they going to reopen or close? Did they have insurance? Could they afford to reopen?"

Amid the turmoil, the Broners received an offer they couldn't refuse. The church next-door was thinking about expanding and wanted to know if they were selling their building. The family sold and moved the business to Ferndale, keeping their workers onboard. Relatives, including Harry and Goldie Broner and an aunt and her husband who lived in the building, moved to Oak Park. In 1978, the company relocated to Troy.

Now called Broner Hat and Glove, with a division known as Broner Glove and Safety, the business employs 60 people and is based in Auburn Hills. David's son, Bob, and daughter, Stephanie Miller, are the fourth-generation owners.

"[The riot] set everything back," Broner says. "It set people who lived in those neighborhoods back, many lost jobs. They had no place to shop. It set businesses back because they had all this damage."

DODGING BULLETS

Stanley Imerman, owned a business called Imerman Industries that manufactured auto parts, brake products and more. It also had a government contract to make bomb fuse adaptors. As a result, paratroopers guarded the factory during the riot, preventing any damage.

"We were Up North and, as we flew in, I saw through the window that the city was on fire, everything was burning," recalled Douglas Bloom of Birmingham, Imerman's nephew. "When I got to work in the morning, I had to call up the Chrysler missile plant and tell them we needed protection. This big Army truck showed up and they dropped off these paratroopers and we cooked food for them. They didn't have ammunition in their guns, but nobody knew that."

The 100,000-square-foot, two-story building at Lafayette and Mount Elliot was not damaged. But, Bloom, a graduate of Mumford High School, had his own brush with danger one evening while driving home from work.

"I was driving home on Jefferson and they were shooting from a building on the right side of the street," he said. "A bullet went right above my car — I heard it zing by — and I was in traffic. The police said, 'Get out of your car and get behind it,' which I did. They used rifles to take out the shooter. They just shot into the window [where the gunfire was coming from] and there was no more shooting in the street. I got back in my car and went home."

Within a few days, the family had decided to move their entire operation to Mack and Conner, where they had another building. But, they made a conscious decision to remain in Detroit.

"A lot of our employees took a bus to work," Bloom says. Making it easy for them to get to work "was important to us. We already had a factory on Mack and Connor, so that's why we chose to stay in Detroit."

The company went out of business in the 1980s, but Bloom took all the workers and formed another manufacturing company, Bar Processing, which he sold in 1999. §

Historical data was taken from *Violence in the Model City* by Sidney Fine (Michigan State University Press; 1989).

Image credit: Michigan.gov

Income inequality in Michigan: Biggest gap is not in metro Detroit

Stephen Henderson | WDET

The top one percent of the nation's earners make more than 25 times that of the bottom 99 percent. That's an average yearly income of about $1 million versus about $46,000, according to the Economic Policy Institute. The issue of income inequality in America has sparked major protests in recent years and has shaken up political campaigns. Bernie Sanders waged a serious challenge to Hillary Clinton's bid for the Democratic nomination on a message of "political revolution" predicated on closing the income gap.

Here in Metro Detroit, we see the stark contrast between rich and poor all over the place. A new report from the Economic Policy Institute shows in one area in Michigan, the rich make about 25 times more than the poor.

But it's not in Southeast Michigan, which includes Detroit. It's in Grand Rapids.

Grand Rapids Urban League president and city Commissioner Joe Jones said, like Detroit, Grand Rapids is seeing, "substantial growth within the city, particularly in the urban core where you have a renaissance of sorts." But he says that's forcing low-income people out of their neighborhoods.

"What we see is I think what's being seen around the country, which is poverty changing zip codes," said Jones. People outside of Grand Rapids sometimes paint too rosy a picture of what's happening. "We have abject poverty here. We have pockets of poverty that equate to, or if not greater than, inner-city Detroit... I think the resources are here to create a greater sense of equity. But it's going to take work."

Michigan League for Public Policy Vice President Karen Holcomb-Merrill noted that one reason the report shows a larger income gap in Grand Rapids is simply because the top one-percent of earners in Grand Rapids is making more money than the top one-percent in Detroit.

"These are both cities in Michigan, and the widening gap isn't an accident. And a lot of it is tied in to statewide policy and decisions that have been made," said Holcomb-Merrill. She cites Michigan's "regressive" tax structure as an example.

"As long as we have this huge gap of haves and haves-not, we continue to have here in Michigan a lot of folks that are not a part of the so-called economic recovery or not a part of what Gov. Snyder calls 'the comeback state.' There are a lot of families and folks in both Detroit and Grand Rapids that are not experiencing that comeback," she said. §

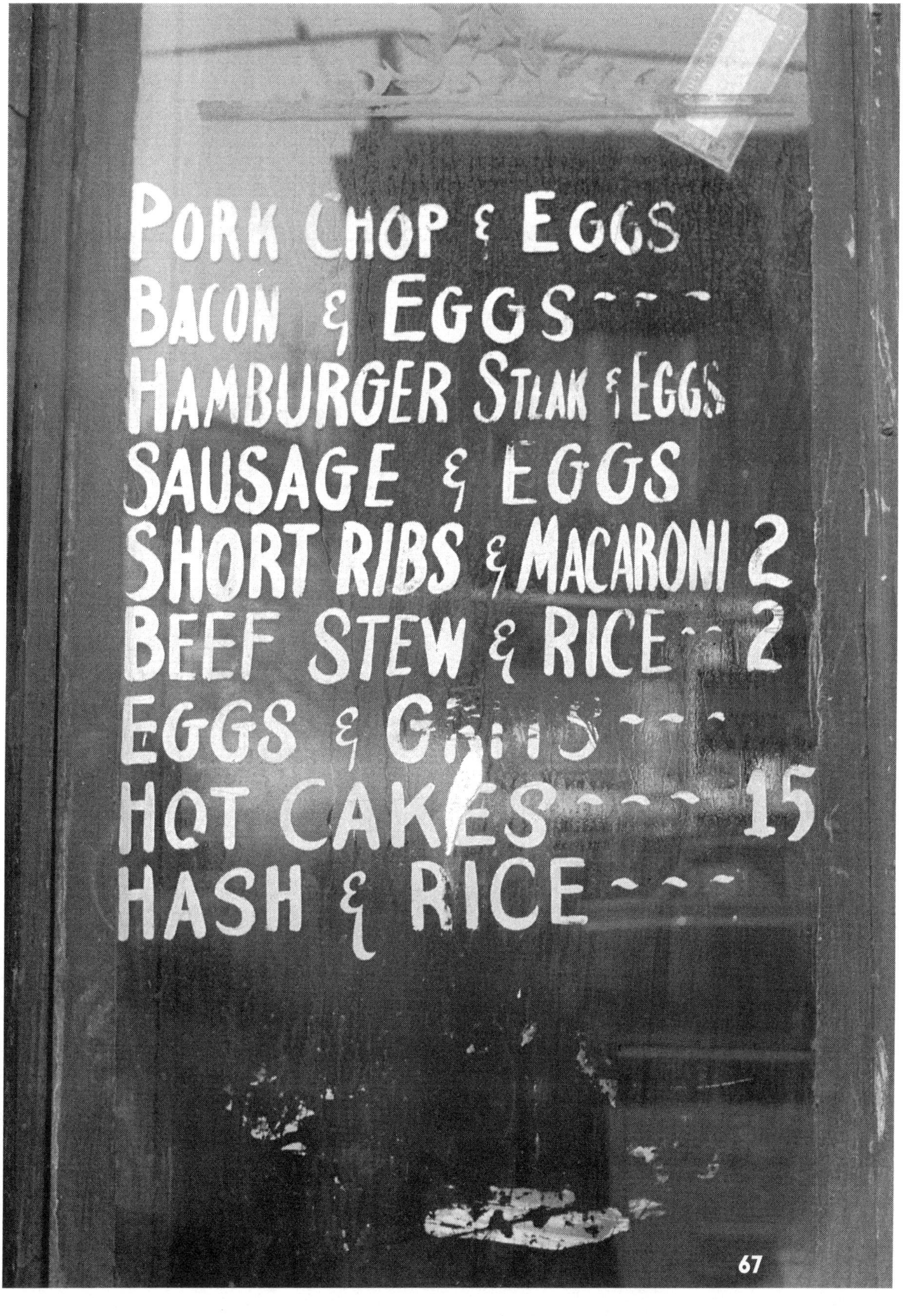

PORK CHOP & EGGS
BACON & EGGS~ ~ ~
HAMBURGER STEAK & EGGS
SAUSAGE & EGGS
SHORT RIBS & MACARONI 2
BEEF STEW & RICE~ ~ 2
EGGS & GRITS~ ~ ~
HOT CAKES~ ~ ~ 15
HASH & RICE~ ~ ~

CHAPTER 4

GRACE

"The events of the summer of 1967 are in large part the culmination of 300 years of racial prejudice…(T)oday's problems can be solved only if white Americans comprehend the rigid social, economic, and educational barriers that have prevented Negroes from participating in the mainstream of American life." – Kerner Commission

DJC Poll: Black and white optimism on Detroit-area race relations

By Bill McGraw | Bridge Magazine

Though their sprawling region had long wrestled with segregation, and racial violence has dominated national headlines, about half of all metro Detroit residents say local race relations today are generally good, according to a summer 2016 survey on racial attitudes by the Detroit Journalism Cooperative.

Seven-in-10 metro Detroiters say they believe race relations in the greater Detroit area are getting better or at least have stayed the same over the past 10 years, the poll found, a significant contrast from results of national polls, in which most Americans say race relations nationally are volatile and getting worse.

Despite the relative optimism, the poll also reveals differing perspectives between metro Detroit's white and black residents, especially when it comes to the ways African Americans perceive how race continues to affect their daily lives, from suspicious looks directed their way to being unfairly stopped by police.

More than half (57 percent) of blacks interviewed said they have had an experience within the past year in which a person acted suspicious of them because of their race. Only 8 percent of whites reported a similar race-based incident. And one-in-three African Americans reported being unfairly stopped by police in the past 12 months — again, they said, because of their skin color.

Though generally positive on overall progress on race relations in the region, African Americans are slightly more pessimistic than whites in the local poll. While 56 percent of whites say race relations are currently good, 47 percent of blacks feel that way.

CHAPTER 4
RACE

A region evolves

Reynolds Farley, a retired University of Michigan sociology professor and expert on the city's racial demographics, said one reason local blacks and whites appear to be getting along better might be that metro Detroiters of all races and ethnic groups are increasingly working, living and socializing together.

"I think it's easier for people in the Detroit area to have some familiarity with race relations than people in a state like Maine, where there's virtually no black population at all and the information comes from seeing violent incidents on television," Farley said.

"We have a higher degree of integration in metro Detroit, believe it or not, than a lot of metropolitan areas."

Tama Smith, a 57-year-old white woman from Livonia who was part of the survey, said in a follow-up interview that she based her belief that race relations are improving on what she sees when she visits Detroit.

"The feeling I get in Detroit — it seems like a much closer community," she said. "Black and white people hanging out together in the casinos, Greektown, sporting events."

By large margins, metro Detroiters say the region has made progress in race relations since the violence of 1967, which devastated large swaths of the city 49 years ago this week, altering the course of Detroit's future and changing the city's image in the eyes of the world.

Dozens of cities across the United States were hit by disorders that summer, though Detroit's was by far the most serious in terms of lives lost — 43 — injuries and damage. People in the poll are split on how Detroit has recovered from that summer compared with other cities; about four in 10 overall say Detroit's recovery has been worse.

The poll, of 600 Macomb, Oakland and Wayne County residents, was conducted by the Lansing-based EPIC-MRA survey-research firm from July 14-19, during the ongoing national furor over police shootings of African-American civilians, and retaliatory attacks on officers in Dallas and Baton Rouge. The poll had a margin of error of plus or minus 4 percent.

The survey's sponsor was the John S. and James L. Knight Foundation, a major funder of the Detroit Journalism Cooperative, which includes The Center for Michigan's Bridge Magazine, Detroit Public Television (DPTV), Michigan Radio, Detroit public radio station WDET and New Michigan Media, a partnership of ethnic and minority newspapers.

Walter P. Reuther Library of Labor and Urban Affairs

72

A long view on race

According to the poll, fewer than three-in-10 metro Detroiters believe race relations are getting worse in their region, a significant difference from a New York Times/CBS poll in July 2016, a few weeks before the DJC survey, in which six in 10 Americans overall said race relations nationally were deteriorating.

Another national survey by the Pew Research Center earlier in the same summer also found Americans more pessimistic than metro Detroiters. Pew, like the New York Times, found six-in-10 African Americans believe race relations are generally bad; 45 percent of whites agreed.

In the local poll, fewer than three-in-10 African Americans and only three-in-10 whites said they believe race relations in metro Detroit are generally bad.

The poll found that while black and white respondents agree race relations are an important issue, neither group put race at the top of their societal concerns. By a wide margin, the people surveyed ranked two other areas — education along with crime, drugs and violence — as the region's most critical issues.

Race joined the economy and jobs as issues on a second tier of priority, though African Americans, Arab Americans and Hispanics placed slightly more importance in bettering race relations than whites.

Notably, a majority of black and white metro residents said that black Detroiters have made progress on economic conditions and jobs since 1967. In fact, as the DJC previously reported, the city's poverty and unemployment rates are worse in 2016 than at the time of the disturbances.

Farley, the demographics expert, predicted the lack of jobs will continue to be an obstacle to improved race relations in Detroit, a city whose downtown core is buzzing with new businesses and development as its overwhelmingly black and impoverished neighborhoods outside downtown struggle.

"We once had in the Detroit area a stable black middle class based on the auto industry jobs and other auto industry jobs," Farley noted. "And those jobs are still around, but they are far less numerous and as a result the overall economic status of blacks has hardly improved in the last 30 or 40 years."

"How do you create more jobs for people who have moderate level of skill?"

Two worlds, separate and unequal

But the hopefulness found in parts of the metro Detroit poll is tempered by the findings of how race continues to play a painful role in the daily lives of many African Americans.

Sixty-five percent of blacks polled said their race makes it harder to succeed in life, though slightly more than four in 10 of the African Americans said they had not personally experienced discrimination in recent years.

Still, large numbers of black residents say they have experienced negative encounters because of their race even within the past year, including people treating them as if they are not smart because of their skin color.

Seven-in-10 African Americans said they believe blacks are treated less fairly than whites while applying for a loan or mortgage, and a similar number said discrimination plays a role in restaurants, the workplace or in searching for a good job. Strikingly, and by large margins, whites were less likely to say blacks receive more negative treatment.

In keeping with Farley's theory that proximity eases racial strains, metro Detroiters offered generally sunny views of workplace harmony. When asked to describe how people of other races treat them at work, nearly 70 percent of African Americans, 64 percent of whites and 75 percent of Hispanics and Arab Americans agreed that relations were very or somewhat friendly.

EPIC-MRA President Bernie Porn noted several reasons for cautious local optimism generally on race relations — Detroit has emerged from bankruptcy, the central city is booming, and mostly black Detroit elected to look past race by electing a white mayor, Mike Duggan, in 2013.

"That speaks to a more positive view of racial issues," Porn said of Duggan's election. "Things have changed. People are very positive about the direction of Detroit in our surveys."

Shirley Stancato, president and CEO of New Detroit Inc., the racial justice coalition formed immediately after the violence of 1967, said she wasn't surprised to see a different assessment of progress on race from Detroit-area residents.

"I think this community has really worked harder at getting to know people who are different and getting to know them. Worked harder at it because I believe folks have felt we needed to work harder."

Neighborhood changes

Another factor could be demographic trends: black Detroiters continue to move to the suburbs, which are far more integrated than they were 20 years ago, a development underscored by the establishment of an NAACP chapter this summer by black and white residents of the increasingly diverse Grosse Pointes, for decades a nearly all-white stronghold bordered by Detroit on two sides.

Add to that whites trickling into Detroit to live and work, a reversal of a 60-year-old trend of white flight that resulted in Detroit being more than 80 percent African American and 12 percent white. That flight produced the most unusual demographics in big-city America: All other major cities have a much more balanced mix of races and ethnic groups, with generally less acrimony between city and suburbs.

While many metro Detroiters in the poll said race relations have improved since 1967, it is difficult to compare sentiments today precisely with the way southeast Michigan residents felt five decades ago.

Sidney Fine, the late University of Michigan history professor whose 1989 "Violence in the Model City" is an influential book on the riot, wrote that the difficulty arises because pollsters of that era used different samples of people and asked different questions.

In June 1968, one survey of Detroiters found that 42 percent of black respondents and 42 percent of whites thought the two races had grown "closer together" in the year since the riot.

Two decades later, another survey found 59 percent of blacks and 47 percent of whites felt the races were "closer together."

Writing in the late 1980s, Fine concluded: "Detroit remained a racially polarized community twenty years after the great riot."

With this new survey, there are signs that Detroit and the region that surrounds it has made halting progress in the ensuing years.

Excerpts from polling on racial attitudes in metro Detroit

A survey on race by the Detroit Journalism Cooperative in metro Detroit revealed a rough consensus among African-American and white residents that progress has been made on racial attitudes in the region since the violence that convulsed the city in 1967; and further, that there is optimism for more progress in the future. But the survey of 600 residents in Wayne, Oakland and Macomb counties in July 2016 also exposed a chasm in the race-related biases and slights that infiltrate the lives of black residents, yet barely register in the daily experience of most whites. Here are some questions asked of metro residents, 90 percent of whom identified as either white or African American:

OVERALL, WOULD YOU SAY THAT RACE RELATIONS IN THE GREATER DETROIT AREA ARE GENERALLY GOOD OR GENERALLY BAD?

	WHITE	BLACK
Generally good	56%	47%
Generally bad	27%	31%
Both/neither	13%	17%
Undecided/refused	5%	5%

THINKING ABOUT THE PAST 10 YEARS, DO YOU THINK THAT RACE RELATIONS IN THE GREATER DETROIT AREA HAVE BEEN GETTING BETTER, GETTING WORSE, OR STAYING ABOUT THE SAME?

	WHITE	BLACK
Better	33%	22%
Worse	23%	28%
About the same	42%	47%
Undecided/refused	2%	4%

DO YOU THINK THAT RACISM AND RACE RELATIONS IS AN IMPORTANT, SERIOUS CONCERN JUST AMONG BLACK PEOPLE, MOSTLY AMONG BLACK PEOPLE, AN EQUALLY IMPORTANT CONCERN AMONG BOTH BLACK PEOPLE AND WHITE PEOPLE, MOSTLY A CONCERN AMONG WHITE PEOPLE, OR IS IT A CONCERN JUST AMONG WHITE PEOPLE?

	WHITE	BLACK
Among blacks	17%	40%
Equal in both races	78%	55%
Among whites	1%	2%

COMPARED TO 10 YEARS AGO, DO YOU THINK THAT WHITE PEOPLE HAVE BECOME MORE POSITIVE IN THEIR ATTITUDES TOWARD BLACK PEOPLE, MORE NEGATIVE, OR, HAVE ATTITUDES OF WHITE PEOPLE TOWARDS BLACK PEOPLE NOT REALLY CHANGED ONE WAY OR THE OTHER OVER THE PAST 10 YEARS?

	WHITE	BLACK
More positive	44%	26%
More negative	13%	25%
No change	36%	43%

COMPARED TO 10 YEARS AGO, DO YOU THINK THAT BLACK PEOPLE HAVE BECOME MORE POSITIVE IN THEIR ATTITUDES TOWARD WHITE PEOPLE, MORE NEGATIVE, OR, HAVE ATTITUDES OF BLACK PEOPLE TOWARDS WHITE PEOPLE NOT REALLY CHANGED ONE WAY OR THE OTHER OVER THE PAST 10 YEARS?

	WHITE	BLACK
More positive	23%	24%
More negative	30%	26%
No change	31%	42%

OVER THE NEXT FIVE YEARS, DO YOU THINK THAT RACE RELATIONS IN THE GREATER DETROIT AREA WILL IMPROVE, GET WORSE, OR STAY ABOUT THE SAME?

	WHITE	BLACK
Improve	50%	41%
Worse	16%	24%
Same	27%	29%

OVERALL, WOULD YOU SAY THAT YOUR RACE OR ETHNICITY MAKES IT HARDER TO SUCCEED IN LIFE, MAKES IT EASIER, OR, WOULD YOU SAY IT REALLY DOES NOT MAKE A DIFFERENCE ONE WAY OR THE OTHER?

	WHITE	BLACK
Harder	14%	65%
Easier	27%	2%
No difference	56%	30%

OVER THE PAST FEW YEARS, WOULD YOU SAY THAT YOU HAVE PERSONALLY EXPERIENCED DISCRIMINATION OR BEEN TREATED UNFAIRLY BECAUSE OF YOUR RACE OR ETHNICITY? IF YES, WOULD YOU SAY THAT IT HAS HAPPENED REGULARLY, OCCASIONALLY FROM TIME TO TIME, OR ONLY ONCE?

	WHITE	BLACK
Regularly	5%	15%
Occasionally	13%	37%
Once	4%	3%
Never	77%	43%

PLEASE TELL ME IF YOU BELIEVE YOU HAVE EXPERIENCED ANY OF THE FOLLOWING THINGS IN THE PAST 12 MONTHS BECAUSE OF YOUR RACE OR ETHNICITY...

PEOPLE ACTED AS IF THEY WERE SUSPICIOUS OF YOU?

	WHITE	BLACK
Yes	8%	57%
No	91%	41%

PEOPLE ACTED AS IF THEY THOUGHT YOU WERE NOT SMART?

	WHITE	BLACK
Yes	11%	55%
No	88%	43%

YOU WERE TREATED UNFAIRLY IN HIRING, PAY OR PROMOTION?

	WHITE	BLACK
Yes	11%	28%
No	87%	66%

WOULD YOU SAY THAT YOU HAVE MANY FRIENDS WHO ARE OF A DIFFERENT RACE THAN YOU ARE, ONLY A FEW FRIENDS, ONE OR TWO, OR, DO YOU NOT HAVE ANY FRIENDS OF A DIFFERENT RACE AT ALL?

	WHITE	BLACK
Many	45%	39%
Few	40%	41%
One or two	7%	10%
None	8%	10%

FOR EACH OF THE FOLLOWING PLACES OR SITUATIONS, PLEASE TELL WHETHER YOU AGREE OR DISAGREE THAT BLACKS ARE TREATED LESS FAIRLY THAN WHITES IN EACH ONE...

IN THE WORKPLACE?

	WHITE	BLACK
Agree	26%	68%
Disagree	58%	25%

IN STORES OR RESTAURANTS?

	WHITE	BLACK
Agree	27%	65%
Disagree	62%	29%

WHEN VOTING IN ELECTIONS?

	WHITE	BLACK
Agree	14%	44%
Disagree	72%	46%

IN FINDING A GOOD JOB?

	WHITE	BLACK
Agree	33%	73%
Disagree	50%	21%

AS YOU MAY KNOW, THERE IS AN ORGANIZATION CALLED "BLACK LIVES MATTER" THAT HAS BEEN PROTESTING SEVERAL SHOOTINGS OF BLACK MEN OVER THE PAST FEW YEARS, INCLUDING RECENT SHOOTINGS IN THE PAST COUPLE OF WEEKS, BY POLICE OFFICERS. BASED ON WHAT YOU KNOW OR HAVE HEARD OR READ ABOUT BLACK LIVES MATTER, DO YOU SUPPORT OR OPPOSE THE ACTIVITIES OF THIS ORGANIZATION?

	WHITE	BLACK
Support	34%	79%
Oppose	44%	7%
Undecided	22%	14%

A NUMBER OF CITIES OTHER THAN DETROIT WERE STRUCK BY WHAT HAS BEEN DESCRIBED AS RIOTS DURING THE SUMMER OF 1967. BASED ON WHAT YOU KNOW FROM PERSONAL EXPERIENCE, OR MAY HAVE HEARD OR READ, COMPARED TO OTHER CITIES, HOW DO YOU THINK DETROIT RECOVERED FROM THE RIOTS?

	WHITE	BLACK
Better	27%	24%
Worse	37%	44%
Same	28%	28%

BASED ON WHAT YOU KNOW FROM YOUR PERSONAL EXPERIENCE, OR HAVE HEARD OR READ ABOUT THE EVENTS THAT TOOK PLACE IN THE SUMMER OF 1967 IN DETROIT, WHICH OF THE FOLLOWING TERMS BEST DESCRIBES WHAT YOU THINK TOOK PLACE — A RIOT, A REBELLION, AN UPRISING, OR SOME OTHER WORD?

	WHITE	BLACK
Riot	61%	34%
Rebellion	12%	27%
Uprising	12%	24%

COMPARED TO 1967, HOW MUCH PROGRESS DO YOU THINK THERE HAS BEEN IN TERMS OF RACE RELATIONS IN THE GREATER DETROIT AREA?

	WHITE	BLACK
Progress	73%	63%
Little/none	22%	34%

COMPARED TO 1967, HOW MUCH PROGRESS HAS THERE BEEN IN TERMS OF ECONOMIC CONDITIONS AND JOBS FOR BLACK PEOPLE IN THE GREATER DETROIT AREA?

	WHITE	BLACK
Progress	60%	55%
Little/none	29%	41%

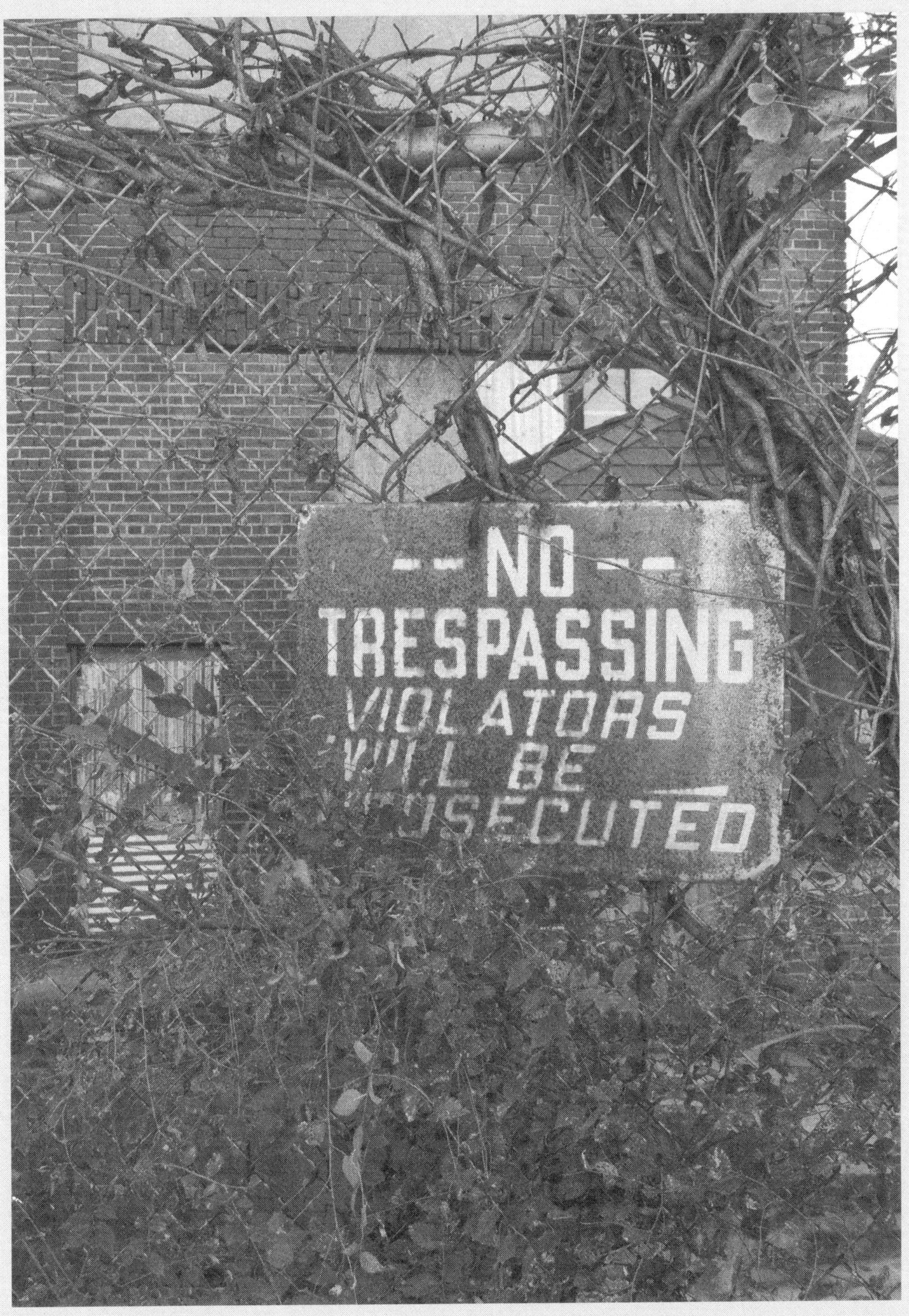
NO
TRESPASSING
VIOLATORS

Metro Detroit racial divide is widest over police

By Bill McGraw | Bridge Magazine

Nearly one-in-three African Americans (31 percent) in the metro area reported being unfairly stopped by police in the past 12 months, they said because of their skin color. By contrast, 5 percent of whites reported an unfair, race-or-ethnicity-based interaction with law enforcement.

While black and white metro Detroiters are finding common ground on racial progress, there remains a gulf, shaped by vastly different experiences, in how the two groups view police.

And nowhere are those differences laid more bare than in the divergent views on the protest movement known as Black Lives Matter.

Roughly eight-in-10 African-American residents in metro Detroit express support for Black Lives Matter, according to a survey on racial attitudes conducted in July 2016 for the Detroit Journalism Cooperative. BLM arose three years earlier in reaction to the killing of unarmed blacks by police. Black support for the group (79 percent strongly or somewhat support BLM) is more than double that among white metro-Detroiters, 34 percent.

HOW TO EXPLAIN THE DIFFERENCE?

Both blacks and whites have been witness to heavy media coverage, including video, in recent years of police killings of African Americans, as well as the apparently retaliatory killings of police officers. But as DJC polling reveals, blacks in and around Detroit report far more personal experience being unfairly treated by police than whites.

One Detroiter surveyed, a 52-year-old African American from the city's east side who asked to be identified only as LaMar, told the DJC that police regularly hassle him when he ventures to the suburbs to shop at stores not available in Detroit.

"I don't experience the harassment within the city limits nearly as much," he said. "In fact, it's rare. In the suburban areas, where unfortunately I'm forced to shop, I am accosted by police, and I fear for my life."

The survey shows that nearly one-in-three African Americans (31 percent) in the metro area reported being unfairly stopped by police in the past 12 months, they said because of their skin color. By contrast, 5 percent of whites reported an unfair, race-or-ethnicity-based interaction with law enforcement.

The poll, of 600 Macomb, Oakland and Wayne County residents, was conducted by Lansing-based EPIC-MRA and had a margin of error of plus or minus 4 percent. The poll's prime sponsor is the John S. and James L. Knight Foundation, which is also a major funder of the Detroit Journalism Cooperative.

The split along racial lines echoes polling nationally, sentiments apparently fueled by vastly divergent experiences interacting with police in white and African-American communities. The differences stand in contrast with the general consensus among black and white metro Detroiters that there has been progress in race relations in the region and that it will continue into the future.

Only seven percent of African Americans in metro Detroit said they oppose Black Lives Matter, a movement that has also become a contested rallying cry, which whites often replace with "All Lives Matter" or, when it comes to memorializing police officers, "Blue Lives Matter." Many whites (and some blacks) have taken issue, too, with what they believe are overly militant tactics by BLM protesters.

Forty-four percent of whites and 30 percent of Arab Americans and Hispanics voiced opposition to the BLM movement in the local survey.

"There's a huge pushback in this country on Black Lives Matter," said Shirley Stancato, president and CEO of New Detroit Inc., the racial justice coalition, who is African American.

"It's unfortunate that in the county, if you say something like, 'Black Lives Matter,' then people think that you think that no other lives matter. Black Lives Matter was created to say that of all the things happening to African Americans in the country, our lives matter, also. It doesn't mean that our lives matter separately."

While the DJC poll was taken during a violent summer nationally and a contentious presidential campaign, southeast Michigan has been mostly spared the divisive, often videotaped accounts of police shootings that have roiled the country. As the DJC has reported, many suburban Detroit police departments have failed to keep pace with the racial transformation of the communities they protect.

In Detroit, abuse of the black community by the overwhelmingly white police was considered one of the chief reasons behind the violence in Detroit and many other U.S. cities in 1967.

In 1968, a report by the National Advisory Commission on Civil Disorders, known as the Kerner Commission, created by then-President Lyndon B. Johnson to study the causes of urban unrest, said: "(T)o many Negroes, police have come to symbolize white power, white racism and white repression."

With the 1973 election of Coleman Young, Detroit's first black mayor, the Detroit Police Department personnel and management slowly began to reflect the city's racial makeup. Mistreatment of citizens did not end, however.

It was not until earlier in 2016 that Detroit Police emerged from 13 years of oversight by the U.S. Justice Department over the shootings of suspects, unconstitutional investigative techniques and mistreatment of prisoners — some of the same issues that propel Black Lives Matter today.

The current Detroit chief, James Craig, has made further changes to try to better ensure police respect the rights of residents. Craig, who is African American, has enjoyed sky-high popularity among residents, previous polls have shown.

Still, as the DJC survey shows, police-community relations remain a sticking point for many African Americans in the region.

Asked if they thought police in their communities treats blacks better, worse or about the same as they treat white people, three-quarters of whites, but only half of African Americans, responded "about the same."

Nearly four-in-10 African Americans said "worse." There was little difference in responses between African Americans living in Detroit or the suburbs.

African Americans' feelings of being treated unfairly also extend to other parts of the criminal justice system in metro Detroit. Fifty percent of blacks surveyed in Wayne, Oakland and Macomb counties said the court system treats blacks worse than whites. §

Survey excerpts on police, Black Lives Matter

Roughly 1-in-3 black metro Detroiters said they have been unfairly targeted by police based on their skin color in just the past year. Perhaps as a result, far more African Americans voice support for Black Lives Matter than whites.

PLEASE TELL ME IF YOU BELIEVE YOU HAVE EXPERIENCED FOLLOWING IN THE PAST 12 MONTHS BECAUSE OF YOUR RACE OR ETHNICITY: YOU WERE UNFAIRLY STOPPED BY THE POLICE?

	WHITE	BLACK
Yes	5%	31%
No	95%	69%

OVERALL, DO YOU THINK THAT POLICE OFFICERS IN YOUR COMMUNITY TREAT BLACKS BETTER, WORSE, OR ABOUT THE SAME AS THEY TREAT WHITE PEOPLE?

	WHITE	BLACK
Better	1%	2%
Worse	15%	37%
Same	74%	49%

AS YOU MAY KNOW, THERE IS AN ORGANIZATION CALLED "BLACK LIVES MATTER" THAT HAS BEEN PROTESTING SEVERAL SHOOTINGS OF BLACK MEN OVER THE PAST FEW YEARS, INCLUDING RECENT SHOOTINGS IN THE PAST COUPLE OF WEEKS, BY POLICE OFFICERS. BASED ON WHAT YOU KNOW OR HAVE HEARD OR READ ABOUT BLACK LIVES MATTER, DO YOU SUPPORT OR OPPOSE THE ACTIVITIES OF THIS ORGANIZATION?

	WHITE	BLACK
Support	34%	79%
Oppose	44%	7%
Undecided	22%	14%

Robert Cattone (17), Anthony Saraceno (18), Armando Mastantuono (20) and Aldo Trani (16) wait in a Detroit Police Station. The youths were convicted in the murder of Moses Kisks, an African American man, during the 1943 race riot.

Kisks was gunned down as he waited for a streetcar at the corner of Chene and Mack on Detroit's East Side. The racially motivated murder was particularly heinous due to a lack of remorse from the youths and their statements that they simply "wanted to have some fun."

Walter P. Reuther Library of Labor and Urban Affairs

White people find it hard to talk about race

By Lester Graham | Michigan Radio

A Washington Post-ABC News poll shows the majority of Americans think race relations are getting worse. Concern about race relations spiked shortly after the reports of white police officers killing black men. Since the poll, two black men have targeted and killed police.

If you're white, you might be surprised by increased racial tensions. If you're black, you know there's been tension all along.

"Prior to the video phones and video taping of police murder, it had been happening continuously from one generation to the next," noted Kwasi Akwamu, a small business owner in Detroit.

He said the only difference is technology and the internet.

"There has never been a period when we've never been lynched, we've never been slain in the streets for the suspicion of an act. I mean, those things — it's part of our history. It hasn't changed. It's just changed form," Akwamu said.

Police data bear that out. Police are not killing any more or any fewer black people than they have in the past. Cell phone video and the internet have just made us all more aware with sometimes gruesome scenes.

"For people of color, we always knew that happened," said Lauren Hood, who works with companies on diversity training.

"I've been stopped by the police for no reason. My mom referred to it as 'Driving While Black,' DWB. The media attention to those stories just brought it out to everyone who wasn't a person of color. Like, welcome to our world. We've always known that that was a problem. Now, everybody else knows," Hood said.

She said for many white people, no matter their politics, race is a very difficult thing to discuss.

85

"It's a place most people aren't willing to go and particularly people that are liberal and think they're doing the right thing all the time. So, if you think you've already arrived at some point of consciousness and someone tells you you're not quite there yet, you're not ready for it. You get defensive," she explained.

One of the tools to avoid that defensiveness is an online test. The Harvard implicit bias test takes about ten minutes and helps determine if you are unconsciously biased.

"When you present the data to people that way, it absolves them from responsibility. So, you say, 'Ah, see what the data have shown: that you have an unconscious bias. It's not you; you're not choosing this way of thinking. It's something unconscious that existed operating in the background that you might not be paying attention to when you're making decisions and it shapes how you see the world, but you're not conscious of it all the time,'" Hood said.

But, only a fraction of the population is going to take that test, resulting too often in a failure to understand the plight of others.

"Especially right now with so much national news and conversation happening around these topics too, you'd think more people would be plugged in, but personally my experience is that some of my closest friends, who I think are progressive, don't necessarily spend a lot of time thinking about these issues," said Claire Nelson.

Nelson runs an organization called Urban Consulate. The facility is housed in a historic house in Midtown Detroit. The Urban Consulate brings together economic developers and investors with people who want to start new small businesses in Detroit. Recently it also began to invite the people who live in those neighborhoods. The idea is to sit down and talk. Nelson calls the discussions "parlors."

"Often times when you're talking about development and investment, the people speaking about that are the people who are representing the banks or commercial interests," Nelson said. Most of those voices are white.

"And so, we're trying to flip that a little bit and have the voices leading conversations be more community based, or who are creative artists, or who've been around a little longer, can share some history and context," Nelson said.

Nelson says including more diverse voices — people of color, people who live in the neighborhoods, hearing their concerns about economic development — has been an eye-opener for some people, including her.

She says in the past, she saw segregation as a matter of the white suburbs versus the black city.

Now she says she can see segregation up close, at the neighborhood level because of those talks.

Supporting new stores and other developments in the fast changing area of Detroit has been her work for several years. She says she'd been blind to some of the problems that would cause the neighborhood problems such as rising rents.

"I think it's been a growing awareness and an ongoing conversation that's helped me see things that I didn't see five years ago. Examples, I guess would be sources for stories or speakers that we've had who've for whatever reason have had a lot of courage in order to call out some stuff, some BS, and some hypocrisy that I think I've been immune to, perhaps, before this," she said.

Nelson says being closer to people of color, having private conversations about race, noting their observations have helped her grow.

Longtime Detroit residents such as Kwasi Akwamu want to know whether the new white residents and business owners truly are going to be invested in the city.

"How many people are living in the neighborhoods where black people are going through it? I mean, are their children going to the schools, the same challenged schools that we are going to? Are they really experiencing what we experience and ready to mobilize for real change because of that experience," Akwamu asked.

He wants the new white population to recognize the struggles of the current residents.

"It's a frustration which sees the disparities, but doesn't fully understand them," he added.

Lauren Hood said the only way to fix racism is to talk to people who are subject to it. "In order to move forward, we just have to be fearless in having these conversations." §

Real talk about race

By Chastity Pratt Dawsey | Bridge Magazine

It's not easy to talk about race in America. Even in this post-Obama election era, or perhaps in reaction to it, candid conversation about racial attitudes can be like dancing across a minefield. Bridge Magazine and the Detroit Journalism Cooperative asked Detroit metro-area elected officials and activists to discuss race in their region. Some declined. But others, including activists who deal with race in their work, as well as a mayor who has seen the complexion of his community change, agreed to address racial attitudes, including their own.

Matthew Jaber Stiffler

MATTHEW JABER STIFFLER, 37, is research and content manager at the Arab American National Museum in Dearborn. His father is white. His mother was born in America and is of Lebanese descent. Stiffler said he was raised as, and thought of himself as, a white child. Other than noting that he was once followed around a mall for wearing a high school letterman's jacket that signaled that he lived in a working-class white neighborhood, not a rich one, Stiffler said he has never been the target of discrimination. That is, he said, until he reveals his heritage, where he works, or shows support for Arab causes.

IN ORDER TO IMPROVE RACE RELATIONS, IS IT MORE IMPORTANT TO FOCUS ON WHAT DIFFERENT RACIAL AND ETHNIC GROUPS HAVE IN COMMON, OR WHAT IS UNIQUE ABOUT EACH?

STIFFLER: Tough one. I think trying to build common ground sometimes is easier for the majority population because they feel better when they're told how everybody is like them. But it actually can do more harm to minority populations who are made to feel that they are only valuable in that they reflect the majority population. So I would say a starting point is rather to be more educated about the differences and where they come from and what they are.

DOES THE COUNTRY NEED TO CONTINUE MAKING CHANGES FOR BLACKS TO HAVE EQUAL RIGHTS WITH WHITES AND, IF SO, ARE YOU SKEPTICAL THAT SUCH CHANGES WILL EVER OCCUR?

STIFFLER: Not skeptical they will occur, but skeptical about the timeline. We'll probably get to black-white equality at the expense of other minorities, increased xenophobia against immigrants especially from Muslim countries, I think. Whenever you have an enemy or a perceived enemy in a majority population ... it's a shame there always has to be some sort of scapegoat.

ARE RACE RELATIONS BETTER NOW THAN IN 1967?

STIFFLER: No, they're not. I'm a historian. I deal in narratives. I'm not from (Michigan) but I've been here for the last 12, 13 years. I hear people talk about what Detroit used to be like mostly from a white perspective. "Oh, we used to go to Detroit on Saturdays and go shopping and eat at these restaurants and then all of sudden we couldn't go anymore." They mourn that as a loss. Unfortunately, they mourn it as a loss because they think it

was taken away from them by black people and black people's inability to manage the city or, you know, play nice. We applaud revitalization of Detroit, the idea that progress is through new freeways, progress is through new investments in certain industries that only reach a small section of the people, not thinking broadly about the region. I see a really bad trend where we're at now in the so-called revitalization of Detroit that allows people to capture this nostalgia for what Detroit was in the pre-1967 — or what they think it was pre-1967 — and they think the movements we have now happening in the city will somehow get us back there.

WHAT WILL GET US BACK THERE, TO A MORE VIBRANT AND PROSPEROUS DETROIT?

STIFFLER: There's a palpable racism that operates now that assumes the population living in Detroit right now could not possibly fix it on their own. The story should be we need to give the residents that are there, the residents that have stuck it out, give them the tools and the abilities to prosper instead of letting them die out so that land speculators can come in and buy up entire neighborhoods for future potential use.

SO RACIAL ATTITUDES HAVEN'T CHANGED?

STIFFLER: No, I think people are still in this idea that it's black people's fault that Detroit is the way it is and only through reinvesting in certain industries that are run by a small cadre of people is how we're going to get to the Detroit they think they remember from pre-'67.

WHERE DO WE GO FROM HERE? HOW DO WE GET HONEST DIALOGUE? ARE WE EVEN HAVING DIALOGUE?

STIFFLER: I think honest dialogue is happening with what people call the movable middle. The portion of the people that either haven't formed an opinion yet or have formed an opinion, but with accurate information are willing to alter that opinion. You're never going to reach the hard liners through dialogue. You might not ever reach them in any capacity.

HOW DO PEOPLE ACHIEVE PROGRESS IN SUCH A STRATIFIED COMMUNITY?

STIFFLER: You have to be intentional about it. That's the problem with our school districts, our school districts are based upon tax revenue so the nicer the area, which tends to be the whiter the area, the better the schools and those people don't interact with other ethnicities. You see that in Dearborn. Fordson High School is like 98% Arab American; those kids don't hang out with African Americans and Latinos who live just across the street in some cases. As a society you have to be very intentional about fighting through the structural racism boundaries and barriers that are enacted. I don't think it's racist to want to hang out with people that have the same experiences as you. The racism comes in when you think that everyone else is inferior.

Jim Fouts

JIM FOUTS, 73, is the white mayor of Warren, in Macomb County just north of Detroit. In 1967, many residents in Warren feared violent disturbances in Detroit would come to their neighborhoods if African Americans moved there, he said. African-American Detroiters in recent years have moved to Warren by the thousands, but they didn't bring riots with them. The formerly white city now also is home to at least four mosques, said Fouts, a former high school teacher. He talks about what it was like growing up in Warren in the 1960s, and taking office after controversial Mayor Mark Steenbergh, who was charged in 1996 with racial intimidation and assault for allegedly choking an African-American teen and calling him the N-word. He was later acquitted.

WHAT KIND OF CHANGES DO WE NEED HERE TO MAKE SURE EVERYONE IS ON THE SAME, EVEN PLAYING FIELD?

FOUTS: There has to be a focus and an infusion of public funds and private funds to rebuild the neighborhoods in Detroit and then have more police presence so that people feel safe and they want to stay in the city. Now, if the city builds up, it becomes a model. Then that eliminates some of the stereotypes that exist today amongst whites about the city of Detroit.

A few weeks back, I went to see a concert at the Detroit Symphony Orchestra to salute (composer and conductor) John Williams. And on the way back, I took I-75 home. There was construction. I got off on McNichols, which people call Six Mile. I took McNichols east. I was shocked about how bad it was. I didn't' see one police car on McNichols.

I saw a lot of abandoned homes and I saw some unsavory characters. I even saw one (white) woman who obviously was a crackhead walking. It was pretty dismal. I then took Ryan Road to Eight Mile Road. Same thing. Now if you want people to achieve equality, then you need to take care of your neighborhoods and you need to give some hope. And hope in the neighborhoods come in two things: blight and crime. If you will not clean up the neighborhoods, there will not be pride ... that affects the people in the neighborhoods and that affects the perception of the city of Detroit.

The last several (Detroit) mayors, in my opinion, have been mayor of downtown Detroit. They have not been mayor of the city of Detroit. By the way, I have a radio program that I do on WADL and I get listeners who are mostly African American and say to me, "Mr. Mayor, what you said about your trip, the other mayors should've said. They don't care."

WARREN IS FAR MORE DIVERSE NOW THAN IN 1967 — UP FROM NEARLY 200 AFRICAN AMERICAN RESIDENTS TO 15-TO-20 PERCENT AFRICAN AMERICAN. HOWEVER, THE HIGH SCHOOLS ON THE SOUTHERN PART OF TOWN ARE MOSTLY BLACK. WHY?

FOUTS: I would say all the schools in Warren are integrated. You're right, the two south (Warren) high schools are heavily African American, but that is because of the population change. A lot of Detroiters have become refugees. I know the mayor of Detroit probably wouldn't like me saying that. I asked them, "Why did you move to Warren from Detroit?" Schools, blight and crime. They need to clean up the neighborhoods in Detroit. The state and the federal government need to have some sort of Marshall Plan.

> The biggest problem for people is the fear of the unknown. When you know your neighbor and your neighbor is Arab American, Muslim, Chaldean, African American, Asian American, it's hard to dislike someone you know. It's easy to dislike a group. It's not easy to dislike an individual.
>
> —— Jim Fouts

IT APPEARS THAT WHEN THE BLACK STUDENTS MOVED INTO WARREN FROM DETROIT, WHITE STUDENTS USED (THE STATE'S) SCHOOL CHOICE (LAW) TO MOVE TO OTHER SCHOOLS.

FOUTS: Don't confuse all black schools with necessarily the absence of white neighborhoods. The schools are hard up financially so they're taking kids from Detroit and Hazel Park and wherever.

DOES THAT MAKE THE WHITE WARREN RESIDENTS SAY, "WE DON'T KNOW THEM, THEY'RE FROM DETROIT, LET'S NOT GO TO SCHOOL WITH THEM; LET'S GO TO SCHOOL A LITTLE FURTHER NORTH?"

FOUTS: That I don't know. I can't hypothesize on that. What I can do is answer this way: Southeast Warren tends to be older people. And they no longer have children and those schools had to advertise and open up to Detroiters because the schools were becoming depleted. You have a lot of students who are from Detroit. Not all, but a significant number. So I cannot say that that's racism.

ARE RACE RELATIONS GENERALLY GOOD, OR GENERALLY BAD?

FOUTS: Today, I can say that I do not know someone who would openly say a racially disparaging word. I can say that among young people there is an acceptance. If you compare today with even 20 years ago I think there's been great progress. If anything inflamed racial attitudes it was the (1967 Detroit) riots. As time has evolved, things have changed. Racial disparity is just not acceptable. Now what's in the heart and mind of every person, I can't say.

I go back to Warren. I appointed the first African-American fire commissioner. Right now, four out of nine members of the planning commission are African American. This city is changing. If a Warren mayor 30 or 40 years ago had appointed an African American it would've been an uproar. Today, I did it and that was it. Now, my predecessor Steenbergh said some pretty harsh statements. He said that he wanted to build a fortress to keep people of Detroit out of Warren. He also wanted to prevent Arabs (actually, Iraqi refugees) from moving into Warren.

YOU HAVE A RADIO SHOW ON WADL WHICH BILLS ITSELF IN DETROIT AS THE LARGEST VOICE FOR AFRICAN AMERICANS, SO YOU HAVE CONSISTENT INTERACTION WITH AFRICAN AMERICANS FROM DETROIT. GROWING UP, HOW WERE YOU TAUGHT ABOUT RACE RELATIONS AND HOW HAS THAT EVOLVED OVER THE YEARS?

FOUTS: Let me start with some criticism about my upbringing and some positive things. Number one, in education we didn't learn a lot about African Americans and that was the fault of the education system. I heard about (George) Washington Carver and people like that, but for the most part African Americans were missing from the history books. That was wrong.

Watching television, not a lot of African Americans. The positive thing is my mother was a saleswoman at Sears in Highland Park. I never heard my mother say anything disparaging about African Americans and I really didn't hear my dad, although I think my dad was conservative.

We didn't grow up with the N-word or anything like that, but I don't think my dad would've openly welcomed African Americans. I don't think if they moved in the neighborhood he would've been the first to greet them and tell them, "Welcome to the city." In general, there was an absence of African Americans in my life except my mother had friends who worked with her at Sears. I went away to college and had friends who were African Americans. At that time there was civil rights (protests) and Vietnam. I think my sister and I grew up with an absence of intolerance. I think college and mixing with other students and growing up in a turbulent time period affected my thinking.

WHAT SITUATION OR CURRENT EVENTS CRYSTALLIZE THE TRUTH ABOUT RACE RELATIONS TODAY?

FOUTS: Integration is best when it's an evolving and comfortable thing. I have African Americans in my neighborhood. I have some Muslims. The whole secret to people getting along is getting to know each other. My mother way back in the '50s got to know black people she worked with. She became good friends with a black woman. It wasn't my mother's idea, but she worked with her and became good friends. That's what does it, not government mandates.

SO IN WARREN, THE FEAR OF THE UNKNOWN, OF OTHER RACES, IS BEING ERODED BY FAMILIARITY DUE TO PROXIMITY?

FOUTS: Familiarity breeds understanding and open-mindedness. The biggest problem for people is the fear of the unknown. When you know your neighbor and your neighbor is Arab American, Muslim, Chaldean, African American, Asian American, it's hard to dislike someone you know. It's easy to dislike a group. It's not easy to dislike an individual. Individuals make a difference in changing group attitudes. America is becoming multicultural, multiracial. It's evolving and I would say, maybe not in my lifetime, but that's going to happen.

Kenneth Reed

KENNETH REED, 48, spokesman for the Detroit Coalition Against Police Brutality, is African American and a resident of Detroit. This interview took place in the midst of the recent spate of police-involved killings nationwide — after police killed an African-American man in Baton Rouge and another in Minnesota and after a shooter in Dallas killed five police officers; but before another shooter, in Baton Rouge, killed three police.

ARE RACE RELATIONS GENERALLY GOOD OR GENERALLY BAD NOW?

REED: Generally, bad, at this point. Whenever our (African American) children come down into the downtown area — be it (the Detroit) RiverWalk or inside downtown or in other places, Cass Corridor — which I call Cass Corridor, I'll never call it Midtown — they're made to feel uncomfortable in their own city and that is a problem.

WHO MAKES THEM FEEL UNCOMFORTABLE?

REED: Well, I think some of it is the merchants, some of the residents and policy in terms of law enforcement.

DO YOU THINK RACE RELATIONS IS A MAJOR CONCERN JUST AMONG BLACK PEOPLE OR OR IS IT EQUALLY AS IMPORTANT TO WHITE PEOPLE?

REED: With black people it is a very big concern, particularly in the city. When they go to venture into the inner-ring suburbs, more often than not they're profiled by law enforcement agencies. As far as with whites, I think it may be a concern. I think their concern is more out of fear of the unknown. If you get to know someone you're not comfortable being around every day then I think some of those fears would be alleviated.

DO YOU THINK WHITE PEOPLE'S ATTITUDES TOWARD BLACK PEOPLE HAVE BECOME MORE NEGATIVE OR MORE POSITIVE?

REED: I think particularly in the last 18 months it's become more negative because of mainstream media. I think a lot of rhetoric that has been espoused by the candidates, particularly by the Republican Party and (Donald) Trump in particular has made it popular to espouse feelings that may have otherwise been kept to themselves. He seems to have made it cool to say what we really feel. What we really feel.

DO YOU THINK BLACK PEOPLE'S ATTITUDES TOWARD WHITE PEOPLE HAVE BECOME MORE POSITIVE OR MORE NEGATIVE?

REED: I would say black people are a very forgiving race, not that we always go seeking friendship or what have you. We tend to be more open minded in terms of wanting to have good race relations overall. That's not always the case on the other side. I think it's a thing where blacks would not be opposed overall to having good race relations but it comes to a trust factor. There's a lack of trust in terms of blacks being able to trust whites, because history depicts (justification for mistrust).

SO YOU THINK THE RIFT BETWEEN WHITES AND BLACKS IS THAT WHITES FEAR BLACKS AND BLACKS DON'T TRUST WHITES?

REED: It's a trust factor. A lot of it stems from law enforcement and the inner-ring suburban enclaves. And when you feel left out in your own city, you feel as if you've been colonized all over again.

HOW HAS THE RELATIONSHIP BETWEEN DETROITERS AND POLICE CHANGED SINCE 1967?

REED: Only through our work where we got federal intervention through the (U.S. Justice Department obtaining a) consent agreement (to monitor and curb police abuses), the way the Detroit Police Department works has shifted. It has changed to the extent where we're not being clubbed upside the head. A deaf man is not being killed because he's holding a rake in his hand. That portion has stopped. (I'm) cautiously optimistic in terms of moving forward. There's more of an open dialogue, but I think it's only because there was federal intervention.

YOU SAY THE FEDERAL INTERVENTION CHANGED THE WAY THE DETROIT POLICE DEPARTMENT WORKS. HOW? WHAT SPECIFICALLY HAS HELPED MAKE EACH SIDE MORE TRUSTING?

REED: It's an uneasy trust. I believe what has happened is with the federal oversight some of the policies have changed. You're not housing people who are witnesses to a crime against their will at the lock up; things mandated through the consent agreement are being carried out by the department. That has brought about a certain degree of trust between the citizenry and the department. I think also when the Detroit Police Commission got their full powers back, we got police commissioners now who are out in the community more. That has helped as well. The commission is mostly black.

WHAT ABOUT THE ADVENT OF COMMUNITY POLICING?

REED: We had officers assigned to community policing. They would get to know the residents, the children, the block club presidents, your community organization presidents. They would be known in the community. And bear in mind when it was really going well that's when we had the residency requirement (where city employees had to live in the city). When I was growing up, I had a police officer live next door to me. We had police officers living in the community.

SO THEY WERE NOT UNFAMILIAR WITH THE COMMUNITY?

REED: Now with residency (requirement) gone in the year 2000, you got police officers who may not look like me or you. They don't understand the culture, they don't understand the youth as well as they should and that is what led to the problem.

YOU'VE SAID IN THE PAST THAT SOME OFFICERS TODAY HAVE REPLACED "PROTECT AND SERVE" WITH "COMMAND AND CONTROL." WHAT ARE THE LEADING CAUSES OF POLICE BRUTALITY?

REED: Now you have command and control. It used to be when officers come on shift they may be 50-150 calls in the hole from the previous shift. If you go from scene to scene you don't have time to decompress, everybody reaches a breaking point. And if you already have a predisposed bias in terms of the people in the city you're supposed to serve and protect, if you already have preconceived biases and you're not really accustomed to being around black people you might believe the stereotypes that they're poorly educated, they already don't like cops, that these people, they're animals more or less. They may not even view us as human. And they bring that on the job. That's a recipe for for disaster.

COULD WHAT HAPPENED IN DALLAS — POLICE BEING TARGETED AND KILLED — HAPPEN HERE?

REED: Absolutely. Come around my house on New Year's Eve and you'll know what I'm talking about.

SO THERE'S A LOT OF AMMUNITION AND GUNS IN THE NEIGHBORHOODS, BUT IS THERE AN ATTITUDE THAT IF THERE'S ONE MORE INCIDENT WITH THE POLICE SOMEONE IS GOING TO SNAP AND GO AFTER POLICE HERE?

REED: Unfortunately you have young people who may not necessarily have the economic opportunities, they might not have the educational opportunities. They may have already been exposed to the criminal justice system.

PEOPLE WHO DON'T HAVE OPPORTUNITIES DON'T HAVE ANYTHING TO LOSE AND COULD CHOOSE TO TAKE DRASTIC ACTIONS AGAINST POLICE TO MAKE A POINT?

REED: Once you get that felony on you, your employment opportunities generally just dry up. Who's to say? A crew out here might just decide, "Let's take it to them (police)."

Bear in mind in 1967 you had lack of economic opportunity. Housing was a problem. Police brutality, harassment was a problem.

THE KERNER COMMISSION (A PRESIDENTIAL COMMISSION APPOINTED TO FIND THE ROOT CAUSES OF DISTURBANCES AND RIOTS ACROSS DOZENS OF AMERICAN CITIES IN 1967) SAID THAT WE WERE MOVING TOWARDS TWO NATIONS: ONE WHITE, ONE BLACK, SEPARATE AND UNEQUAL

REED: We're looking at this again today. What's changed?

YOU TELL ME.

REED: We're going right back into that.

HOW IS THAT TRUE WHEN WE HAVE PLACES SUCH AS WARREN WHICH HAD 182 BLACKS IN 1967 AND NOW IT'S 15 OR 20 PERCENT BLACK? THERE'S SO MUCH INTEGRATION, AT LEAST IN THE INNER RING SUBURBS. HOW ARE WE STILL MOVING TOWARD A NATION DIVIDED, SEPARATE AND UNEQUAL?

REED: Look who's left behind when the middle class left the cities. Those who can't get out. The poor who can't get out. Then there's those of us who have an undying love for Detroit. We're going to be here regardless. We stayed and prayed. Now with the new Detroit, a lot of (African-American) people are made to feel they're not even welcome in their own city. Those attitudes from the parents sometimes they permeate right down to the children and young adults.

YOU SAID YOU WEREN'T SURPRISED BY WHAT YOU SAW IN DALLAS — IS THAT BECAUSE VIOLENCE BEGETS VIOLENCE?

REED: You have some young people who have the mindset that, "I'm not going to sit there and let you put a billy club upside my head. You're not going to sit up here and just tase me for no apparent reason and you're not going to just sit up here and continuously shoot us without some type of repercussion." So everything reaches a boiling point and it's starting to boil over. As they say, pressure busts the pipe every time.

DO YOU THINK WHAT HAS HAPPENED WITH THE POLICE INVOLVED SHOOTINGS (OF BLACK CIVILIANS) WILL MAKE PEOPLE CONFRONT THEIR OWN BIASES OR MAKE THEM MORE BIASED?

REED: I think it will make people more biased. The outright racist-type attitude towards black people is going to escalate. I strongly feel that. So we could be in for a long, hot summer. There's going to be some hardened attitudes behind this.

FIVE YEARS FROM NOW, WHEN THERE ARE EVEN MORE WHITES LIVING IN THE CITY, AFTER YOU SEE MORE PEOPLE FROM DETROIT WHO ARE BLACK MOVING OUT PUTTING PEOPLE IN CLOSER PROXIMITY TO EACH OTHER, WILL THAT HELP RACE RELATIONS?

REED: Leadership has to make the commitment that people get to know about each other. The fear of the unknown — that's where we're at. We're so fearful. I think some of it comes from the past in terms of what we learn from our forefathers and a race of people who have been oppressed as long as black people have since they came to the shores of America continue to be singled out.

You have a (state) legislature that comes with policies centered on the city of Detroit. A legislature that would split up a school district, withhold money; a legislature that will go out if its way to take away opportunity for children to have quality education all under the guise of reform. Reform what? I think people have a right to live out what their destiny is. They have a right to elect those who they want to govern them. Revolution is the hope of the hopeless. The times, things are not looking good right now. It's not a whole lot different (from '67). My uncle is 95 years old. He was working at Mack stamping in the middle of the rebellion (in 1967). He had to show his work ID to be able to move through the streets and not get shot. It could very well come back to that.

Adonis Flores

ADONIS FLORES, 28, is an immigrants rights organizer with Michigan United and a resident of Detroit. He said generations of his relatives found work in America under the Bracero Program, which allowed Mexican workers to come to America to help alleviate the labor shortage that occurred during World War II. Flores was born in Guanajuato, Mexico and was brought illegally to Detroit when he was nine. He supported the Dream Act, a bill that failed in the Senate in 2010. It would have granted undocumented immigrants who came to the U.S. as children the chance to become citizens if they attended college or joined the military. After the bill failed, President Obama signed an executive order that gave people like Flores a temporary work permit that allows them to remain in the U.S., though a recent Supreme Court stalemate may put that status in question.

ARE RACE RELATIONS GENERALLY GOOD OR GENERALLY BAD?

FLORES: Generally bad. I come from a very organizer-oriented definition of racism. I believe that there's structural racism and it is composed of three types of racism: personal racism, institutional and cultural racism. Overall, institutional racism and cultural racism are very prevalent. People let personal prejudices take over when making day-to-day decisions. We all do it. People do it unconsciously.

EXAMPLE?

FLORES: The school to prison pipeline. It's very, very obvious in schools where there are people of color whether Latinos or African Americans.

And in the immigration system, immigrants from countries that are usually populated by people of color tend to have a very difficult process to immigrate legally to the U.S. In Mexico, it takes 20 years. In countries in Europe people can get a visa to come to the U.S. in weeks or months or sometimes they don't need even need a visa they can come on a European passport. That's institutional racism. The Immigration and Naturalization Act put a limit on the numbers of persons admitted from each country. European countries had high limits, Latin American and African countries had very low limits.

GIVE ME AN EXAMPLE OF CULTURAL RACISM.

FLORES: When people have prejudices against an entire culture. For example, I was knocking doors when I first started working with Michigan United. I came across an

> It is definitely a very dark time in this country especially if you are a person of color. It doesn't matter what your educational attainment is. It doesn't matter what your zip code is. It doesn't matter that you obeyed all the rules and you've never been arrested. If you find yourself in the wrong place, at the wrong time, under conditions of an antsy, anxious police officer, this could be your last day. That is a reality our children see play out day after day.
>
> —— Monica Lewis-Patrick

undocumented immigrant who was really upset about Immigration and targeting the Latino community for deportations. One of the comments he said was, "I don't know why they are coming after us. We are just here working hard. They should go after the Arabs because they are the real terrorists." I don't think the person disliked all Muslims, but I think (American) culture overall is creating this picture, this message that Muslim Americans are terrorists.

IN ORDER TO IMPROVE RACE RELATIONS, IS IT MORE IMPORTANT TO FOCUS ON WHAT DIFFERENT RACIAL AND ETHNIC GROUPS HAVE IN COMMON OR WHAT IS UNIQUE ABOUT EACH?

FLORES: I think it's more important to focus on what we have in common. Low-income white Americans and low-income African Americans and low-income Latinos, most of the populations in these groups are blue-collar workers who are being exploited by multinational corporations. And instead of uniting our efforts for better working conditions, better wages, we're falling into the politics where we focus on our differences. That tends to create a fear between us and fear of each other. Divide and conquer.

HAVE YOU EXPERIENCED DISCRIMINATION OR BEEN TREATED UNFAIRLY BECAUSE OF YOUR RACE OR ETHNICITY?

FLORES: Yes, definitely. The most obvious was when I was applying to college back in 2006. I was a 4.0 GPA student, honor roll, lots of community service, dual enrollment at Wayne County Community College and a really good resume. I was accepted to all the universities I applied to, U of M in Ann Arbor, Michigan State, Wayne State. However, when it came to the interview with the admissions counselors, I didn't have a social security number and my application didn't have one (because he had entered the U.S. illegally). I was honest, I told them, "I am an undocumented immigrant. Can I still attend your institution?"

WHAT WAS THE RESPONSE?

FLORES: Their answer was, "You have to be admitted as an international student and pay three times a much." That was pretty much a nice way of saying, "No." It was institutional racism. If you are not a white American it is more difficult to get accepted.

In this instance, the excuse was my immigration status even though I'd been living here all my life, working, paying taxes and my great grandfather used to work here as a bracero (guest worker). We had a long, long heritage of living in the U.S. and working here and paying taxes in the U.S. I did not qualify. The laws make it extremely difficult for me to get documented. This was explicit, it wasn't hidden. When I hear comments like, "We are a country of laws," what I am hearing is a hidden message of, "A country of laws for white people that excludes people of color."

DOES THE COUNTRY NEED TO CONTINUE MAKING CHANGES FOR BLACKS TO HAVE EQUAL RIGHTS WITH WHITES AND, IF SO, ARE YOU SKEPTICAL THAT SUCH CHANGES WILL OCCUR?

FLORES: Definitely, changes need to happen to allow people of color to actually have the same rights as whites. I don't think these changes are going to happen soon. This is a generational commitment. Slavery was abolished in the 1860s. The Civil Rights Act was not signed until the 1960s. It's been over 50 years since the Civil Rights Act and there's still lots of disparities and discrimination. I'm skeptical change will happen for multiple generations.

CAN WHAT HAPPENED IN BATON ROUGE — POLICE KILLING SOMEONE, AND THEN A SHOOTER KILLING POLICE — HAPPEN HERE?

FLORES: I think it can happen anywhere. There's always going to be a loose radical. It's completely valid to be angry about people dying. If you're not, you're not human. The challenge is, how you deal with that? Do you seek structural change that will prevent further people from dying?

DO YOU SEE DIALOGUE HAPPENING THAT WILL BRING ABOUT CHANGE?

FLORES: I see honest dialogue coming from one side. Black Lives Matter is saying this (police killings) is a racism problem. The police say it's a training problem or lack of education in the community problem. It's the same with immigration. Latinos say (U.S. Citizenship and Immigration Services) is ripping families apart. They say, "We're a country of laws." That's not being honest.

ARE LATINOS BEING UNFAIRLY LEFT OUT OF THE GROWING CONVERSATION ABOUT HOW DETROIT TODAY COMPARES WITH DETROIT IN 1967 WHEN THE RIOTS HAPPENED?

FLORES: No, the Latino population was not nearly as large then as it is now.

Monica Lewis-Patrick

MONICA LEWIS-PATRICK, 50, president and CEO of We the People of Detroit, is African American and has lived in Detroit for the past decade. The group advocates for water rights, workers' rights and housing rights, among other issues, and opposes the state's controversial emergency manager law. Her family has lived in Detroit since 1952. Her uncle is Willie Horton, the famed former Detroit Tigers' star. We the People was among of 42 researchers and activist groups that collaborated on the upcoming book, "Mapping the Water Crisis: The Dismantling of African American Communities in Detroit," which is expected to be released Aug. 14.

ARE RACE RELATIONS GENERALLY GOOD OR GENERALLY BAD?

LEWIS-PATRICK: Generally bad because a majority of African-American cities in this state have been under what I consider a reptilian law called emergency management that … extracted from them not only their voting rights but their property, their pensions, control over their schools and now what we see playing out is the ability to even access clean, safe affordable water.

COMPARED TO 10 YEARS AGO, DO YOU THINK WHITE PEOPLE ARE GETTING MORE POSITIVE IN THEIR ATTITUDE TOWARD BLACK PEOPLE, MORE NEGATIVE OR NOT REALLY CHANGED?

LEWIS-PATRICK: I have seen a combination of persons who understand their privilege in being white in America and have been willing to take that privilege and set it aside to come in as an ally and supporter of the work that's being done at the community level. I have seen people come in — not only white, but black elitists — that have come

> I call Detroit beloved. When you see water hoses running from house to house, that's belovedness.
>
> — Monica Lewis Patrick

in and it's been more of extracting and examining and commentating as opposed to collaborating and working with Detroiters. And when I reference Detroiters it's the ones that live in the neighborhoods.

FLIP IT, COMPARED TO 10 YEARS AGO, DO YOU THINK BLACK PEOPLE ARE GETTING MORE POSITIVE IN THEIR ATTITUDE TOWARD WHITE PEOPLE, MORE NEGATIVE OR NOT REALLY CHANGED?

LEWIS-PATRICK: They're tremendously getting worse. We are constantly bombarded with negative messages, this whole narrative about Detroit being the murder capital, about black-on-black crime and our schools are failing and our inability to lead ourselves. All of these mantras are actually creating an atmosphere of more divisiveness, and a targeting of our community and our people. It is definitely a very dark time in this country especially if you are a person of color. It doesn't matter what your educational attainment is. It doesn't matter what your zip code is. It doesn't matter that you obeyed all the rules and you've never been arrested. If you find yourself in the wrong place, at the wrong time, under conditions of an antsy, anxious police officer, this could be your last day. That is a reality our children see play out day after day.

WHICH IS THE BIGGER PROBLEM – INSTITUTIONAL RACISM OR RACISM AGAINST INDIVIDUALS?

LEWIS-PATRICK: Institutional racism is the bigger problem because systemic processes have a broader reach. An individual being racist does not have the capacity to extract my grandmother's pension away from her. Or take my city into bankruptcy. Or deny my voting rights. But an institution does.

HAVE YOU EVER BEEN TREATED UNFAIRLY BY THE POLICE?

LEWIS-PATRICK: I can't say that I have. As a matter of fact, I've been treated very well by the police, especially those that understood that our activism was supportive of them keeping their pensions.

WAS THE RACIAL MAKEUP OF YOUR COMMUNITY A DECIDING FACTOR IN YOUR CHOICE TO LIVE THERE?

LEWIS-PATRICK: Not at all. What was a deciding factor to me was that I wanted to be part of repopulating the city with people who really care about the city. I wanted to work with people that were about creating land trusts and co-ops and opportunities to keep Detroiters invested in the comeback of the city so they weren't being excluded. And we wanted to do it through cooperative work and self-determination not wait for somebody to help us, not waiting on some rescue. I live on the east side off Outer Drive and Seven Mile.

I know on my block alone 22 people have had their water shut off. I have a mixture of white, Asian and blacks in my community.

IF HALF OF THE PEOPLE WHO MOVED INTO YOUR NEIGHBORHOOD WERE PEOPLE OF A DIFFERENT RACE FROM THE CURRENT RESIDENTS, DO YOU THINK YOUR NEIGHBORS WOULD MOVE?

LEWIS-PATRICK: No, I don't. It's my understanding from what I learn from ethnic groups that aren't black that one of the reasons they moved here was to be in a more diverse, more culturally-rich area.

SINCE 1967, WHAT PROGRESS DO YOU SEE IN THE DETROIT AREA? WARREN HAS A SIGNIFICANT AFRICAN-AMERICAN POPULATION, ISN'T THAT PROGRESS?

LEWIS-PATRICK: That was progress created by the pushout (of residents from the city). The progress I see is more at the grassroots level where we are growing our own souls, we are reimagining what community and policy should look like and unashamedly approaching entities with a boldness I don't think they'd seen before.

Our organization is led by five black women. Over 50 percent of my volunteers are young white kids from all over the state of Michigan. They come in once a month to participate in activities we are doing around water, education, freedom schools. To me that's where the connectivity is going to happen, not missionary acts of cutting grass and picking up trash. I think these are well-intentioned people, but it's still a missionary, privileged mindset that, "I'm going to do good in the 'hood," and then you go back to where you live. (Change) is going to be from people really connecting and understanding and allowing people in the community to lead and not be led.

HOW DID YOU DEVELOP YOUR RACIAL AWARENESS?

LEWIS-PATRICK: Growing up in northeast Tennessee, in Kingsport, I think my first encounter with racism was when I was 14 years old and they were attempting to get rid of African American studies and African American history in our high school. We mobilized and one of the things our teacher talked to us about was, "Don't just mobilize the black students because it's not enough of you to save the class. Mobilize with your white friends."

And through that initiative we were able to encourage our white friends not only to join the African American studies classes, but they also joined the social clubs. The Ebony Teen Kings and Queens, every black talent show, black history events, sit-ins we had in the school. I saw them be able to actually set aside their own issues and embrace the fact that (African Americans) were being disenfranchised or marginalized in our own school.

WHAT'S WRONG WITH MICHIGAN? HOW DO WE COMPARE TO OTHER STATES? IS THIS MICHISSIPPI?

LEWIS-PATRICK: It's Michissippi. As a matter of fact, it's Michissippi, goddam.

I call Detroit beloved. When you see water hoses running from house to house, that's belovedness. So when I talk about this city, I don't talk about its failures or inadequacies. I will speak on it if asked, or if you want my opinion for an analysis. But for me Detroit is still beloved in spite of what other people say. With its inequities, it's still beloved.

HOW DO WE TURN THE TIDE?

LEWIS-PATRICK: My job is to help black folk deal with internalized racism and oppression that keeps them from being all that they are capable of being. It has to start with us as ethnic groups doing some healing work and dressing each other up instead of dressing each other down. White people's problem is dismantling white supremacy because they are the only people that can practice that. §

Joe Louis Monument, Detroit.

Activists, academics, and authors on racial attitudes

By Lester Graham | Michigan Radio

"Dealing with the set of issues we still haven't figured out how to deal with is: what racism, what personal prejudice, what institutional racism means, what the connection is between poverty and race. There's nobody living in the suburbs, in my opinion, or even in the wealthy neighborhoods of the city who's white who hasn't benefitted from this idea of white skin privilege. That is a set of ideas that needs to be explored. It is a conversation that in my experience white people don't want to have. They just don't want to have it."

Sheila Cockrel, former member of the Detroit City Council

A presidential commission blamed white America for the racial uprisings and riots of the 1960s. The findings of the National Advisory Commission on Civil Disorders (the Kerner Commission) shocked many white Americans when they were released in 1968.

"What white Americans have never fully understood — but what the Negro can never forget — is that white society is deeply implicated in the ghetto. White institutions created it, white institutions maintain it, and white society condones it," the report stated.

Nearly five decades later we're still coming to grips with attitudes about race. We interviewed several people who either live in, write about, or study Detroit. We asked them about racial attitudes then and today...

"While there have been some advances, we can see in the present divisions of America right now between North and South, between Republicans and Democrats, between conservatives and so-called liberals or progressives, that many of the attitudes that were responsible for the racial explosions that the Kerner Commission was founded to help examine and hopefully prevent in the future, I mean, those attitudes are still with us."

PAUL LEE, historian and resident of Detroit

"If you looked at polling data from 1968, the year that the Kerner Commission report comes out, the level of white misunderstanding of the African-American experience and the level of racist stereotypes the whites carried about African-Americans was way higher than it is today. White attitudes have improved. The idea that whites, not all whites, but, a lot of whites could actually talk today about the idea of white privilege is a remarkable change from 1968 when most whites would never have thought of that concept. So, actually, white attitudes have changed. The remarkably depressing thing is they haven't changed as dramatically as they ought to have had over this extended period of time."

KEVEN BOYLE, Professor of History, author of "Arc of Justice," and Detroit native

....

"One of the conclusions of the Kerner report was that white racism was at work, was the cause of the upsets and the uprisings that we had. In fact the report stated that white society created it, perpetuates it, and sustains it. Those conclusions really upset many people throughout the country who felt they were being accused of being racist by a presidential commission. People still resist the notion that they are racist because they opposed desegregation. When we attempted to implement the remedies necessary to correct historic discrimination, there had to be some impact on the status quo. White persons who had established their positions and their conditions did so, in part, as a result of denial of rights to others."

NATHANIEL R. JONES, Assistant General Counsel of the Kerner Commission

....

"One of the astounding things that happens after this wave of civil rights rebellions is that even though the Johnson administration is passing civil rights legislation, he is simultaneously erecting an entire apparatus by which a war on crime is going to be fought for the next 40 years…and, so, for whites in places like Detroit they didn't have to come out in the streets and run a black family off of a block by 1972 because there were so many policies in place, policing policies and school district policies, that made white privilege cement in a way that allowed many white citizens to not see their own complicity in this racial injustice."

HEATHER ANN THOMPSON, author of "Whose Detroit?"

....

"In the past few years I've always assessed the white return to the city in the terms of how many people are living in the neighborhoods where black people are going through it. I mean, are their children going to the schools, the same challenged schools that we are going to? Are they really experiencing what we experience and ready to mobilize for real change because of that experience? Or are they coming with their padded positions, you know, good jobs where they can buy up these properties for dirt cheap and pay the back taxes, the back water bills because they already had the money saved up because they start from a good position. It's a frustration which sees the disparities, but doesn't fully understand them."

KWASI AKWAMU, former journalist, activist, small business owner

....

"The potential for the place to explode again exists because the grievances are still there. And they get worse sometimes because there is no avenue that is reliable for those who have these grievances to get them addressed in a way that they'll feel confident that they'll be treated as they should. No city at this point that I know of has something in place that is controlled by the civilian population that when you have a grievance against any situation involving the police department you can get your grievances addressed and you can trust the process that's engaged in those grievances to try to solve them. That doesn't exist. The Kerner Commission recommended that. It hasn't been done."

—— Joe T. Darden, professor of geography researching segregation, and inequality

Wait...there's an NAACP in the Grosse Pointes? Seriously?

By Keith A. Owens | Michigan Chronicle

Greg Bowens, the newly elected president of the newly created Grosse Pointe/Harper Woods NAACP, has become amusingly accustomed to that reaction. His vice president, John Clark, a retired white Detroit police officer who served on the force for more than 30 years beginning in 1971, has also experienced his share of raised eyebrows. But more importantly, both men have experienced a significant amount of support from fellow Grosse Pointers who are beginning to recognize the importance of diversity and inclusion in an area that doesn't exactly enjoy a reputation for either.

"I attended the Black Caucus sponsored by the Michigan Senate back in June, and there were a number of chapters from throughout the state there. We all had to go around and introduce ourselves, right? So I stand up in my blue blazer and club tie and say 'Hi, I'm John Clark from the new chapter in Grosse Pointes/Harper Woods. And it's like, 'you've got a chapter in Grosse Pointe Harper Woods?" said Clark, adding that after the initial shock, he received a warm welcome.

One of the first to sign up as a member, Clark confessed that his son describes his political leanings as somewhere to the left of Rachel Maddow. To Clark, who laughed when recounting the discussion, it's simply a matter of what's right versus what's not.

"For me it goes from something that can be accomplished to something that must be accomplished. The ongoing viability of diverse neighborhoods depends on there being, in my estimation, a resource like the NAACP available. It's important for the folks who are discriminated against, but it's also important for the rest of the community to have a place to go to when something has happened, or to report it."

The evidence of change, both Bowens and Clark agree, is that so many more residents now feel compelled to report incidents of discrimination and racism, as opposed to looking the other way.

"I think generationally the Pointes have changed," said Clark. "I like to believe my adult kids have a broader view, and a more open view, of social issues than the generation that I came from. But you can't take anything for granted. You can't just assume that change is going to occur. You have to be aware of events in the community that give you indications that well, you know, maybe we're not that bright shining city on a hill that we thought we were

According to Bowens, the impetus for the creation of Michigan's youngest NAACP branch came from Grosse Pointer Elaine Flowers who was one of the first black females to join the Detroit police force in the '70s. Becoming frustrated with her inability to find an organization that she felt could be used as a vehicle to help create programs for young people to come together around issues related to race relations, she reached out to Bowens for his assistance in establishing a local NAACP branch. Bowens agreed to help, and the two reached out to their contacts, creating a nucleus of like-minded individuals who would join them. Clark was one of the first to sign up. But then Flowers leaned on Bowens a little harder, urging him to consider becoming the first branch president. Once again Bowens agreed. Much of what bound them together was a belief that the Pointes had enough good people living there who believed in racial equity and who were equally anxious to help the area grow and divorce itself from its well-known racist and unwelcoming past.

As fate would have it, two separate and unrelated tragedies that took the lives of two young women last December during the holiday season served as an unexpected catalyst toward racial healing, not only for Grosse Pointe but for Detroiters as well. Paige Stalker was 16 years old, white, and a resident of Grosse Pointe. Christina Samuel was 22, black, and a resident of Detroit's east side. Stalker was killed on Dec. 22. Several days later, on New Year's Eve, Samuel was killed.

"She (Paige Stalker) was the young lady who was a senior at Grosse Pointe South and was in a car with a bunch of kids. White kids. And they went across…they were in Detroit, on the east side of Detroit…reportedly smoking weed, I don't know for sure, and the car was shot up and she was killed. And, at that same time, that was around the holidays, that same night, there was a young woman, she was a college student, about the same age, and she was murdered on the east side of Detroit, around Gratiot and 8 Mile. And people were saying that there was a lot of attention that had been paid to Paige Stalker's death, and that folks had stepped forward and offered a substantial reward leading to the person's capture …And so people all across the region were asking the question 'why are we paying so much attention to this one life and not the other?" said Bowens.

"It looked like this incident at first might increase the divisions in the area, but instead the two families got together and rose above the nonsense, and said we believe that both of our daughters' lives have value. I think it touched a lot of people to see how they were able to cut across lines of race, class and geography to say that there's enough love out there for everybody. And that was another example of the kind of spirit that was floating around in the Pointes that would allow people to come together under the banner of the NAACP."

Unfortunately, a more recent event in Grosse Pointe, also involving young people, involved a group of Grosse Pointe South high schoolers who created a racist video that circulated throughout the YouTube universe. Ironically, the school's principal, Moussa Hamka, is the first Arab American, who also happens to be a Muslim, to serve in such a capacity in any of the Pointes. When Hamka was first appointed he received death threats and racial taunts from around the country. Still, Bowens said he was encouraged by the response of the community which chose to confront the issue. And for the Pointes, Bowens said, this is progress.

"I'm gonna tell you the truth, man. Six years ago, five years ago when my oldest first went to high school? That kinda thing woulda never happened. They would have never said anything about it… The onus would have been on the black and Hispanic and white kids who would have been offended by seeing that and want to say something in class or in the hallway. And it would have been about their reaction as opposed to the incident itself that gave rise to it. The way that the community rose up and spoke out this time speaks volumes about the progress made."

But it isn't only among white Grosse Pointers where progress is required. According to Bowens, there is still too much attachment to symbolism over substance among some black critics who persist in viewing the Pointes through a 1950s lens as opposed to where the community is today. What happened not that long ago at the Grosse Pointe Farmers Market is a perfect example, he said.

"The brouhaha was that Grosse Pointers are doing things to keep Detroiters out. And there were people from both sides who hung onto that narrative and said 'that's the deal'. Now, I make no judgment about what's in people's hearts or anything like that. But I will say that while sometimes we can get distracted by symbols, and the symbolism involved in something, that we lose sight of the big picture.

"People put a kids' wagon in the middle of Kercheval with a sign on it that said 'Welcome to the Farmers Market'. And some people said, 'well that's just another example of Grosse Pointers trying to keep Detroiters out'. It was a welcome sign on a wagon."

"And so while we're going to be incensed about a wagon in the middle of the street and the symbolism that it represents. Even though it says 'welcome'. You're not incensed that there are no black cops on the police force for any of the five Grosse Pointes. There's not one black judge in any of the five courts for the Grosse Pointes. Or Harper Woods. You're not upset that there's only two teachers of color in the school system. You can have a kid that starts in kindergarten and goes all the way through 12th grade and never has a black teacher. Never see a black administrator. Never see a black secretary.

"I get the symbolism. What I'm saying is you're incensed about this over here, but you're comfortable with the real racism and the real discrimination. We can do something about this wagon, but teachers? Aw man, that's hard. The fact that the U.S. Supreme Court is more diverse than every elected body in the Pointes ought to have those same people coming out in the streets and registering people to vote." §

Arabs and African Americans: A complicated relationship between solidarity and bigotry

By Ali Harb | Arab American News

DETROIT — Arabs and African Americans appear to have a common struggle against white supremacy.

But when former State Rep. Rashida Tlaib participated in a protest demanding account-ability for the fatal shooting of an unarmed black man by a Dearborn police officer in December 2015, she received disparaging messages from prominent members in the Arab American community.

"Why are you there? Why are you against Chief (Ronald) Haddad? This makes the Arabs look bad. You guys shouldn't be there. This isn't your issue," Tlaib said she was told.

Tlaib was demonstrating after the death of Kevin Matthews. A month later, Dearborn Police fatally shot Janet Wilson, a black woman they accused of using her car as a weapon to run over an officer who stopped her.

"No one, I don't care what color, what faith, should be dehumanized like that," Tlaib told The Arab American News.

According to Tlaib, there is an anti-black attitude in Arab societies, even in the Middle East. "The anti-blackness that's happening across this world is real. It's very painful," she said.

She called for sincere efforts among Arab Americans to empathize and understand the state of Black America and when there are instances of police brutality.

The former state representative also urged individual Arab Americans to be self-aware and check their own bigoted instincts.

Relations between Arabs and blacks in Detroit are complicated and vary across generations and political leanings.

Racial tensions in Detroit exploded into riots in 1967. The Kerner Commission Report blamed "an increasingly disturbed social atmosphere" for the unrest. The report, which highlighted the roots of violent protests that broke out across several American cities, slammed racist patterns in white-black relations that date back to slavery.

Almost half a century later, complaints of racism and fears of white-led gentrification are rising in Detroit. Meanwhile, Arab Americans who gained a foothold in the city by expanding their small business ownership after chain stores left continue to struggle with their own identity, with some unsure of their place in the race construct and power structure.

In 2014, a prominent Arab American activist from Dearborn was arrested during a protest against police brutality in Ferguson, Missouri. Simultaneously, local Arab-American social media users were calling the protesters thugs.

A TRANSACTIONAL RELATIONSHIP

Amer Zahr, a comedian and adjunct law professor at the University of Detroit Mercy, said Arab-black relations have improved over the past few years as more Arab Americans are identifying as people of color.

"It's not where it needs to be yet," he said. "It needs to get a lot further, but I think that we're moving in that direction."

Zahr said there is terrible anti-Black racist trends among Arab Americans, who are counted as Caucasians on the U.S. Census.

Some of the anti-black bigotry in the Arab American community stems from that designation, Zahr said. "One of the main characteristic of whiteness in this country has been anti-blackness," he said. "So if you try to be white, you manifest that through racism."

He said that Arab Americans mainly interact with African Americans in a business setting. Local Arabs own hundreds of gas stations and liquor stores in Detroit. They serve a mostly black customer base.

"When you own a business in a low-income community that's not very mobile, and people have to come to you, that creates a position of power structure that's not very healthy for creating relationships that are good to social justice," he said.

Zahr added that the uneven, transactional nature of the interactions has fueled bigotry on both sides.

He urged businesses to contribute and invest in the neighborhoods they profit from. He rhetorically asked about the number of

gas station owners who are helping revamp neighborhood parks or sponsoring a local baseball team.

"If we did that, it shows that we respect the communities that we're in," he said.

Detroit is the Motor City, but 26 percent of its households are without a vehicle, according to a 2014 study by the University of Michigan. In the absence of a reliable public transportation system, that leaves gas station and party stores as the sole destination for some needed commodities.

"We do have a responsibility," he said. "We shouldn't just be crazy capitalists in an urban society. That's how you create more poverty, not less."

Zahr said that some Arab Americans try to overstate their Americanism by showing more solidarity with law enforcement agencies than their own communities.

"For black people, their skin color is their blackness," he said. "For us, our names are our blackness. Sometimes people might not know we're Arab until they hear our name. That's when the conversation changes with us. We are seen as 'other'; we are seen as foreign, as people who don't belong here."

A PERSONAL RESPONSIBILITY

Rana Elmir, the deputy executive director of the American Civil Liberties Union, said Arabs and African Americans have complicated interactions that vary among individuals because of the two groups' diversity.

"It's a fractured relationship," Elmir said. "Ultimately, it's a relationship that's based on transactions, as opposed to true understanding, solidarity, empathy."

Elmir has been outspoken in her calls for alliances between the communities.

She said building understanding takes time. Elmir encourages Arab and African Americans to ask themselves one question — "What would our joint community look like if we had solidarity, if we had effective partnerships?"

"My estimation is that we would be powerful," she said.

Elmir said she feels a personal responsibility to call out and correct bigotry within the Arab-American community, as an Arab-American activist.

"Racism, xenophobia, Islamophobia, homophobia, all come from the same pathology," she said. "It's all about ignorance and fear creating hate. If we can say anti-Arab sentiment is on the rise, but we can't see how racism, particularly anti-black racism and structural racism, has impacted black communities, it's difficult for me to justify how to ask other communities of color to come and support us."

Concentrations of Arab and black residents in Southeast Michigan are segregated by geographical frontiers. For example, Tireman Avenue, which marks Dearborn's northern border with Detroit, is also a demarcation line that separates the mostly Arab neighborhoods in east Dearborn from the mostly African American Aviation subdivision in Detroit.

Elmir suggested the communities have shared concerns that could be used to break down the invisible barriers of segregation.

"Arab Americans," she said, "understand educational inequities. Arab Americans understand being targeted and profiled. Arab Americans understand a militarized police force. Arab Americans understand a criminal justice system that is stacked against us."

BREAKING THE WALLS

Dawud Walid, the executive director of the Council on American Islamic Relations, described interactions between Arab and African Americans as tenuous. He said the two communities remain segregated despite relations between leaders and activists.

"There's not a lot of deep connections socially," he said.

Walid, a black Muslim, said the lack of social rapport fuels misconceptions and bigotry because people are afraid of what they don't know.

A quarter of violent crime in Detroit happen within 500 feet of gas stations, according to city officials.

Gas station and liquor store owners have been targeted and sometimes murdered by robbers who happen to be black, igniting racial animosity.

"We should stand by our principles and recognize the authority of the law. Arab store owners in Detroit are being killed for $10 and $20 sometimes," an Arab American engineer told the Arab American News in 2014, with underlying racial tones. He was stating that he stands with the police against Black Lives Matter protesters.

Walid said violent crime in Detroit is a security, socioeconomic problem, not a racial one. He added that extreme poverty and the breakdown of community can make parts of the city unsafe.

"There are black people who get shot and killed in Detroit on a daily basis," he said. "I caution people against centering Arab life as if it's more important than the overwhelming majority of people who get shot in Detroit who are actually black residents."

Walid pointed to the discrepancy in police presence and response time between the greater downtown area which is more affluent and the mostly black, deeply impoverished neighborhoods on the east and west sides, where Arab Americans own gas stations.

"That's a part of the institutional racism that's related to policing in Detroit," he said. "Arab American merchants unfortunately have to suffer from slower response time."

Walid added that some gas station owners are reluctant to engage their customers beyond their purchases. "Bulletproof glass tends to dehumanize people — dealing with people basically as commodities, not as people," he said. §

Freedom Monument, Detroit.

Mich Central Station, 2011

Photo by Aivoges

CHAPTER 5

EDUCATION

"Education in a democratic society must equip the children of the nation to realize their potential and to participate fully in American life … But for many minorities, and particularly for the children of the racial ghetto, the schools have failed to provide the educational experience which would help them overcome the effects of discrimination and deprivation." – Kerner Commission

School choice, metro Detroit's new white flight

By Chastity Pratt Dawsey and Mike Wilkinson | Bridge Magazine

When the high school in Eastpointe recently welcomed the football team from Lakeview High, it was a homecoming of sorts.

That's because nearly 700 students from Eastpointe actually attend school in Lakeview, a public school district five miles away in St. Clair Shores. As it happens, many of the students who left Eastpointe for Lakeview are white.

So it was that on a cool September evening, most students and fans on the home team's side of the football field were African American, while many of their white neighbors filled the Lakeview side. It was a sight that saddened Jennifer Ward, head of the band boosters.

A lifelong Eastpointe resident, Ward, who is white, graduated from the high school in 1988, when almost everyone in the district looked like her. Eastpointe was called East Detroit back then, but residents soon changed its name to distance this blue-collar city in Macomb County from the crime-soaked image of its neighbor to the south. The only vestige of its old name is in its schools, which are still called East Detroit Public Schools.

Ward said she thinks half of those who left East Detroit schools choose other districts for racial reasons. Others, she said, probably did so because the Lakeview schools have better test scores, more funding and better facilities. She admits there is likely no way to know for sure. But she also believes that when neighbors don't go to school together, they don't get to know each other as well as those who do.

"East Detroit is diverse. It's the real world," Ward said. "Everybody should go to school where they live."

CHAPTER 5
EDUCATION

East Detroit High cheerleaders pepped up the crowd at a recent football game versus Lakeview High, a school in St. Clair Shores. East Detroit Schools have become majority African American as more black students enrolled as many of their white classmates now attend school in St. Clair shores.

....

The white flight seen in Eastpointe is playing out in districts across metro Detroit and around the state. In the past 20 years, as African Americans have moved out of Detroit and into the suburbs, white parents have, whether by chance or design, used the state's schools of choice program to move their children to less diverse, more white traditional public schools. At the same time, some black families have chosen historically white suburban school districts to send their children, while others are choosing charter schools that are strikingly more segregated and black.

As a result, school districts across parts of the state are ending up more racially segregated than the communities from where they draw students.

Such is the case in Eastpointe.

Consider: The East Detroit school district is only 19 percent white, even though 40 percent of school-age children living there are white. And the flood of East Detroit students to Lakeview, which is 80 percent white, has produced yet another shift: the loss of students prompted East Detroit to solicit students from other cities, mostly Detroit.

"School choice has accelerated segregation by race, by class, by ability, by special education status and by language," said Gary Miron, an education professor at Western Michigan University who has reported widely (and often critically) on Michigan's school choice policies.

But defenders of school choice say the policies produce more good than harm by empowering parents — black and white — whose local schools are failing their children.

Gary Naeyaert, executive director of the Great Lakes Education tion Project, is one of the staunchest defenders of school choice in

Michigan. He acknowledges that choice can financially harm the districts that are losing students.

But he and others contend that education policy should err on the side of supporting parents who want to move their children to schools that are better performing or safer.

Naeyaert said many more families would be hurt if the program was curtailed in an effort to reduce segregation that can accompany generous choice policies. He argues that, if anything, the state should make school choice less restrictive so poor families have more flexibility to take advantage of school options.

"I don't know if it's possible to rewrite the rules to (change) social behavior without eliminating options for people," he said of segregation trends. "We can't legislate morality and good intentions."

50 years later: still separate and unequal

Almost 50 years ago, the Kerner Commission, formed to study the causes of urban unrest in Detroit and other cities, concluded that African-Americans and whites in the United States were moving toward "separate and unequal" societies, including in the classroom.

Today, Michigan's school choice law has led to several districts that are far more majority white, while creating additional districts in which minority students are in the majority, a Bridge analysis of state enrollment records shows.

The number of so-called majority-minority school districts statewide — where white students are in the minority — rose from 38 a decade ago to 55 last year. Meanwhile, the number of majority-minority charter schools went from 119 to 182.

Some critics of school choice argue that the state doesn't necessarily have to get rid of choice programs to discourage segregation in schools. Some strategies, such as locating magnet schools in communities of color, would promote diversity (which researchers see as a positive for students of all races), while giving parents quality options outside their neighborhoods.

But these same critics say the state's current system has few safeguards.

Consider:

- Blacks comprise half of the school-age population within East Detroit schools, yet nearly 70 percent of the district's enrollment.

- Across the state in Holland, white enrollment has plummeted in the last decade, with the top charter destination, Black River, educating 430 Holland students last year. The charter is 74 percent white, compared with a 38 percent white population for the city at large. Nearly half the students remaining in city schools are Hispanic.

- Statewide, more than 93 percent of African-Americans students who attended a charter school last year were in charters that were predominantly filled with minority students. That number reached 97 percent in Detroit's Wayne County, as well as in neighboring Oakland and Macomb counties.

"Diverse schools foster both academic and non-academic benefits," said Dr. Roslyn Arlin Mickelson, sociology professor at the University of North Carolina-Charlotte who studies school choice and segregation patterns in Charlotte and across the nation. Students in diverse settings learn better, are more likely to be exposed to different ideas and get better grades, she said.

Those findings echo what the Kerner Commission, established to look at the causes of the 1960s riots that roiled Detroit and cities across the nation, wrote in 1968:

"We support integration as the priority education strategy; it is essential to the future of American society. In this last summer's disorders we have seen the consequences of racial isolation at all levels…It is indispensable that opportunities for interaction between the races be expanded.

"If existing disadvantages are not to be perpetuated, we must drastically improve the quality of ghetto education. Equality of results with all-white schools must be the goal."

But that vision has been a hard sell to parents for decades. They see changes within a school and become uncomfortable with the differences, complaining of increased friction or fears of lowered academic standards. Some have, like students in school lunchrooms or playgrounds, opted to self-segregate.

"They don't want to make their children the sacrificial lambs on the altar of social science," Mickelson said. She said it's up to policy makers to recognize the benefits of diversity —and take steps to minimize the segregationist tendencies of school choice. But she also said she is skeptical that leaders will make different choices than those of the parents who, after all, elect them.

"I would like public policy to be informed by science," she said. "It's not."

A stampede for choice

School choice has been a popular option in Michigan for more than two decades. A byproduct of the 1994 adoption of Proposal A, which radically altered school finance in the state, students were able to switch to any district that opted to open their doors.

Today, over 300,000 students — more than 20 percent of all taxpayer-supported K-12 students in the state — are educated in either charter school or a traditional public school district other than the one in which they live.

Whether choice benefits students academically is subject to debate.

Researchers found that Michigan's choice students typically do no better on state tests than similar students who stay in their home districts. And many students who leave for another district often come back. Findings for students who attend charter schools are more favorable, with Stanford researchers saying that charter students in Michigan typically perform better than those in traditional public schools, at least for those who attend the state's better performing charter operators.

Choice transforms Macomb schools

Perhaps nowhere in the state are the links between school choice and race more vivid than Macomb County, where East Detroit schools are located.

It is the state's third largest county and had long been nearly all-white. As recently as 1990, blacks comprised only 1.4 percent of Macomb's population, despite bordering the largest majority-black city in America. By 2015, its black population had risen to 11.4 percent.

But as African-Americans moved north from Detroit into southern Macomb, thousands of white students used school choice to attend class elsewhere, in districts whiter than the ones they left.

"You'd have to have your head in the sand to not see that some of it is racial," said Ryan McLeod, the superintendent in East Detroit.

Before Proposal A, parents wanting to switch schools had few options: They could pay tuition at a private school, or they could move their family to another district. With the passage of Prop A, families could remain in their homes and still change their children's school, few strings attached.

Last year, 11 of Macomb County's 20 districts lost more students to choice than they received. For each of those 11 districts, the No. 1 destination was a traditional public public district more white than the one they left. And the Macomb district gaining the most choice students was Lakeview.

As white districts get whiter, other Macomb districts are turning increasingly black. In 2003-04, two Macomb districts were majority black. Now, there are four, including East Detroit.

Taken together, white and black, three-of-four Macomb students who took advantage of school choice last year moved to a district that was less diverse than the one they left.

That pattern is being repeated across Michigan.

In the 2009-10 school year, roughly 64 percent of choice students across the state moved to a less diverse district. That rate is now approaching 70 percent, a Bridge review of student residency and demography data shows, changing the face of classrooms from Holland to Jackson.

"The data suggests that might be happening; that some people are leaving because other people are coming," said Sarah Winchell Lenhoff, an assistant professor of education at Wayne State University who has studied student demographic changes in metro Detroit schools.

The tug of segregation

Lenhoff and fellow Wayne State researchers Ben Pogodzinski and Michael Addonizio examined U.S. Census and state school enrollment data. They found that the 10 school districts that took in the highest number of Detroit students since school choice began saw hundreds of local students leave their districts. And those who left moved to schools with a higher percentage of white students.

Likewise, data compiled for Bridge by a Michigan State University researcher showed that white students used school choice in greater proportions in East Detroit.

Enrollment trends in St. Clair Shores show how choice can impact segregation among white and black students.

While the Lakeview district is 80 percent white, the face of South Lake Schools in St. Clair Shores is markedly different. Records show that 23 percent of the school-age population in South Lake is black, but its schools are 47 percent African American.

Alice Tolan, volunteer aide Mrs. Lillian Hodge, Cornell Askew and Debrah Anne Ross read a book together at the Adams H. Sarver Building, 9780 Quincy, a branch of the Boys' Clubs of Detroit. A day care center was established at the building to assist children displaced by the civil unrest of 1967.

....

Walter P. Reuther Library of Labor and Urban Affairs

Similarly, in Warren, another changing Macomb County community, just under a quarter of students living within the Fitzgerald school district are black, but district enrollment is 40 percent African American.

Dan Quisenberry, president of the Michigan Association of Public School Academies, which represents the state's charter school industry, said quality, not race, is the critical factor for most families taking advantage of school choice policies.

Parents may very well opt for a more diverse school district for their children, if all other factors are equal, he said. But quality is paramount, with segregation an unintended byproduct of school choice.

"It's parents finding a place that works for their children," Quisenberry said.

Still, support for choice remains solid, and there have even been efforts to make choice policies stronger.

In 2011, Gov. Rick Snyder proposed removing all restrictions between districts. His "Any Time, Any Place, Any Way, Any Pace" choice plan would have made it impossible for districts to deny a seat to a non-resident student if space was available.

His proposal went nowhere, Naeyaert said because even supporters of choice didn't like the idea that districts would be required to open their borders, rather than keeping that decision optional.

Currently, districts get to decide if they want to accept outside students. Which is why districts like Dearborn and Grosse Pointe, which border Detroit, can decline to enroll students from outside their district.

116

Echoes of the past

The debate over race and school choice goes back decades in metro Detroit.

In 1971, U.S. District Court Judge Stephen J. Roth found that the city's public schools had for years illegally separated whites and black students in violation of the landmark desegregation ruling of Brown vs. Board of Education. Among Roth's findings was that Detroit school officials:

- Created "alternative" school zones in racially mixed neighborhoods that allowed white students to transfer to nearly all-white high schools.

- Bused white students past black schools with available space so whites could attend other white city schools. And, similarly, bused black children to other black schools.

- Built new schools in all-white and all-black neighborhoods, ensuring that segregation continued.

What caused a bigger uproar, however, was Roth's proposed remedy: busing students between Detroit and more than 50 suburban districts in Wayne, Oakland and Macomb counties, areas where many white former Detroiters had moved.

Roth's busing plan sparked protests and even more flight: From 1972, when Roth first announced his plan, to 1975, the suburban districts targeted under his plan lost 45,000 students; while suburban districts outside his plan gained 15,000 students, according to a Bridge review of historical enrollment data.

But two years later, a divided U.S. Supreme Court struck down the Roth plan in a landmark ruling that curtailed desegregation busing plans across the county. The majority concluded that the suburban districts should not be compelled to take part in cross-district busing because they did not cause the segregation in Detroit. As a result, districts across the metro region remained largely segregated.

> Parents may very well opt for a more diverse school district for their children, if all other factors are equal, he said. But quality is paramount, with segregation an unintended byproduct of school choice.

Winners and losers

East Detroit's superintendent, Ryan McLeod, said it's too simple to say race is the sole reason students leave the district. Some parents opt for districts with more resources — resources that tend to expand as more choice students transfer in, bringing with them education funding dollars.

On that point, at least, Naeyaert, the school choice advocate, agrees.

"I don't think this is motivated by race. I think the motivation is getting my child from a district that is doing less well to a district that is doing better," Naeyaert said.

At Lakeview High, juniors last year had an average ACT composite score of 19.8, well above East Detroit's 15.8 score, and its elementary school students were far more likely to score proficient than East Detroit youngsters on the most recent M-STEP assessment tests.

That is not much of a surprise, considering that just a third of Lakeview students struggle with poverty, compared with 7-in-10 East Detroit students who live in poverty. Research has consistently shown that more affluent students typically perform better academically than low-income students.

As a result, said McLeod, of East Detroit, school choice will inevitably produce "winners and losers" among school districts. "There are some communities that have benefited from school choice; communities that have the means to take care of basic needs are the winners."

Under this scenario, East Detroit is not a winner. Indeed, earlier this year, the state stepped in and named a CEO to take over the academic programs at four of East Detroit's six public schools.

Which is likely to produce more uncertainty: Will parents support the next millage when most East Detroit district residents do not enroll their children in their schools? Will they continue to run for school board? Join the PTA?

"With school choice, people don't have to invest in their local community schools," McLeod said. "They have the ability to simply send their kids to some place where other parents have made the decisions."

Is there a better way?

Is it possible to provide choice and stability? Yes, say some researchers, who argue that giving families options for sending their children to school does not have to lead to cuts or racial segregation.

Choice "can be a tool rather than an end in itself," said Kevin Welner, a researcher at the University of Colorado who has studied the issue. "It's a question of how you set the rules."

His study argues that choice should be "grounded in our larger societal goals for our schools, including the valuing of diverse communities." That would include, as Naeyaert of GLEP suggests, policies that help poor families to get their children to the same schools chosen by more affluent families.

Miron, the Western Michigan University professor, said he agrees that changes to Michigan's school choice policies can help redeem them.

"We look at Detroit and metro Detroit as the poster child for failed school choice," Miron said. "School choice is not being used as a tool for alleviating segregation. But it could be, if it was designed for that purpose."

Mickelson, the UNC-Charlotte professor, said one way states can use choice to foster diversity is to locate magnet schools in minority communities.

"Inter-district choice plans are the best strategies to address choice," Mickelson said.

In the 2009–2010 school year, roughly 64 percent of choice students across the state moved to a less diverse district. That rate is now approaching 70 percent.

Tempted to go, choosing to stay

As the sun set and a cool breeze swept over the East Detroit football game against Lakeview earlier this month, Ward, the band booster, draped a thick blanket over a fellow parent, Loretta Price, who is African American.

Both mothers have daughters in the marching band and concede they have considered transferring their children to Lakeview, where there's been no budget deficit, nor a threat of state takeover. But transportation remains a barrier.

And, Ward added, her daughter is a sophomore with roots in Eastpointe, stellar grades and a list of school leadership positions. Starting over in a different school in a different city holds less appeal.

"Over there, she'd be just another kid," Ward said.

So the family stays.

So does Angelia Mitchell, an African American with two children at East Detroit High. Though she, like Ward, is conflicted. She notes that the high school has seen more fights and disciplinary problems in recent years. Racial tensions, rarely discussed, hover over a community that's changed from majority white to majority black in a decade.

"As parents, we're all looking for possibilities for our children to go farther. I don't think there's anything wrong with that," Mitchell said. But she added that whatever decision a family makes, people need to be more accepting of racial differences.

"Education has no color," she said. "How do you get to acceptance? That's the hard part."

"As parents, we're all looking for possibilities for our children to go farther. I don't think there's anything wrong with that.

Education has no color. How do you get to acceptance? That's the hard part."

— Angela Mitchell

Walking back segregation in Ferndale schools

By Chastity Pratt Dawsey | Bridge Magazine

Blake Prewitt, superintendent of Ferndale Public Schools, said the district's decision this year to merge a majority white elementary school with one that is majority black is "what's best for kids."

....

One suburban Detroit school district is embracing school choice while taking steps to reduce segregated classrooms.

In Ferndale, an inner-ring suburb of Detroit, the city's two elementary schools were mirror opposites: At Kennedy Elementary, 57 percent of the students were white and 27 percent black; at Roosevelt Primary, where most students lived in poverty, 54 percent were black, 32 percent white.

But in 2015, Ferndale's school board decided to combine the two elementary schools. It was a tough decision that didn't please everyone, the superintendent said. Some, including a few educators, warned that desegregating the schools would hurt the district because more white families would leave.

But Ferndale stuck by its decision. As the 2016-17 school year opened, there were still two elementary school buildings: One is the K-2 "lower elementary" and the other is an "upper elementary" with grades 3-5. Young students will cycle through both schools.

The district did it, Superintendent Blake Prewitt said, because the board felt the best way to prepare children for a global society was to educate them in a diverse setting.

"I will give my community credit and school board credit. We didn't shy away by saying, 'There might be white flight so we won't" desegregate," Prewitt said. "We really kept pushing on what's best for kids."

The next step: integrating Ferndale's all-black high school with its other high school.

Ferndale's University High School is comprised almost entirely of black students coming from Detroit through schools of choice. It was created in 2005 with grants and collegiate partners to be a college preparatory school and targeted students from Detroit, who had suffered through a rash of school closures and low graduation rates. University High is 96 percent black, with just two white students last year among its 400-plus student body.

Meanwhile, at Ferndale High School, which has not been available to choice students, blacks were 56 percent of the student body last year, while the white population stood at 30 percent.

The district already has moved to merge some sports teams at University and Ferndale high schools.

Prewitt acknowledged that a few parents have told him they were leaving the district because they didn't want their children to go to school with African-American students from Detroit.

"It's socioeconomic, it's racial," he said. "It's 'I don't want my students with those kids.' Or there's the perception that a certain population of kids is going to drag the education down so (parents) are prone to go somewhere for lack of a better term, where other kids look like (their) kids." §

In the 1970s, then NAACP General Counsel Nathaniel R. Jones argued for a desegregation plan in the Detroit region. Today Jones is a retired federal judge and works at a law firm in Cincinnati, Ohio.

....

Photo by Lester Graham

A Moment that Sealed the Detroit Schools' Fate

Lester Graham | Michigan Radio

The U.S. Department of Education says kids at mostly black or Latino schools don't get as good of an education as kids at mostly white schools.

Generally speaking their teachers are not as experienced and their buildings are in worse shape. You can see that in Detroit, Flint, and other Michigan cities.

There was a major Michigan court case that could have ended segregated schools and made it possible for children to have a good education no matter where they lived.

From the 1950s on, white people started leaving Detroit and moving to the suburbs. By 1970, only one-in-three students at Detroit Public Schools was a white kid. And those white kids were concentrated in mostly white schools.

Detroit schools were segregated. The school board was trying to come up with a plan to fix that, but it was getting push back from white parents who didn't want to send their kids to black schools. There was also pushback from forces within the black community who wanted to keep majority black schools and have more of a say in hiring more black teachers and administrators in those schools.

The school board tried to find a compromise plan, but in the end no one was happy with the modest desegregation that included busing kids in Detroit. It got so bad someone threatened to kill a school board member. There were bomb threats, and students held walk outs.

The Michigan legislature stepped in and passed a law that Senator Coleman Young sponsored. Young was later Detroit's first black mayor. The law did give more neighborhood control over schools. But, it also legalized segregation in the Detroit schools by allowing white kids to leave their neighborhood school that had a growing black population and transfer to one that was more white and vice versa.

The 1954 Supreme Court decision in Brown versus the Board of Education ruled that the idea of racially separate, but equal was anything but equal. In the South, government began enforcing school integration.

In the North it was a different story. By the 1970s, segregation in schools was growing.

"While the decisions in the Southern states, the Southern school districts, were moving toward implementation, the segregation and isolation, racial isolation in the North was increasing," Nathaniel Jones explained.

In 1969, Jones had just been hired as the top lawyer of the NAACP. With the new law in Michigan, Detroit became a target for a desegregation lawsuit.

The case became known as Bradley versus Milliken. Ronald Bradley was a young student in Detroit and the first named in the suit. William Milliken was Governor of Michigan.

The case went to the U.S. District Court and ended up bouncing up to the U.S. Court of Appeals for the Sixth Circuit a couple of times.

Joyce Baugh is the author of *The Detroit School Busing Case*. She says when the U.S. District Court Judge Stephen Roth decided there were not enough white students in Detroit for any meaningful integration. He decided the only way to end segregation was by busing black Detroit students to the white suburban districts and suburban kids to Detroit. White suburban residents were outraged.

"They were basically saying that they didn't think that their kids should have to go to schools with these black kids because there would be all kinds of problems and, you know, more racial problems, their kids wouldn't get a good education, they would be subject to violence. All of those kinds of things," Baugh said.

To give you an idea of how unpopular busing was, at about the same time a lawsuit to integrate Pontiac schools had argued for busing. A woman named Irene McCabe organized a group called that National Action Group (NAG). She rallied thousands of white parents and their kids who took to the streets to protest. Attorney L. Brooks Patterson represented NAG and launched a political career that eventually led to him being the long-time and current County Executive of Oakland County. Before the school year started in 1971, the Ku Klux Klan used dynamite to blow up ten empty Pontiac school buses.

In the Milliken versus Bradley case, lawyers for the suburban districts argued they were not the cause of segregated schools in Detroit.

But Joyce Baugh says the trial court found that white people were leaving Detroit for the suburbs and keeping blacks out of the suburbs which contributed to the segregation.

"And the fascinating thing to me is if you look at the census data from 1970, there were 2,668,000 people living in the suburbs. Only 97,000 of them were African American," she said.

The NAACP's lawyer, Nathaniel Jones, argues redlining by banks and real estate agents, past policies by federal and state government agencies all contributed to segregated housing and segregated schools.

"That situation and phenomenon was not the result of happenstance. It was not accidental. It was not a matter of choice. It was a result of policies and practices that had been pursued by public officials in the North over time," he said in a recent interview with the Detroit Journalism Cooperative.

Jones also argued that school districts were auxiliary units of state government since the state had authority over them. So, they didn't have to prove an individual school district was segregated. State policies led to segregation throughout the Detroit region.

The Appeals Court agreed.

The State of Michigan and the mostly white suburban districts appealed to the U.S. Supreme Court.

In the arguments archived by Illinois Institute of Technology, Jones laid out the case for the lower court's busing plan to desegregate the schools in Detroit and the suburbs.

"A plan that promised to realistically work now and hereafter, a plan that would eliminate the vestiges of state imposed segregation, that would eliminate the core of state imposed black schools," Jones argued before the court in 1974.

The Michigan Attorney General at the time, Frank Kelley, argued the state was not responsible and that the plan to bus students was out of line because the suburban districts did not cause segregation.

"The trial court ordered a desegregation plan including 53 school districts involving 780,000 students and requiring at least 310,000 of them to be bused daily on the school days so that each school, each grade, and each classroom would reflect the racial make-up of the entire 53 school district area," Kelley told the justices.

When the Supreme Court handed down its decision in the summer of 1974, it ruled Detroit schools with its 35 percent white student population would have to figure out how to desegregate itself without the help of the ring of white suburbs surrounding it. Nathaniel Jones said the decision meant there would not be real desegregation in America's northern cities.

"We argued the case to the Supreme Court and in a 5 to 4 decision they reversed the Sixth Circuit and the trial judge, saying that we had not proven that the suburbs had participated in creating the segregation in Detroit," Jones recalled.

Among justices who disagreed with the majority, was Thurgood Marshall. He saw the ruling in Milliken versus Bradley as a dismantling of the landmark ruling of Brown versus the Board of Education which he had won just 20 years before.

"Our nation, I fear, will be ill-served by this court's refusal to remedy separate and unequal education for unless our children begin to learn together, there is little hope that our people will learn to live together and understand each other," Marshall said from the bench, reading from his dissent.

Today the Detroit Public School District is 84 percent black.

The district has been a financial mess with deteriorating schools for decades.

African Americans have made inroads into the suburbs. Some of those suburban schools change into majority black schools as many whites move or use school-of-choice laws to send their kids to a majority white school district.

There is no sign the laws that allow these shifts to continue will soon change. §

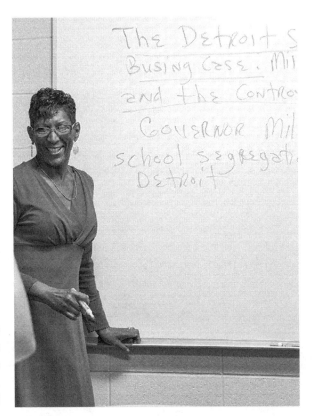

Joyce Baugh is the author of *The Detroit School Busing Case* and a Professor in the Department of Political Science and Public Administration at Central Michigan University.

Courtesy photo

[Left to right] Vivienne, Wynton, Kristen, Dana, Justine, Melvin, and Sterling Dacres. All five children go to Burton International Academy.
....

How Detroit Parents Pick Schools

WDET Production staff

For Detroit parents, the decision-making about where to send their children to school sometimes begins even before they are born.

It's a complicated conversation informed by school conditions and demographics, parents' own educational experiences, where people live, what transportation options families have and other factors. Politics play a part as Detroit Public Schools (DPS) has been controlled and reformulated by the state, charter schools open and close and nearby districts offer open enrollment for Detroit youth.

WDET talked with some Detroit parents about how they decided where their children would go to school.

THE DACRES FAMILY

Dana Dacres says her children could succeed at any school. It's what she does with them at home that makes a difference.

Dana and Melvin Dacres have four kids in elementary school and one in pre-school. All of their children go to Burton International Academy.

The Dacres like that their kids have had the same principal since their oldest first started going to the school. They like that children outside the neighborhood have to test to get into Burton and they like that it's a public school.

But there are issues, too. The parents say there is a lack of funding for after-school activities and that copper-contaminated drinking water discovered during the last school year was not fixed in a timely manner. Meanwhile children drank lukewarm water in 4-ounce cups laid out on tables.

But overall, the Dacres say they are satisfied with the school. And besides, Dana said, there's no perfect school.

Patty Lare (center) attended Detroit Public Schools until 8th grade. She now attends International Academy in Troy. Her parents, Lisa Schlicker and Ron Lare, say they are strong public school advocates.

"Racial division is probably the No. 1 historic theme in U.S. history, and it's reflected in every aspect of our lives. I wanted her to know something firsthand about the variety of people. What is an education? It's not only what you learn in books, it's relating to other people, too."

—— Ron Lare

"Well here's the deal: my kids could go anywhere, okay? And they can even stay here and be educated, home schooled. It's not so much where my children go to school, it's about what we do with them after they leave school."

Before graduating from the University of Michigan, the Dacres attended Detroit Public Schools for elementary and middle school. While Dana went to high school at Cass Tech, Melvin received a scholarship to Cranbrook in one of Detroit's most affluent suburbs and boarded there for high school. Going to the private institution did not affect his support for public schools, but he would like to see them improve.

"I know there's people who really don't want the public school system to survive," he says. "But if they understand that this is an option that, [for] a lot of people... that's the only thing they have."

HIGH SCHOOLER PATTY

Lisa Schlicker and Ron Lare have raised their daughter, Patty, in Detroit. As parents, they are both strong public school advocates. But Lisa admits that as their daughter got closer to school age in the early 2000s, she wasn't sure if she wanted to send Patty to a DPS school. She just hadn't heard very good things about the district. But her hesitation also troubled her.

"I really struggled with, if we were living in Livonia or Royal Oak, would I even question sending my daughter to public school? And my answer was, 'no,'" she says. "And I thought the only way to know whether DPS was truly broken, whether there was nothing that would work for us, was to try it."

After talking to neighbors and meeting with teachers, the family decided to send Patty to Golightly Education Center, a pre-K-8 public school in Detroit. They also liked the woman who would be Patty's first teacher.

"She was wonderful, enthusiastic… was very well-organized and really seemed to love what she did," Lisa recalls.

Still, Lisa was still a little nervous about sending Patty to school there.

"My husband and I are Caucasian, my daughter is Chinese in ethnicity, and most of the DPS schools are over 90 percent African American. Golightly was no exception, it was mostly African American. So, I wasn't sure — neither my husband nor myself are native Detroiters — I was not sure how we would be received in the school setting."

But, she said, "people get used to you." Lisa describes herself as "a chatter" and says she became friends with a lot of the other parents. Most important, she said she felt like the students accepted Patty.

Patty remembers sometimes being made fun of by the other students.

"Basically people would squint their eyes, pull their eyes back to create an image of an Asian person through different stereotypes," she recalled.

This upset her, but she said she got through it because of the support of her parents and the close circle of friends she'd developed at the school.

In sixth grade, Patty moved to Bates Academy, a pre-K-8 public school that aims to attract high-performing and gifted students who are screened through an application process. Patty says a math teacher there, Mr. Byas, helped improve her skills. And her sixth-grade English teacher, Miss Curley, had Patty's class read books like "The Outsiders," "The Pigman," and "Romeo & Juliet." Patty said this helped her become more prepared when she re-read "Romeo & Juliet" as a high-school freshmen.

Patty's father, Ron, says in all Patty's years in DPS he only encountered two teachers he didn't think were very high quality.

"I'd like to know any suburban district where a parent would say that," he says.

Overall, Patty says she feels good about her pre-K-8 experience in Detroit Public Schools.

"The people I've met along the way, the teachers I've made acquaintances with, the different administration processes that I've adapted to, they've all helped me and they've all been mostly positive," she says.

Ron, a union activist, says it was and still is important for him to expose Patty to diverse populations.

"Racial division is probably the No. 1 historic theme in U.S. history, and it's reflected in every aspect of our lives. I wanted her to know something firsthand about the variety of people. What is an education? It's not only what you learn in books, it's relating to other people, too," he says.

But for high school, Patty has left the district.

"The teenage years are sort of a special time, right? And I wanted her to be in a school where there was a little more diversity. She'd always been a minority, and I wanted her to be in a school that was strong academically but where there were all different sorts of students," Lisa says.

With Patty's input, they picked International Academy in Troy. The school offers the International Baccalaureate program. Patty says she's excited to learn about her Chinese heritage, which she doesn't know much about. She is also, for the first time, finding herself in the majority as Asian-Americans make up the largest demographic at the school. Patty says she wishes the school had its own sports teams, but overall it feels like a good fit for her. She's currently starting her sophomore year.

Lisa is happy with her daughter's high school so far but she says she does feel a little bit guilty that they took Patty out of the Detroit system.

"Because I feel so many people say bad things about the system, that it isn't working, and I feel like it did work for Patty for pre-K-8, and I think it would have worked through twelfth grade," she says.

Patty had tested into Renaissance High School, a public school in Detroit, which was the family's second choice.

> "Although I was the only African-American in the classroom, I was invisible at Osborn. One third of your grade depended on class participation. So they always marked me down a third because they said I never participated."
>
> — Darlene Alson

Darlene Alson chose integrated, neighborhood schools for her daughters.

Alston says she grew up "in the projects" on Detroit's east side. In 1967, her family moved, and Darlene attended White Elementary, a predominantly white school in a predominantly white neighborhood. She remembers experiencing racism and prejudice but she just took it in stride and did not let it break her self-esteem.

"Back then, in the 1960s, your parents built your self-esteem. Your church built your self-esteem. We didn't look to school teachers to necessarily build your self-esteem," she says. "Unless they did. But if they didn't, we understood that, 'That's just the way things are.'"

Alston had a very different experience in junior high. She went to Cleveland Middle School in Detroit, which was predominantly African-American. She describes her teachers as being "like mothers." She says they were very domineering and always telling Darlene and her fellow classmates, "You need to be a credit to your race."

Alston says back then she didn't understand what they meant. She thought:

"What are they talking about? A credit to my race? Are they kidding me? I'm just here to learn."

According to Alston, the three best Detroit high schools at the time were Cass Tech, Denby and Osborn. Cass was too far away from her home for her to easily attend, but Osborn was on a convenient bus line. Alston's older brother enrolled at Osborn, which she says was mostly white and had not yet been integrated. Some people didn't like that the student population was "changing" — adding African-American students — so they set up a barricade in the road to try to block black youth and their parents from getting to school. Darlene went with her mother to pick up her brother.

> "I think one of the reasons we love living in Detroit is the engaged, diverse, creative environment, and so [we're] thinking about a school that really reflects those same things for our son."
>
> — Rachel Perschetz

"They had Molotov cocktails. They had clubs. They were throwing rocks. They were rocking buses, and so, I mean, it was horrifying," she says.

And yet two years later, in 1972, Darlene chose the same school to attend herself.

"I had to go there, I wanted to go there because I wanted a good education," she says.

The experience was a far cry from the encouragement she had felt in middle school.

"Although I was the only African-American in the classroom, I was invisible at Osborn," Alston says. "One third of your grade depended on class participation. So they always marked me down a third because they said I never participated. And so I got into a discussion with the teacher about that. He said, 'Well you never participate.' And I said, 'I raise my hand every day. I'm the only African-American,' or I probably said 'black person or colored person in this class. You have to be able to see my hand. Because I'm the only one here.'"

Alston says despite never being called on in that class, she still received a good education.

"I got a good education at Osborn because it's predominantly Caucasian," she says. "Whatever you're telling them, you gotta tell us."

By the early 1980s, it was time for Alston to find a school for the first of her three daughters. At the time, the Detroit Public Schools system was becoming less integrated due to "white flight."

Alston says her children had access to some good public schools in their Detroit neighborhood. There was a math teacher who tutored one of her daughters in his home just so she could pass his class. The school counselor knew every student's name. The law program at Redford High School enabled one of her daughters to meet Johnnie Cochran, OJ Simpson's lawyer. Alston says if there were distractions in the classroom it was usually because teachers were trying to teach students whose parents didn't "set them up" to learn.

"I think it's hard to teach children who don't come from a home where education is paramount," she says.

Decades later, Alston says there were a lot of those kids in the schools her daughters attended.

"If the parent isn't teaching, it's hard for the children to behave in a way that's conducive to a school setting because they don't see it at home," she says. "Sometimes I would see, at the parent-teacher conference, the behavior of the parent reflects in the child."

Alston remembers hearing a parent yell at a teacher because her child, who had only been to school 15 days out of the semester, was failing.

Alston remembers thinking, "'Your child, who's supposed to be in school, has not been here, and did you know where he was for the rest of the time?' Because that would have been my concern."

The way Alston sees it, however, there was value in having her daughters in the classrooms with the kids whose parents may have set a bad example at home.

"They weren't going to live in a box," she says of her daughters. "You have to live in the world. So, is the majority of the world nice, kind, sweet, ordered, structured people? No. You have to learn how to navigate in the world. If I've put you somewhere where everybody's nice, everybody's great, everybody's fantastic, and you come out into the world, you're going to have culture shock."

Alston says her daughters know how to navigate the world because they went to their neighborhood schools. She doesn't understand the logic when parents send their children elsewhere.

"So you say, 'Well I'm gonna put my child in a better school?' Why not make the school that your child is in better? As opposed to saying you're gonna do something better [somewhere else]? And then your school closes down, then that's blight because then they got this vacant building that people are vandalizing," she says. "You don't know what's going on in there, and the children don't have people in their neighborhood who care."

Alston says when parents send their kids to neighborhood schools, it helps keep the community strong. That said, she understands that the neighborhood school model is dying in Detroit and she admits she rode a bus to go to a better high school.

Still, she stayed in her local public school district.

129

Saige Jones will be attending Detroit Prep for Kindergarten this year.

....

KINDERGARTNER SAIGE

Saige Jones's parents say, diversity was the deciding factor in choosing where to send her to kindergarten.

Five-year-old Saige will tell you herself where she is heading off to school this year.

"I am going to kindergarten, Detroit Prep," she says.

But after that the details about her education get a little sketchy.

"They told me all about it, but it was too boring so I couldn't listen to all of it because I was drawing stuff in a drawing room," says Saige.

Her mother, Shirel Jones, has been paying more attention. She says, in choosing where to send Saige, diversity was the deciding factor for her family.

"We wanted to make sure that she wasn't going to a school that had all white kids or all black kids or all Hispanic kids. Because I grew up in New York City, so that was really important to moving here, to make sure that she saw different people," Shirel Jones says.

As a high schooler, Jones attended the performing arts school in Manhattan that was the inspiration for the film and television show "Fame."

She and her husband were looking at the Boggs School for their daughter but it was full, so they were deciding between the Detroit Waldorf School, which is private, and the Detroit Achievement Academy, which is a free public charter school that Shirel Jones said she liked for its scores, though it isn't as diverse as they wanted. But then Detroit Prep opened up and ended the debate.

BABY BONNIE

Bonnie's parents want quality schools she can walk to so they're moving to Grosse Pointe Park.

Bonnie may only be a 1-year-old, but her family's life is already being affected by deciding where she will go to school.

"We didn't want to move twice in the next couple of years so even though we would love to live in the city for the next three or four years until she's in school, we thought that probably the charter schools and the public schools wouldn't be at a point that we were excited about by then and we couldn't really afford to do private schools long term," says her father, Ian Studders.

Studders and his wife decided they will move to Grosse Pointe Park. Ian says he wants a school for Bonnie where there are parents they can relate to as well as learn from.

"Having it be close to where our house is is also important to me because I grew up like two blocks from our elementary school, my high school," says Studders, who is from a northwest suburb of Chicago. "So, the idea of being able to walk her to school is pretty cool."

The family had been eyeing the Friends School, a private Quaker school in their neighborhood, but then it shut down for financial reasons. They also looked at Chrysler Elementary, a public school in their neighborhood school, but Ian says it doesn't seem like it will get to the point that he and his wife are comfortable with by the time Bonnie is ready for school.

TODDLER ARTHUR

Arthur's parents see the value of raising children in the city.

"There's not really anything about a suburban lifestyle that necessarily appeals to me," says Rachel Perschetz, who works with the Community Investments Team at Rock Ventures.

Her husband, Sean Mann, founded the Detroit City Futbol League, which pits co-ed neighborhood soccer teams against each other. He's also a co-owner of Detroit City FC, the city's minor league soccer team. By day he's a multi-client lobbyist in Lansing.

Rachel and Sean just finished renovating their southwest Detroit house and say they have no plans to leave the city. They're already thinking about where they might want to send their 1-year-old son, Arthur, for school.

"I think one of the reasons we love living in Detroit is the engaged, diverse, creative environment, and so [we're] thinking about a school that really reflects those same things for our son," Rachel says.

At this point, nothing really is off the table. But Sean says, for him, sending Arthur to a neighborhood school would be ideal.

"I think it creates the fabric of the neighborhood. It's another way that neighbors engage and get to know each other. So, I certainly see the value in that," he says.

In their southwest Detroit neighborhood, Maybury has a good reputation for very engaged parents, Sean says. But he says the school's test scores aren't as high as he'd like. And yet, Rachel points out, scores aren't everything.

"You know, if there are gaps in the actual academic education, there's a huge amount of things that a city offers that make up for that," she says.

In terms of any kind of perceived fear about a lack of safety in Detroit Public Schools, Rachel had this to say:

"I think statistically you're probably more likely to be injured in a car driving 30 minutes to a school in the suburbs than you are actually going to a public school in the city." §

Legacy of teaching: From mother to daughter

Keri Guten Cohen | Detroit Jewish News

Flo Paterni of West Bloomfield may have retired from teaching violin in the Detroit Public Schools in 2012, but that doesn't mean she lost touch with some of her previous students and their parents or grandparents.

For many years, Paterni, an instrumental music teacher who started teaching in Detroit in 1975, invited students and their families for a picnic she hosted in the summers. One grandparent became a traveling buddy. And a brother and sister came to play for her at her home when she was recovering from cancer.

"I wanted to teach in Detroit because I went to school in Detroit," Paterni said. Her family, however, moved to Livonia in 1965, two years before the rioting in Detroit in 1967.

"My parents never told me why," she said. "I wanted to go to Cooley High, but things were happening. The year we left, someone's hair was set on fire. My parents wanted to be near Jewish people, and there was a significant amount in Livonia." Still, Detroit was the only place Paterni applied for a teaching job. In her job, she floated from school to school. And she had to find instruments for her students because they were not in the budget.

At one point, she started Suzuki group violin classes for preschoolers whose parents would commit to coming to lessons. "No one

had this in the Detroit schools," she said. "I got to know the families and became invested in the whole family." That's when she started her picnics.

"I had no fear of being in Detroit," she said. "Most of my students were black. I taught in schools in the previously all-Jewish area. There was one principal who got rid of every Jewish teacher in his school, including me, but the school I went to is the place that changed my career forever because it's where I started the Suzuki program.

"I did feel racial tension from paraprofessionals and the assistant teachers because I was white, but not from students or parents.

"I really know that teaching in Detroit was what I was supposed to do; it was a good match for me. I feel I had a positive influence on the children and they on me. I talked about Jewish holidays and did Chanukah songs, and I created a Christmas song CD they could play with at home.

"I was involved with the families, and some of them are my best friends now," she said. "They absolutely became part of my life, too."

Paterni's daughter, Lydia, 27, of Waterford is keeping up the family tradition. She's a kindergarten teacher at Coleman A. Young Academy, rebuilt on the location of a little schoolhouse called Stratford that her mom used to attend as a child.

"When I was younger, I used to go to work with my mom during vacations and breaks," Lydia said. "I always really felt at home and very invited. I felt comfortable. When I decided to be a teacher, I always wanted to work in an urban setting. Once I did my interview at DPS at Coleman Young, I instantly felt at home like when I went with my mom to work." Lydia just started her third year at the school.

"It was a valuable experience when my mom's students would come out to our house," she said. "It was interesting to see the different cultures on a more informal, personal level. We went to their homes and birthday parties and different functions and they to ours. It was very cool to see.

"I think it's easier for my generation, but in reverse — people in Detroit accept us as teachers. Black history is a very big deal in February, and there are times when I'll have my black teacher's aide step in and talk. It's cool to have it from both sides.

"In kindergarten, we have to talk a lot about race," she said. "The kids mention it all the time. My hair, my skin. I've also had a couple little girls say, 'I wish I was white like you.' I tell them 'I'm not white, but more peach like a beach. You're more like peanut butter.' It's cool to talk about this because they are so little."

Lydia says a lot of things are changing now as DPS has become the Detroit Public Schools Community District. "There are new policies and teachers are struggling; but within my school, we have a passionate principal, and we all decided we would stick together for the kids."

But the job hasn't come without some hassles.

"I have been pushed by parents," Lydia said. "I usually can de-escalate things quickly, but it is scary. There are times when parents have not been dealing with discipline in a good way. I've talked to the principal in tears, but there's only so much you can do. But it feels rewarding, especially when I can help parents learn ways to discipline. Parents 100 percent want the best for their kids. This is a different culture, and it's built on respect. They will respect you if you respect them."

Lydia says she believes she's giving her students a good foundation. "I incorporate art and music in the classroom. I have little instruments — xylophones and maracas. My mom comes in and teaches songs and tells stories. They call her Mama Paterni.

"I think I'll stay in Detroit for a while," she said. "I love my school." §

DJC Poll: Education one of top concerns for region

By Sandra Svoboda | WDET

Bernie Porn, of EPIC-MRA, conducted the poll for the Detroit Journalism Cooperative.

....

Photo by Lester Graham

BLACK AND WHITE RESIDENTS IN SOUTHEAST MICHIGAN ARE SPLIT WHEN IT COMES TO THEIR OPINIONS ABOUT THE QUALITY OF THEIR SCHOOLS, ACCORDING TO A POLL THE DETROIT JOURNALISM COOPERATIVE COMMISSIONED IN 2016.

A majority of whites — 56 percent — say they are "very" or "somewhat" satisfied with the education provided by local schools in their communities, but just 29 percent of African Americans say the same.

When it comes to being dissatisfied, 69 percent of African Americans report they are "somewhat" or "very" dissatisfied while just 38 percent of whites agree.

Detroiter Vanita Robinson, a African-American nurse practitioner, who says education is her main concern for the region, sees the problem as one that only makes itself worse.

"Our schools systems, with the low scores that we have, we can't attract more students to come in because the success rate is so low," she says. "It's almost like a system set up for failure."

The poll was conducted for the Detroit Journalism Cooperative partners by EPIC-MRA, based in Lansing, and included 600 residents of Macomb, Oakland and Wayne counties.

Questions throughout the survey focused on racial attitudes and race relations, and results were reported earlier this summer. But the survey also included education-related queries. Overall, the poll has margin of error of plus- or minus-4 percent.

As an issue for the region, metro Detroiters ranked "education" and "crime" as being of the highest importance. No difference existed between the races, with about a quarter of people surveyed naming either of those issues as tops.

But when other questions dug into opinions about local schools, whites and blacks answered differently, most notably in judging their local schools.

"Since we have done so many surveys in school districts — more than 130 throughout the state — I can tell you from our experience and just measuring metrics about the local school districts … that there is significant difference between the perception of communities that are mostly or all-white as opposed to communities that are either mixed or that are predominantly black," says Bernie Porn who conducted the poll at EPIC MRA. "That is not only from this survey but also what we have done in surveys for Flint schools and for predominantly African-American and all-white schools."

Porn attributes the difference in opinion about the quality of schools to "a whole collection of issues."

Collection indeed: Renaissance High School Junior Imani Harris has criticized the overcrowding, building malfunctions, moldy food, large class sizes, teacher turnover and lack of books in Detroit schools; the state has fined a charter school because of unlicensed administrators; some schools are chronically low-performing.

For Lisa Bryant, students not having adequate resources — like books — is a main concern. Bryant attended school in California and New York and now lives in Westland, and she also named education as a top problem for the region when she was surveyed.

"To me, these kids are being cheated," she says. §

WDET's Gabrielle Settles and Melissa Mason contributed.

Researchers find Detroit Public Schools have struggled from the beginning

By Lester Graham | Michigan Radio

Illegal scrappers removed the windows, lockers, and wiring from the Hutchins Intermediate School shortly after it was closed.

....

One of the gymnasiums at Hutchins Intermediate just four years after the school was closed.

....

Photos by Lester Graham

This spring, I was led through an abandoned building in Detroit.

"The first time we came in here in 2013 it was still relatively intact. The power was off, but pretty much everything else was in decent shape. It wasn't in great shape, but just a matter of months and this place was completely destroyed," one of my guides told me.

So, who walked away from a perfectly good building and then failed to secure it well enough to keep metal thieves out?

THE DETROIT PUBLIC SCHOOL DISTRICT

"We're inside Hutchins Intermediate School," said John Grover with Loveland Technologies. The doors were open. All the windows had been removed. The only barriers were piles of broken concrete and bags of leaves dumped on the property.

"Hutchins was built in 1922. It was actually one of a few prototype schools. It was very innovative for its time. In the early 1920s, the education system as we know it was really starting to come together, in particular public education," Grover explained as we walked on broken glass and fallen ceiling tiles.

John Grover and Yvette van der Velde co-authored the report, "A School District In Crisis." We were walking through Hutchins because the authors think it's a classic example of how the closure of nearly 200 buildings over two decades have harmed neighborhoods and left the Detroit Public Schools to continue its spiral downward.

"Hutchins was one of the first purpose-built intermediate schools," Grover said. "Before, a lot of junior high schools and high schools were just old, converted elementary schools. But Hutchins and its twin on the other side of the city, Barbour, were designed for junior high school students. So, it had a number of innovations. It had gymnasiums, swimming pools. It was also one of the first schools designed specifically for community use. They envisioned it not only as a place for education, but also for the neighbors to come in and use the auditorium for meetings, or to use the gymnasiums or the swimming pools after hours. So, Hutchins really was the center of this neighborhood."

Hutchins was shut down in 2012.

"The damage that you see here was done in maybe six months," he said. "Some of it was longer term. The weather does a lot of it. The tiles coming off of the ceiling, that's just the result of water getting in. But, these used to be lockers here, you know, this giant gap in the wall. The scrappers would just come in and rip out the entire bank of lockers and walk straight out the door with them," Grover explained.

Looking at the remnants of this grand three-story brick and stone building, the oak paneled library, the gyms, and swimming pools, and auditorium, you wonder why the school district walked away from it. They don't build them like this anymore.

Grover told me it's all about numbers.

"Around 2006 there were only about 380 students going to school here. So, the school district was faced with a choice. You have a successful school academically, but it's designed for 2,200 students. It only has 380 in there. What do you do? So, what they ended up doing is they closed the program that was in this school, the Hutchins Intermediate program. They moved it to another school about 10 blocks to the south called McMichael Intermediate. And that became Hutchins at McMichael. And the feeling was you could just pick up all the students, all the teachers, the program that was so successful here and transplant it into another school," Grover said.

But many students wouldn't be transplanted. They left the district. It was either that or walk 10 blocks through rival gang territory to go to the new school. They went to charter schools. They went to inner-ring suburban schools.

This is not new. Since 2000, the Detroit Public School District went from 162,000 students to 47,000 — a loss of 115,000 students. Back at the Loveland Technologies office in downtown Detroit, John Grover explained what they found as they studied the history of Detroit schools.

Grover said it was thought closing schools was necessary because of the shrinking number of students. Actually, closing schools exacerbated the problem.

"Studies found that about 30% of the students from a closing school would leave the district altogether and go to different schools. With each student having a price tag on their head of between $6,000 and $7,000 a year in student funding, the loss of those students is a tremendous financial hit. You're talking about losing hundreds of thousands of dollars just by moving the school from one location to another," Grover said.

"Then there were the follow-up costs. When they were doing some of the closings in 2004 and 2005, they found that the anticipated cost-savings from closing those schools was actually more or less wiped out in the first year by the one-time costs of moving everything out, the logistics of moving the students to a new building, preparing the building to receive them, then securing the old building, and maintaining the old building," Grover said.

"And as the years went on, the amount of money that they sank into securing the buildings — especially after the scrappers started to come in, they would break in, damage the water pipes, start ripping out the electrical wiring — the cost of keeping up with the scrappers, keeping the building secure, dispatching the police every time that they had a burglary alarm going off was extremely high as well. And then, after the building became essentially a rotted-out husk, now they have to come up with money to demolish them which can range anywhere from $130,000 for a small school building to upwards of a half-million to a million dollars for a larger building," Grover continued.

"Those costs, all those costs after the closure were not factored into the anticipated savings. And the loss of students, the permanent loss of 30% of students when you close a school as well as all of those after-the-closing costs have essentially made closing the school building not practical anymore. And that's why Detroit Public Schools haven't closed any schools since 2013. They know that the benefits of closing the school are outweighed by the costs of closing it," the Grover said.

John Grover and Yvette van der Velde co-authored a Loveland Technologies report on the decline of the Detroit Public Schools District.

....

Photo by Lester Graham

He explained that for the entire history of the Detroit Public School District, it's struggled to get it right. The Loveland team looked at data back to the year the district was founded, 1842.

"Some of the problems that the Detroit Public Schools are facing today have their roots dating back to the 1850s, the 1860s. Issues that they had then, including segregation, are still being felt today. So, rather than taking a look at just a slice of the school district's history, we took a look at the entire history to see how we got to where we are today."

The study found there was only one short period of time the Detroit Public School District was able to hit the sweet spot. It wasn't long, though, before white flight and the slow decline of the auto industry started to affect the district.

"It's a tale of extremes. The school district when it was founded really struggled to provide enough seats and teachers for the number of students that wanted to attend. There were chronic shortages of buildings. The district was underfunded. And that struggle went on through the automotive boom, the First and Second World Wars, but towards the end of the 1950s and 1960s, the school district peaked. And just when they had enough capacity, enough schools, enough teachers, that's when the decline began. And now the school district is struggling with having too many buildings, too many teachers for the number of students that it has," Grover said.

At the district's peak, there were about 300,000 kids going to Detroit Public Schools in 370 buildings. Today 47,000 kids are taught in 91 buildings.

That's 810 kids per building at the peak and 516 kids per building this year.

The Loveland report concludes Detroit Public Schools face a no-win scenario.

With no additional money, already substandard schools will get worse. The 1,700 teachers will get no substantive pay raises. That will lead to a further exodus of experienced teachers and larger classroom sizes.

The cost of trying to monitor and maintain or demolish closed buildings is a continuing drain on finances. The debt — which has continued to grow under state emergency management — is crippling.

The report leaves the residents and government with this question: Are Detroit's public schools worth saving? And if so, how? §

Helping with Homework, with a House

By Laura Herberg | WDET

A construction crew in Highland Park is busy at work, transforming what was once a two-family flat into a community resource.

"They're removing existing walls and installing the proper supports to open up the floor plan," says Project Engineer Gerrajh Surles. Not long ago this house was on its way to the demolition list, says Surles. But now it's being given a new life. "We're turning it into a community resource center, mainly for the youth."

At the renovated house, kids will have a quiet spot to work on homework. But they'll also be able to produce rap music, learn to sew or garden. The house will use solar panels and geothermal technologies as its primary utilities. Outside there will be basketball and tennis courts.

A WATCHED BLOCK

The project is the brainchild of Shamayim Harris, better known as "Mama Shu." You can see the construction of the Homework House from her porch on Avalon Street. It is just the beginning of her plan to transform the entire block into a 21st-Century sustainable eco-village.

"There's a lot of places in Highland Park, different pockets of historical homes that are very, very beautiful, with very nice houses," says Mama Shu. "Some blocks aren't vacant or blighted. This particular part that we're on is terribly blighted."

Mama Shu says she had her eye on this block for a while. Even when she lived down the street, she would watch this block — with its tall grass, abandoned houses, and lack of street lights — and envision how to improve it.

"I did that for about three, close to four years. And it looked the same. It looked the same all that time while I was looking at it," says Mama Shu.

While working as an administrator in local schools, Mama Shu saw that sometimes basic needs weren't being met for students at school or home. She thought these kids could benefit from having a comfortable place to get their homework done, be served a full dinner and have their clothes washed.

The idea for the Homework House was born, but she needed somewhere to make it a reality. So Mama Shu chose this block of Avalon Street.

"It was clear space for me, fertile ground actually," says Mama Shu. "When I looked at it I saw beauty, I saw the Homework House, I saw just all the stuff, putting it back on this block and utilizing all the blank space to put back some of the things that we need and we want and we deserve."

"Nothing to do"

Plumber Christopher Martin lives in the neighborhood not far from where the Homework House is being built. When his five daughters are with him, the younger ones sometimes play with friends down the street, but most of the time they just stay at home.

"I don't really like them to be out too much. There's not a lot of activities for the kids to do in the neighborhood," he says.

His 15-year-old daughter, Samyia, says she rarely goes outside. "Because there's nothing to do."

Mama Shu's hope is that attitude will change when the Homework House is up and running.

HELPING HIGHLAND PARKERS HELP THEMSELVES

There is more on the agenda for Avalon Village. The ambitious project aims to include a cafe, a greenhouse, a meditation garden, a healing house and shipping container storefronts. Mama Shu says the goal of the so-called village is simple.

"Basically to show people how to be more self sufficient… how to take care of themselves," she says.

Close to $250,000 in donations came in for the project on the crowdfunding site, Kickstarter. Mama Shu says that shows people want to help a community that's helping itself.

"We're ignored neighborhoods, and it's plenty of them. Not just over here, there's other blocks, there's other neighborhoods all over Detroit that don't have the attention and don't have love and don't have anybody caring for them," says Mama Shu.

She says the people in these places are waiting on somebody to come and come fix something.

"And I'm not waiting on nobody to come remove a mattress, remove a toilet, and I'm just sitting here on the porch looking like, 'Okay when are they gonna come get that?' That ain't me." A ribbon cutting for the Homework House was set for September, 2016. The next phase of the village was to begin in spring 2017. Mama Shu says she will continue to work to provide services to the people of Highland Park, a city within Detroit, that Highland Park does not offer. Because, she says, at some point, residents really need to take care of things themselves. §

Alycia Meriweather

A fresh start for DPS?

By Keith A. Owens | Michigan Chronicle

In many ways, after all the turmoil experienced by Detroit Public Schools over more than a decade, it seems that the only direction to go is up. With all the headline-grabbing news reports of dead rodents in school hallways and freezing classrooms, not to mention rapidly declining enrollment, it's hard to imagine things getting any worse.

Fortunately, it appears that some steps toward measurable progress are being made. That's the good news. The not-so-good news is that the mountain to climb is so steep — and the resources still painfully limited — that the task ahead cannot afford any missteps or further miscalculations. There is little to zero wiggle room for error.

One of the largest concerns among Detroiters was eliminating emergency management and returning the schools to community control with an elected school board. That long-awaited transition took place during the November 2016 elections when Detroiters were once again given the opportunity to elect their own school board.

"The people of this city want, and are entitled to local control," said Judge Steven Rhodes, who began the first day of his appointed role to serve as DPS Transition Manager by Gov. Rick Snyder in March 2016.

"In order for the promise of local control to be fulfilled, the Financial Review Commission has to have a working relationship with the school board that fully recognizes the school board's democratically mandated role in running those schools.

We in the FRC are still working that out. It's going to be a process. It's going to take time. And when the school board comes in January [1017], it may have to be reset again.

"I understand why the legislature felt that some role for the Financial Review Commission (FRC) was necessary. I supported that role here, just as I did in the Detroit bankruptcy case. But the FRC can't be the school board. It can't be a second school board. It has to play a lesser role. The extent of its role is ambiguously described in the legislation, but what's not ambiguous about its description is that it's not a school board. Its primary function is, as its name implies, to deal with finances."

On a more positive note, Rhodes said that much progress has been made in filling teacher vacancies with qualified teachers.

"And just for the record, to say it the umpteenth million time, we are not going to hire any non-certified teachers, even though the law says we can. Not gonna happen."

Meanwhile, the lives and futures of more than 45,000 Detroit children hang in the balance.

Alycia Meriweather has been an employee of Detroit Public Schools for the past 20 years. She began attending public school in Detroit at the age of four. So it's safe to say that Meriweather knows a few things about Detroit Public Schools.

On March 7, 2016, five days after Rhodes began his tenure, Meriweather was appointed by Rhodes as Interim Superintendent of DPS (now DPSCD). All that experience was scant preparation for the perfect storm of catastrophes that came raining down like a swarm of screeching bats from practically her first day in office.

"So here we are, and when you think about everything that's happened since March 7 to today, it's really incredible," Meriweather said. "When I talk to other superintendents, in their whole tenure – that could be five years, 10 years, even as many as 15 years as a superintendent – they might have had one of the things that's happened in the last five months happen. So when you think about the legislative piece, when you think about the budget piece, when you think about the legal piece, the various indictments, the sickouts, the facilities, I could go on and on. But most organizations have one of those happen in a 10-year period, and we've had all those happen in 5 months.

"I feel like once we got past July 1, and the new district was born, then I felt like we are in a position where we can move forward. We're not distracted with Lansing, and we're not distracted with all of these other things that were taking away from the work. Once we got past July 1, I felt like now we can really, really dig into the work and prepare for Sept. 6."

For example, "I think we do have some real issues related to peoples' pay. We're working on our building issues. We are chipping away. We have three buildings that are getting new roofs. We've got boilers that are being installed at different schools. So we're slowly chipping away at things we know are concerns," she said.

Meriweather also pointed out that 2016 will be the first year the district will get the full per-pupil allocation without $1,100 per pupil going toward the debt. And that is a major hurdle cleared.

Rhodes is also hopeful that the Detroit Public Schools Community District (now DPS Community District), formally created as of July 1, 2016, is on the right path. But he is equally aware of the challenges created by the $50 million gap between what was

"If you were to begin today afresh to allocate school buildings throughout the city of Detroit, based on not only its current demographics and geography of demographics, but what you expect and want it to be in the future, you would not in a million years create the geographic distribution we have now. It is totally irrational."

— Alycia Meriweather

Judge Steven Rhodes
....

requested of the Michigan Legislature and what was granted. Rhodes' term, originally scheduled to terminate at the end of September, has been extended until the end of December, after which he is gone. Had Rhodes not agreed to the three-month extension, yet another emergency manager would have had to be appointed for a single three-month term.

"I went to the legislature, with the administration's support, and said 'we need not only the $515 million to pay the debt, but we need $200 million of transition costs and support to launch this new school district. That was not a number that was just pulled out of a hat. It was a number that this district and the treasury department came up with after a review of the minimum amount that the district would need to launch successfully and we didn't get it. That's a challenge," said Rhodes.

But Rhodes added that it is a challenge that has to be met.

"The governor has promised that he and his administration will continue to find ways and fight for ways to make that additional $50 million available for DPSCD. That money was going to go into buildings. The buildings still need that money. And our children still need for the buildings to be fixed. I am satisfied that the governor and the administration understands this need and is committed to doing what it can to help us. I intend to hold him to his commitment."

Meriweather echoed Rhodes' concern, saying that too many Detroiters still do not fully understand the situation that DPSCD is currently in, even with the money granted by the legislature.

"People need to understand that while $617 million was allocated to the district, we're not sitting on $617 million. When it's all said and done, when the legacy debt was satisfied, when the OldCo obligations were satisfied, when we take care of cash flow needs to get us to October, which is our first state aid note, we were left with basically $25 million. The money that was allocated to the district was allocated to satisfy the debt. We asked for $200 million. We were allocated $150 million."

"So $25 million is what we have to invest. I don't know how to get people to understand, because the story I keep hearing is that we got $617 million, which we should be thankful for, and that we should be able to pay somebody some money now. Or that we should be able to fix all of our buildings. We were really clear from the beginning; we've done intense analysis of our buildings. We said that we needed $65 million just to take care of the buildings.

"When you talk about $65 million, when you're talking about 94 buildings, I mean, if you've done home renovation and you fix the bathroom or a kitchen? And that's at your house. Think of a school building. When you're talking about windows and roofs and walls and boilers and plumbing and electrical..."

In addition to the need for more funds, Rhodes said he still believes strongly that something resembling a Detroit Education Commission still needs to be created that would have control over where and when new schools could be opened. The DEC was removed from the Michigan House version of the bill that was ultimately approved.

"If you were to begin today afresh to allocate school buildings throughout the city of Detroit, based on not only its current demographics and geography of demographics, but what you expect and want it to be in the future, you would not in a million years create the geographic distribution we have now. It is totally irrational. This is nothing against charters, nothing against whatever decisions DPS made about which schools to close, just a reflection of looking at the map and where schools are. It's nuts." §

Students at William Ford Elementary on the first day of school.

....

Photo by The Arab American News

Dearborn Schools leading the way in accommodating immigrants

By Ali Harb | The Arab American News

DEARBORN — Dearborn has come a long way from the days when Mayor Orville Hubbard wanted to keep it white. Now, Dearborn is home to the highest concentration of Arab Americans in the country.

About 30 years ago, Mayor Mike Guido wanted to talk about the "Arab problem". In May, an Arab woman who graduated from the Dearborn Public Schools gave the students' commencement speech at Harvard University.

Dearborn Schools represent the changing demographics and perceptions of Arab Americans. Because Arabs are considered white on the U.S. Census, there is no specific data on the ethnic makeup of the Dearborn Public Schools.

But there is a growing diversity in neighborhoods and the classrooms. In some Dearborn schools, the overwhelming majority of the student population is Arab American.

The district has been increasingly sensitive to the cultural and educational necessities of these students — expanding English programs, providing days off for Muslim holidays and halal food in some schools.

But it hasn't always been this way. The change did not happen overnight.

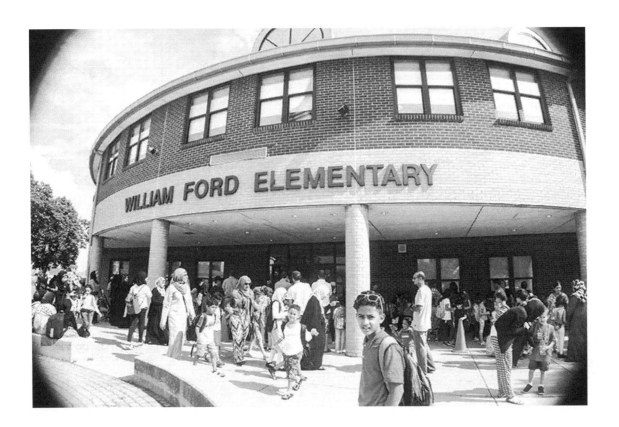

The schools have benefitted from a steady housing market in the city and residents' commitment to the children. In addition to state funding, a renewable 10-year millage amounts to 20 percent of the district's operating budget.

Former School Board President Aimee Schoelles said at a time when districts were shrinking across the state, Dearborn Schools grew partly because of immigrant students.

Despite not participating in the state's schools-of-choice program, Dearborn became the third largest district in the state in 2015; it was the 11th in 2001, according to Schoelles.

She said the increase in student population, coupled with budget cuts, put pressure on the district. "A huge amount of that growth is because of the Arab-American community," she said.

Schoelles added that some teachers and administrators were uncertain about the influx of Arab students, but others stepped up and were able to invest in the growth. She said Arab Americans took an active role in pushing for better schools.

Schoelles recalled how Arab-American activists who had formed a political organization succeeded in voting down a 1999 bond of $50 million because it was not enough to accommodate the expanding community.

Two years later, the Arab American Political Action Committee helped push through a $150 million bond that funded the construction of several schools, Schoelles said.

William Ford Elementary

Photo by The Arab American News

144

The former school board president said school officials did not address the needs of Arab students "out of the goodness of their heart" initially, but over time they became willingly accommodating.

As recently as 2012, the Office of Civil Rights of the U.S. Department of Education had to step in and bring the schools to a settlement where the district pledged to provide material to parents who do not speak English in a language they understood.

"When you educate people, whether it's by choice or not, they can't help but understand," Schoelles said. "It was an education process with the staff in the district. They were resistant at first, but the more they learned about Arab culture, about how students learn, the more willing they were to do what it takes to make things happen."

Dearborn Superintendent Glenn Maleyko said the district is in a great shape academically and culturally, and the schools' finances are relatively sound.

The district has about 20,000 students — a number that grows by the year, according to Maleyko.

"Parents are happy with what we offer at the school district," he said, adding that Dearborn Schools are a model for the state, though "we still recognize that there are still improvements to be made to help our students."

Maleyko said the district has been able to accommodate immigrant students over the past two decades by recruiting teachers who have credentials in teaching English as a Second Language.

In 1997, Salina, an elementary school in a mostly Yemeni neighborhood in the south end of Dearborn, had no certified ESL teachers, according to Maleyko, who worked there at the time.

He said the push for hiring ESL teachers started in 2002.

"Now, 32 percent of our teachers are working on an endorsement or already have the ESL endorsement," said Rose Aldubaily, the district's director of English Language Learning (ELL).

Aldubaily said the ESL endorsement is obtained through post-bachelor's studies that train educators to communicate and convey information to students who are learning English. ESL entails not only teaching language, but also building the background academic knowledge necessary for newcomers to match their grade levels.

"We are giving them that exposure, putting that language in their ear before giving them the content," the ELL director said.

In response to the political movement that demands using English only in the classrooms, Superintendent Maleyko said foreign languages are not substituting for English in Dearborn, but rather used to teach English.

"If I went to Germany and I don't speak German, how would I acquire the German language if I wanted to learn it?" he asked. "If someone could speak to me in English to explain and transfer (information), I'd have a better chance of learning the language."

Maleyko said Dearborn has been leading nationally on teaching English to non-native speakers.

Rose Aldubaily
....
Photo by The Arab American News

Imad Fadlallah
....
Photo by The Arab American News

Youssef Mosallam, director of student achievement, said instructional strategies in the district have changed to meet the needs of all learners, including ELL students.

"When there are instructional strategies that support language development, that language development supports all students," he said.

Mosallam said the district has programs that can serve as support mechanisms for immigrant students, including early college opportunities, community service activities and anti-bullying initiatives.

"We're not only telling students it's not okay to be a bully, but we're also helping and teaching students, as well as parents and other educators, how to be upstanders — how to respond to those who are struggling to stand up for themselves," he said.

Mosallam said diverse students get along in the district with minimal tensions.

"They bring in different cultural aspects; they bring in different perceptions," he said. "But no matter what, they all have the same ultimate goal. They want to be happy. They want to learn. They want to be successful."

LITTLE OPPOSITION

Maleyko said there is "very little" opposition today to Dearborn's ESL programs.

The superintendent said about 15 years ago, there was a clearer demographic split in Dearborn between the mostly Arab east side and predominantly white west end.

"We no longer talk that way; we no longer feel that way," he said. "If you talk to the mayor or chief of police, you'll see one Dearborn."

Maleyko said there might have been a competition for resources on each side of the city, but those lines have been blurred since.

"I'm sure there are still some people out there who have that feeling, but in the school district we don't feel that way any more," he said. "We're going to educate all the children. We've overcome that."

He credited the schools' staff and the city's elected officials for promoting unity.

Although Maleyko spoke of harmony in the schools and at City Hall, the east-west divide is still apparent in the neighborhoods.

The differences are not only cultural and political, but also economic. According to the U.S. Census, the median income in the 48126 zip code, which covers east Dearborn, is $28,524 compared with $76,354 in the west side's 48128 zip code.

Maleyko said the district has shifted the calendar to suit the growing diversity in the schools. Over the past 10 years, the district has added Martin Luther King, Jr. Day and the Muslim Eid holidays as days off.

Maleyko said most complaints about the district's efforts to be culturally inclusive are from out of state. He said such grievances stem from ignorance.

"We try to explain it to them," he said. "It's not really widespread."

Without naming then-Republican presidential nominee Donald Trump, who proposed banning new Muslims from entering the United States, Maleyko said the political climate has caused concerns among Dearborn's Arab American students.

The superintendent sent an internal memo instructing staff to assure children that the schools will always support them and uphold their Constitutional rights.

FORDSON

Despite the progress portrayed by officials, former Fordson High School Principal Imad Fadlallah spoke of both soft and overt bigotry against Arab-American students, which he said he witnessed before retiring in 2012.

Fordson, where almost the entire student population is Arab American, has been called Hezbollah High.

"I came to Fordson and I found it to be disengaged and chaotic to say the least," Fadlallah, who started his tenure at the High School in 2006, said. "It was not in any way shaped or designed around the needs of students."

Asked how the school was performing academically, Fadlallah responded, "It wasn't."

He said an example that would demonstrate the school's poor results in the early 2000s is that only one student attended the University of Michigan in Ann Arbor upon graduating in 2003.

He said the school did not offer ACT tests, assuming that graduates would not apply to universities that require them.

That was a time before the state-mandated M-STEP testing. Fadlallah said some teachers had "retired mentally" and did not teach properly because of lack of accountability.

"You may find a very good and decent individual, who looks at you with a kind of soft bigotry that you (as an Arab immigrant) cannot perform because you come from a race that cannot achieve," Fadlallah said.

The ex-principal said low expectations led teachers and counselors to steer students towards skilled trades.

"They thought an Arab student could never become an attorney or a surgeon or an engineer because he just doesn't have it; he comes from that race," he continued. "There are some people who looked at us in that fashion and they are very well-intended individuals."

Fadlallah said an Arab-American principal at a Dearborn middle school was told by a Fordson counselor to pursue a career as a secretary.

During his six years on the job, Fadlallah said he had to force out some teachers, "who didn't want to teach" to implement a culture of accountability. This, he said, raised the school's academic standards. In 2012, 80 Fordson graduates were attending U-M, and a handful made it to Harvard, he said.

"The kids haven't changed; the kids are still the same kids," he said. "The only thing that changed was the expectations."

But there was a push back. Fadlallah said he faced four lawsuits and smear campaigns.

"They called me a racist; they called it Hezbollah High School. They accused me of cleaning out all the Americans and I'm bringing all the Muslims in," he said. "All the stuff was nonsense."

Without naming then-Republican presidential nominee Donald Trump, who proposed banning new Muslims from entering the United States, Maleyko said the political climate has caused concerns among Dearborn's Arab American students.

147

Fordson High School

....

Photo by The Arab American News

Once, the pulley of the flagpole in front of the school broke. Fadlallah contacted the maintenance department immediately. After a few days, he received a call asking if it is true that he brought down the American flag and installed Hezbollah's.

Fadlallah said he faced unwarranted scrutiny from some administrators and school board members who were putting sticks in the wheel of progress.

"Many issues happened because I was the first Arab-American principal at Fordson," he said. "I never knew it was that political. I went there to do a job. I was under the microscope."

Fadlallah agreed with Maleyko's assessment that local opposition to accommodating Arab-American students is negligible. But he said it is due to the changing demographics.

"Twenty years ago, when we wanted the day off on Eid, they told us no," he said.

The former principal said the holiday was eventually granted because students took the day off anyway, bringing the attendance below 70 percent — the level required by the state for funding per day.

"When the state of Michigan told them they're going to be deducting money, they said, 'Oh oh,'" Fadlallah said. "So they built the calendar around our holidays, also. Those kind of things were not handed to us willingly. They happened because our numbers started to increase."

Fadlallah called for more cultural training. He also stressed revisiting expectations and always aiming higher. He said teachers cannot be color-blind because with the ethnicity, there is a story that is essential to the educational needs of students.

"I will not close my eyes and pretend that this kid is not black or this kid is not white or this kid is not Arab, because I do respect the ethnicity and I do respect the race," he said. "If I don't, I'm shortchanging that child. At the same time, I address their needs as students." §

African-centered schools in Detroit

WDET

Early in 2016, some Detroit children headed to a makeshift school when their parents were fed up with the conditions and finances in the city's public district.

That school, named a Freedom School, is part of a decades-old movement for African-centered education that's grown and shrunk – often with political movements — but ultimately survives in Detroit.

"There was a point when the whole district had committed to African-centric education," says Sascha Raiyn, WDET's education reporter.

Raiyn and Malik Yakini, who formerly operated a school with an African-centered curriculum, discussed the past, future and legacy of this approach to education.

Yakini, now executive director of the Detroit Black Community Food Security Network, founded the now-closed Nsoroma Academy, once one of several African-centric schools in the city.

"We used to say that Detroit was really the capital of African-centered education because there were more schools here than any place in the world, not just the United States. We created this tremendous example and have this tremendous legacy," Yakini says.

African-centered education, by Yakini's definition, is "an attempt to situate black children in their own historical continuums," in part by using classroom materials that portray African Americans in a fair and just way and include their contributions to history, literature, science and other disciplines.

"I don't think there's a unifying definition about what African-centered education is," Yakini says.

There's also a bigger political, civil rights dynamic to it.

"One of the premises, one of the basic understandings that we have to have, that guides African-centered education, is that white supremacy, the system of white supremacy is still a dominant force in American society," Yakini said. "I think the testimonies that you had on your last segment about white flight contin-

ues to speak to that. So African-centered education in some way is a response to this system, which has never really been inclusive to people of African descent. Not only has it not been inclusive in terms of the resources, it has not been inclusive in terms of the intellectual approach to learning."

African-centered education is a resource, an intellectual approach to learning that counters the dominant Eurocentric approach, Yakini said. "School in this country is still very much rooted in the experience of people from western Europe," he says.

Because of that, the experiences, culture and viewpoints of African Americans are not as well represented in education as they should be, according to Yakini.

"Your history and your culture is marginalized. This is what happens historically whenever one people conquers another," Yakini said. "The culture and the world view of white Americans who are the dominant force in society is imposed upon African people."

Raiyn said the other Freedom Schools in Detroit today are a modern-day example of a product of the Civil Rights Movement. "It began to kind of move quickly and powerfully this past spring when there was a threat that by the end of that particular week, Detroit schools would not continue to function," Raiyn said.

In fact, the Kerner Commission report, which attempted to explain the causes of urban violence and protest in the 1960s cited poor educational systems as one of the sources. The report also identified improving education as something that could improve conditions for African Americans.

Today's Black Lives Matter movement and responses to, for example, criticism that the state of Texas is seeking to minimize the horrors of slavery in textbooks, are dynamics that could increase support for African-centered education.

"African-centered education tends to enjoy larger levels of support when we see larger levels of black activism," Yakini says. "As black activism has waned, we see a waning level of African-centered education." §

149

Five African American men are searched by Detroit Police for weapons during the Sojourner Truth Housing Project Riot.

Walter P. Reuther Library of Labor and Urban Affairs

JUSTICE

Detroit House of Corrections.

"The belief is pervasive among ghetto residents that lower courts in our urban communities dispense 'assembly line' justice; that from arrest to sentencing, the poor and uneducated are denied equal justice with affluent, that procedures such bail and fines have been perverted to perpetuate class inequalities." – Kerner Commission

The War on Crime, not crime itself, fueled Detroit's post-1967 decline

By Bill McGraw | Bridge Magazine

Heather Ann Thompson has been in the news recently because of the success of her new book, "Blood in the Water: The Attica Prison Uprising of 1971 and its Legacy," a nonfiction finalist this year for the National Book Award.

But Thompson is also a nationally respected expert on mass incarceration and through her research has reached some provocative conclusions about the role Michigan's criminal laws have played in Detroit's slow-motion economic collapse in the decades following the 1967 uprisings.

For the most part, academics attribute the city's abandonment, poverty and decay to the disappearance of high-paying industrial jobs, white flight, discrimination in housing and employment, and government decisions that favored suburban development.

Thompson, though, argues that historians and others have missed an additional cause of Detroit's unraveling: the rise since the mid-1960s of aggressive policing in black neighborhoods, along with laws that vastly increased prison sentences and the subsequent explosion of Michigan's inmate population. That resulted in large numbers of people — mostly black males — yanked out of Detroit, orphaned children and collapsing neighborhoods.

Thompson, a University of Michigan professor of history who lived in Detroit as a teenager and graduated from Cass Tech, laid out her argument in a 2013 article for the Journal of Law in Society, "Unmaking the Motor City in the Age of Mass Incarceration." She wrote that the nation's War on Crime "undid the crucial strides that Detroit had made when it finally desegregated its schools, its police department, and its places of work. Indeed, countless victories of the tumultuous civil rights era were ultimately undone by the rise of a massive carceral state and the realities of mass incarceration."

The following interview has been edited for length and clarity.

CHAPTER 6 JUSTICE

153

Heather Ann Thompson

BILL MCGRAW: In the mid-1960s, crime appeared to be rising in Detroit, homicides were ticking up, and then 1967 happened. Crime became a big issue, and in 1974, Detroit Mayor Coleman Young took office and homicides hit an all-time high, 714. A lot of people see crime as one of the major reason people left Detroit. You have a different explanation.

HEATHER ANN THOMPSON: I think across the nation, the idea is that cities are emptied out, particularly of their white residents and their more affluent residents because crime goes out of control. And certainly Detroit is seen as Ground Zero where that happened. But as a historian, I had the chance to really go back and unpack this, not just decade by decade, but actually year by year and really ask the question, for example "Was crime really on the rise prior to the rebellion of '67? And was that the reason for why we see an outflux of residents?"

And in fact, it was not. We see very clearly that, certainly under Mayor Cavanagh, it looks for a moment, especially after 1965, that crime is ticking up, but there is whole back story here, which is, number one, the Johnson Administration had incentivized counting crime in such a way with its new war on crime measures, to incentivize showing that you had an uptick in crime.

The mayor himself, the head of the police department himself, both went public and said, "No, it's actually not that we have a rise in crime … we're now reporting it differently." And so the irony of ironies is that we begin this intensive policing that will really lead to the rebellion and we begin these really corrosive practices in cities like in Detroit — in advance of a crime problem. But then, of course, we really do get a crime problem because we get a war on drugs, which, like Prohibition much earlier in the century, illegal economies are dangerous economies, they are economies of desperation, they are accompanied by violence, they are accompanied by crime.

But, notably, when urban Detroiters are most suffering the crime problem, white residents are already long gone. They had already long left the city. So it is a bit of a chicken and egg question, and it's an important one as to what happens when.

BM: You use the term that authorities "criminalized urban space." What does that mean?

HT: Essentially in this country, really in response to civil rights rebellions that preceded Detroit, the federal government began articulating the northern civil rights problem as a crime problem, as a problem of disorder and crime. This is where we get the first clamorings for a war on crime. So it actually begins under Johnson, not Nixon; it is a moment when we start to see urban space in particular, but particularly black neighborhoods, or Latino neighborhoods, as inherently criminalistic. This is where the police are deployed — by the way, not because that's where the most drugs are, not even close to where the most drugs are — but this is the perception that is where the crime/ disorder problem is.

And that process I call the "criminalization of urban space" is because what it literally meant was that things that had not been illegal before become illegal, things that had been illegal before but had very slight penalties start to have much higher and higher penalties, and have much longer time in jail. And pretty soon, cities like Detroit — and Detroit is a mostly black city — but black neighborhoods in other cities, become these sites of intense criminalization, intensive policing that turn creates it own social crisis.

BM: Of all the problems Detroit faced – the deindustrialization, white flight, etc. — is there a way to quantify where mass incarceration fits in as far as a cause of Detroit's decline? How big a problem was that?

HT: We can never underestimate the negative impact of either deindustrialization or white flight. For example, it is deindustrialization that will lead so many impoverished communities to rely on the drug economy, for example. But as important as both of those things are, we have also given short shrift to the punitive turn — the embrace of mass incarceration — had in destroying cities like Detroit. And the evidence is quite clear. If you look at any map of the city and you look at where some of the most intensive policing took hold, they are the most decimated communities.

Because it isn't just about not having jobs, or it's not just about the space being all African American, it's about spaces where all the adults have been emptied out, spaces where even when folks return they are permanently unemployable because of their record, and spaces were without jobs the drug economy again becomes the primary economy, which has its own trauma.

So these are sites of orphaned children whose parents are in the system. It's the sites of newly impoverished children. And frankly what we see is that (in) so many of these families who are losing parents through incarceration, we have created this never-never world where essentially you can never get out of it. Some folks will say, "Well, if they cared about their kids they wouldn't have done whatever it is to land them in the system."

But I want to remind everyone that we only know that they are doing the things because that's where the police are. Other communities who are doing these things never have this presence of law enforcement. But also because we render them permanently unemployable, because of their record, it becomes this vicious cycle (where) devastation is the ultimate result for the city, but also for real individuals and families in the city.

MASS INCARCERATION IN MICHIGAN: A TIMELINE

1965: President Lyndon Johnson launches a War on Crime by signing the Law Enforcement Assistance Act, which, along with subsequent legislation, makes federal funds available for more aggressive policing.

1965: Detroit's homicide total – 188 – is the highest since 225 in 1926, during Prohibition.

1967: Michigan prison population is 7,037 inmates.

February 1967: Detroit Police Commissioner Ray Girardin reports major crimes — including homicide, rape, robbery and assault – rose 40 percent over 1965, but cautions the figures show increases in some categories only because of new rules and methods of crime reporting within the police department.

July 1967: Detroit's civil disturbance leaves 43 dead and 7,231 arrested.

May 1969: The Detroit Free Press reports that major crimes in Detroit have increased 136 percent since 1960.

February 1971: Under Detroit Mayor Roman Gribbs, Detroit Police officials create the STRESS unit – Stop the Robberies, Enjoy Safe Streets – an undercover decoy squad designed to lure potential robbers. STRESS becomes hugely controversial after repeated killings of black youth under suspicious circumstances.

June 1971: President Richard Nixon declares illegal narcotics to be the nation's Public Enemy No. 1, and the War on Drugs begins in earnest.

1974: Detroit's worst year for homicides – 714.

1974: State prison population is 8,630 inmates.

1978: Michigan enacts one of the nation's most draconian anti-drug measures, the "650-lifer law," which mandated a life sentence without parole for anyone convicted of possessing over 650 grams (1.4 pounds) of cocaine or heroin.

1984: Prison population is 14,658.

1985-1992: Michigan builds 23 prisons.

1988: Amid the national War on Drugs, narcotics-related arrests by Detroit Police rise from 3,746 in 1980 to 9,618 eight years later, even as population dropped. Sixty-eight percent of men and 83 percent of women arrested in Detroit for all crimes in 1988 were drug users, according to "Unmaking the Motor City in the Age of Mass Incarceration," by Heather Ann Thompson.

1998: Michigan adopts "truth-in-sentencing" rules that end reduced prison terms for good behavior.

1998: Acknowledging the "650-lifer" law has failed, state legislators remove the mandatory life-sentence provision.

2006: Rate of violent crime in Michigan has dropped 30 percent since 1986, but number of prisoners grew by 250 percent: Prison population is 51,454, the all-time high, a 631 percent increase over 1967.

2011: Michigan, the ninth most populous state, has the second-highest number of adults and juveniles serving life-without-parole sentences.

BM: From virtually the mid-'70s on, Detroit had a black mayor, a black chief of police, a majority black department and black citizens calling for more police as the DPD shrunk. How does that phenomenon square with what you're saying?

HT: On the surface it seems to be contradictory that you could have racialized policing and a war on crime that begins for deeply racialized reasons and then say, at the same time, that it ends up destroying a city led by black officials. Because, of course, why would they participate in that kind of process?

This is where we need to understand a couple of things. By the time we get to Mayor Young, by the time we get to his long reign as mayor, any resources that cities can have are in the criminal justice system. You're not going to find resources in the social service sector, you're not going to find them through health, education and welfare; you're going to find them through the Justice Department. And urban locales, whether they're run by black mayors or white, quickly understand that the way to get support for fiscal management is via essentially crime-fighting dollars.

Number two: police departments are incentivized to become more militaristic, to become more aggressive in their policing because their arrest figures, in turn, command more dollars from the federal government. And, to be honest, the community then ends up in a position of saying, 'Yes: High crime rates! Violence!' There's no one left to call, frankly, but the police. You have a drug-addicted son, and 20 years previously you might have had a social service apparatus where you could get help for that son. But by the time we get to the eighties, and we are dealing with an addiction crisis with crack cocaine, the only one who's going to show up when you call is the police.

So the community is very tortured and very torn about how do we deal with this social crisis when the only tools at our disposal given to us by our mayor, given to us by our president, are really crime-fighting tools, not public health tools, not social service tools.

BM: Did (Detroit Mayor) Jerry Cavanagh and the police chiefs then manipulate crime data when they changed the way they categorized crimes? What's the right way to look at that?

HT: I think that's certainly open to interpretation. What happens after 1965 is that there are newly available resources for police departments. First for states and for cities but quite directly for police departments that had a need, that could show that they needed federal dollars to help fight crime. And for fiscally savvy departments, and ultimately for fiscally strapped departments, arguing that you needed a SWAT team, arguing you needed flak jackets, arguing you needed helicopters is what is going to be heard. So in Detroit, there's a wrinkle that I'm not sure many citizens really thought about: STRESS [the police department's controversial violent-crime unit] becomes one of the most important problems for the black community in the wake of the rebellion.

That's this undercover decoy unit in the police department that black citizens certainly think of as a vigilante force, going out and having far too many fatalities to its credit. STRESS in many respects comes to exist because of this new war on crime. And mind you it's predating a crime problem. This is what allows for funding. This is what allows for those kind of undercover operations, the police operations, helicopter operations.

So did they manipulate the data? I don't know. They certainly became more savvy to understand that if you called it a burglary rather than a larceny, or a home invasion as opposed to a burglary (your department received more money)... Is it a murder? Is it a manslaughter? Is it intentional? These nuances are quantifiable and ... you need to have the arrest figures but you also need to have the crime problem to justify the resources.

BM: Does your research show if Detroit had a true crime problem in the early 1970s, when STRESS was formed?

HT: Not anywhere near what the press would have had you believe. And nowhere near what will become the crisis facing Detroit by the '80s. But yes, crime is ticking upwards as jobs are leaving and resources are leaving. But this too is connected to the policies of the criminal justice system. One of the things that happens between between '67 and '72 is this intensification of policing of black spaces in the wake of the rebellion.

Remember during the rebellion people are rounded up; there are gymnasiums full of people who are arrested, and that pattern, that trend, of arresting potential troublemakers doesn't go away. In fact, one of the reasons we get a new mayor, Roman Gribbs in 1969, is because he is running on a very tough law-and-order program, even though the stats are not showing Detroit is in trouble with crime. But it is certainly coming apart at the seams in terms of race relations.

BM: This subject is more than academic. You grew up in Detroit. But you have written you were late in understanding how mass incarceration played out.

HT: Right. My first book was about Detroit in the '60s and '70s and chronicles the story that will lead to the election of Mayor Young. And it's chock full of stories about policing, arrests, about criminalizing urban space, but I didn't quite see it that way until years later. And one of the reasons that is the case is that I lived in Detroit, and when you're in it, when you're experiencing historical moments and you're in the center of them, you don't have depth perception, you don't quite know what's happening.

2012: A study by The Pew Charitable Trusts finds that, in 2009, violent offenders in Michigan served an average sentence length of 7.6 years, compared with a national average of 5 years.

2013: The state Department of Corrections consumes about $2 billion, more than 21 percent of the state budget, and more than education. In 1980, prisons spending took up three percent of the state budget.

December 2014: Reflecting the growing bipartisan agreement on the need to cut the state's prison population, Joe Haveman, a Republican member of the state House from conservative Holland, pushes a package of criminal-justice reform bills. Warning of "violent criminals" possibly being released "back into our neighborhoods," state Attorney General Bill Schuette urges legislators to reject the legislation, which is weakened in the House and dies in the Senate.

2015: Gov. Rick Snyder signs laws to create a Justice Policy Commission to make recommendations to the legislature on sentencing reform.

2016: Michigan prisons contain 41,413 inmates, a 20-percent drop from 2006.

2016: Despite a 2012 U.S. Supreme Court ruling that mandating life sentences without parole for juveniles violates the U.S. Constitution, many prosecutors in the state drag their feet in holding new sentencing hearings for the 360 Michiganders serving life sentences for crimes they committed as juveniles.

PRISON BOOM SINCE 1967

STATE PRISON POPULATION

1967 || 7,037

2016 || 41,413

NUMBER OF PRISONS

1967 || 4

2016 || 31

MICHIGAN POPULATION

1967 || 8.6 MILLION

2016 || 9.9 MILLION

POPULATION PER INMATE

1967 || 1,222

2016 || 239

STATE PRISON DOLLARS

1967 || $22.7 MILLION

2016 || $1.95 BILLION

% GENERAL FUND BUDGET

1967 || 2

2016 || 19.5

Source: Michigan Department of Corrections

I graduated from Cass Tech High School in 1981, and I can remember the drug war was all round us. Friends of mine were getting arrested; they were going away. These were not people who actually did drugs. These were friends of mine who were just trying to survive on a very, very low level, maybe marijuana transactions, and they were all going away. They were all getting arrested. And it's so ironic, because back in that time we would say, 'So-and-so, what an idiot! Why didn't he get his act together and instead go to college?' We didn't understand we were in the middle of one of the biggest buildups of criminal justice resources in human history.

We didn't understand that we were in the middle of mass incarceration. We didn't understand that we were locking up more Americans than at any other time in our history. So it took me a while as a historian, frankly, to step back from it enough and be able to look at my own city and say, you know, absolutely deindustrialization was a crisis, and so was white flight, but we have missed the elephant in the room. We waged an aggressive war on crime on the most vulnerable population we could have waged it on and destroyed families, destroyed communities and, frankly, emptied out the city of its census population as those people are now all counted at prisons in Jackson or Ionia. And then we said, "Oh my God. Look what happened to Detroit. What did black leaders do to Detroit?"

It took me awhile to have enough depth perception to see that this was a much more complicated problem than even I thought it was.

BM: Do you have any critics about your view of how mass incarceration affected Detroit?

HT: No. Not really. I describe it not as the end-all, be-all solution but as the elephant in the room. I think it's this thing that's happened all around us, it's happened to us. We have only just now begun to understand what the ramifications of it are. I don't think anyone disputes that it is devastating. I leave it to the economists and social scientists and the number crunchers to actually map out exactly what the correlation is in terms of the impact, but nobody disagrees. You just simply need to look at a map of the east side of Detroit, a community like Brewer Park, and you need to get in our car and drive through that area. And you quickly understand that it isn't just that there are no factories or it isn't just that there are no white faces there. That this is about a profound emptying-out of a community in the name of public safety and it has in fact made us less safe, at least in those communities that are suffering and most directly affected.

DJC Poll: Blacks, whites differ in opinions of treatment in local courts

By Gabrielle Settles | WDET

Black and white residents of southeast Michigan differ in their perceptions of how people of color are treated in local courts, according to a poll commissioned by the Detroit Journalism Cooperative.

About half — 49 percent — of African-Americans surveyed said blacks were treated worse in the courtrooms, but just 16 percent of whites agreed. Nearly two-thirds — 64 percent — of whites said they think blacks are treated the same as whites, but only 40 percent of African Americans agreed that treatment is similar.

For Oak Park resident Taneka Jones, a trip to a local traffic court informed the responses she gave in the poll. The African-American woman says while she was in court she witnessed a judge yell at a black man for "getting loud" and "being rude."

"[The man] was like, 'What are you talking about?' to the point where everybody in the courtroom was like, 'What is [the judge] talking about?'" said Jones, who added that she has received similar treatment from this judge.

Jones was one of the 600 respondents in a poll conducted for the Detroit Journalism Cooperative (DJC) by Lansing-based EPIC-MRA in July 2016 of residents in Macomb, Oakland and Wayne counties.

According to the survey, which had a margin of error of plus or minus 4 percent, about seven in 10 metro Detroiters say they believe race relations are getting better or at least have stayed the same during the past decade.

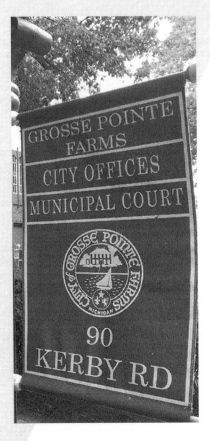

Grosse Pointe Farms Municipal Court

Deborah Shoop, a white resident of Farmington Hills, says she hasn't seen any racial discord toward black people in her local court system. But, she says, she does believe law enforcement uses profiling to discriminate against people and not just because of their race.

"I think that there's profiling also due to age," she says, explaining she thinks older drivers receive more scrutiny.

Retiree Paul Beaudrie lives in Southgate. He says he believes black people in his community get different treatment than white people in the local court system.

"This is a primarily a Caucasian community. There are very few minorities living in this city. And I just have that feeling," says Beaudrie, who is white.

Everyone should be treated equally, he says, but it's not just the fault of the legal system. He says he believes black people shouldn't always use their ethnicity as a defense.

"People, I think are tired of the so-called race card being pulled, and I just think it's a way of what they figure is evening the score," he says. "It may be true in some instances but I can't believe it's true in all instances." §

African Americans wrongfully convicted at higher rates

Lester Graham | Michigan Radio

Tom Boyd is a judge in the 55th District, Ingham County and a member of the Michigan Indigent Defense Commission.

....

In 1967, many American cities were rocked by civil disturbances, including Detroit. Black people rose up against police brutality and unfair treatment. The presidentially appointed Kerner Commission found that among their concerns, African Americans complained that courts administered justice in a discriminatory way and that "...a presumption of guilt attaches whenever a policeman testifies against a Negro."

Today there are more people of color on police forces, in prosecutors' offices and as judges in Detroit, as in many places, but African Americans are still being convicted of crimes they did not commit at a higher rate than white people.

Today, blacks make up 13 percent of the nation's population, but 47 percent of those who are found to be wrongfully convicted.

"What those numbers show is that African Americans are more likely to be wrongfully convicted than white people are," said attorney David Moran with the Michigan Innocence Clinic at the University of Michigan.

People of every race are sometimes sent to prison when they didn't do anything wrong. But Moran said that people of color, especially African Americans, are disproportionately affected.

"The poorest counties have the fewest resources to provide adequate defense and those are counties where you have a lot of minorities."

That was the case for DeShawn Reed from Wayne County. He and his uncle, Marvin Reed, were convicted of shooting a man in the back of the head. The victim identified the Reeds as the men who shot him. Later, he said he was wrong. Despite little evidence other than the victim's testimony, the Reeds were sentenced to decades in prison.

DeShawn spent eight years in prison. He said the worst moments were when he was prepped to be transferred from one prison to another.

"Everybody is butt naked. You got to bend over in front of them, you got to spread them, you got to lift them. You know that was just so humiliating. Then you got to get shackled all the way down and, you know, that was the roughest for me," Reed recalled.

The Michigan Innocence Clinic picked up his case and that of his uncle. The clinic discovered that the gun used in the shooting was found on a man who was killed while trying to steal a car. Witnesses recall seeing that man near the shooting that was blamed on the Reeds. After more than eight years in prison, the Reeds were released.

So, how does the justice system sometimes get suspects wrong?

"There are innocent people in prison because the criminal justice system is not an infallible machine," said Brett DeGroff, an assistant defender with the State Appellate Defender Office, which represents indigent criminal defendants. "It's just a

David Moran is co-founder of the Michigan Innocence Clinic at the University of Michigan School of Law.

....

Photo by Lester Graham

DeShawn Reed was wrongfully convicted of shooting a man. He was in prison for eight years before being released.

....

Photo by Lester Graham

group of people trying to do their best and just like the people who make up the system, the system itself is not perfect. People make mistakes and when people make mistakes in our criminal justice system, that means innocent people go to jail."

Since clinics like the one at U-M started investigating suspect cases across the nation a few decades ago, about 1,900 people have been exonerated. Many of them have a few things in common.

"I think the people going to prison that are actually innocent are disproportionately poor, they're disproportionately living in poor and minority communities that are over-policed in ways that suburban and wealthier communities are not," DeGroff said. "And the people that are getting convicted happen to be in the wrong place at the wrong time, maybe. The scary thing is once you drill deeper, it could be anybody from those communities."

There are several reasons, according to the innocence clinics:

- Eyewitness misidentification is the biggest problem. Studies consistently show people are much better at facial recognition of strangers of their own race than people of a different race.

- So-called junk science is another reason. Some forensic testing methods have been shown to lack sufficient scientific validation.

- False confessions are not uncommon.

- Government misconduct which might be as simple as investigators ignoring a piece of evidence that doesn't fit the case, or more maliciously failing to turn over exculpatory evidence to the defense.

- Witnesses sometimes give testimony against someone in exchange for some kind of incentive. That's not always revealed to the jury.

- And finally... bad defense lawyering.

While every county in the state has a prosecutor's office, few have equally funded public defender offices. Private attorneys are often paid a flat fee to represent criminal defendants who can't afford to hire their own lawyer, which gives them little economic incentive to do more than the minimum that's required, rather than robustly interviewing witnesses, taking statements, filing motions or otherwise thoroughly preparing for a trial. Many don't meet their clients until the day of the trial. Often they encourage their clients to plead guilty to lesser charges and even the innocent feel trapped in these "meet and plead" sessions.

Michigan is trying to tackle that last issue of bad defense lawyering.

"The justice system works best when you have three people really on their game, that's the judge, the prosecutor, and the defense lawyer.

If one of these three people didn't really come to play, we're not sure justice is the final result," said Judge Tom Boyd from the 55th District in Ingham County.

Boyd is a member of the Michigan Indigent Defense Commission which is working on making sure every defendant has a fair day in court. The Commission is working toward better standards for the entire state. Proposed standards include better training for defense lawyers, time and private space for attorneys to meet with their clients, requiring attorneys to investigate the case, and making sure a defendant has a lawyer at an arraignment and all pre-trial proceedings.

"We'll know when these initial standards work when the defendants have more trials and more motions and have their case heard in a true, fact-based way. It would be hard to make an argument that the system today provides defendants with the type of counsel which is guaranteed by the Sixth Amendment of the United States Constitution. Again, you know, the system works best when everybody's on their game," Boyd added.

The initial standards recommended by the Michigan Indigent Defense Commission are considered a first step. Boyd says it's clear more needs to be done.

As noted above, a proper defense is not the only problem. David Moran with the Michigan Innocence Clinic says many police departments, prosecutor's offices and the courts have heavy caseloads which make short cuts tempting.

"It's because of these systemic issues. It's because of under resources for defense counsel in urban courts especially where, frankly, nobody has all the resources. The prosecutor's office doesn't have all the resources and the police department doesn't have the resources to do an adequate investigation. So, it's not just the defense. It's these counties that are under-funded, typically places like Flint, Detroit and Benton Harbor where there are large minority populations. So, there's a systemic problem that leads to wrongful conditions," Moran said.

If you are wrongfully convicted and lucky enough for one of the innocence clinics to pick up your case, it can still take years to resolve. And until recently, if you get out of prison, there was nothing beyond freedom. Those years are lost. Often the wrongfully convicted have no money. It's hard to get a job because their record of conviction is not expunged immediately after release. It can take a few years.

Brett DeGroff with the State Appellate Defender Office says those who did commit a crime and then are released generally have had more going for them.

"If you get released from prison on parole, there's a lot of systems in place to ensure that you're going to succeed. We have a lot invested in that as a community. But, I think because people think of wrongful convictions as a phenomenon that doesn't happen often, we don't have any of those services set up for folks who didn't do anything wrong and went to prison anyway," DeGroff said.

But after decades of legislative efforts, there is finally some help on the way for those wrongly convicted. State Senator Steve Bieda had introduced legislation every session since he was first elected to the legislature in 2003 to change how we treat the wrongfully convicted.

In December 2016, the legislation finally passed in Lansing and was signed by Gov. Rick Snyder to provide $50,000 to inmates for every year they were wrongly convicted.

"The goal of this isn't to make anybody rich," Bieda said before the bill's passage. "Frankly, $50,000 a year is actually kind of a small number, but it is consistent with what at least eight other states have as well as the federal government."

Even with help back into society and reimbursement, the innocent who do time in prison suffer other, more intangible losses.

For DeShawn Reed, it's an uneasiness that haunts him. Even though he's been out of prison for years now, he is wary. No matter where he's at, he wants to make sure his whereabouts are documented somehow. If there's a sign in registry, he signs in and puts down the date and time. He wants to make sure that everywhere he goes he is seen, that it's on the record.

"Wherever I'm at, I'm always looking for the camera, I always want to be on camera because there ain't no telling what somebody else is going to say that I did. I always want to be on camera. Everywhere I go I want to make sure I'm on camera," Reed said.

Tienail Reed sat with his brother DeShawn as he was interviewed. He worked to find proof that his brother and his uncle did not do the crime for which they went to prison. He says since he spent time behind bars, DeShawn has changed.

"Before, he was more silly, I mean, he was more like a jokester. You know, that got taken away," he said.

His brother added, "Yeah. Yeah. I wish I had that, still had that, you know. Silly like everything. I'm just so uptight now. You know what I'm saying? I was more happy and funny, laughing and I'm just more uptight now." §

A conversation with Professor Peter Hammer

By Keith A. Owens | Michigan Chronicle

PROFESSOR HAMMER has been on the faculty at Wayne State University Law School since 2003, and currently serves as the director of the Damon J. Keith Center for Civil Rights. He sat down with the Detroit Journalism Cooperative recently for a discussion on the intersection between race relations and justice in Southeast Michigan.

HOW DO YOU FEEL JUSTICE IS BEING ADMINISTERED HERE IN DETROIT?

So if you ask me about police brutality and the current conflicts going on, I think what's interesting to note is the similarities between the late 1960s and today. And the realization that if you believe, as I do, that structural racism is our generation's civil rights challenge, that we've made almost no progress on structural racism, or the inner cities in the last 50 years.

The important strides in the first civil rights movement were focused largely on the South, and largely institutions of Jim Crow segregation. While Jim Crow was being set up in the South, we were setting up in the North and in western cities systems of spatial racism. The sort of saying that in the South you can be close in social relations but you can't be equal. In the North, you can be equal but you cannot be close. So we have residential segregation, and economic segregation, and the segregation of wealth in the North has been the key factor. We haven't addressed any of that.

So when I see this civil unrest, I see this kind of militarization of police forces. I see the kind of implicit bias within the police officers that are immediately projecting notions of hostility and notions of violence.

WHEN YOU TALK ABOUT UNHEALED SPATIAL RACISM, WHAT ARE YOU SAYING?

If you talk about the unhealed racial divides that exist, particularly in the North, and particularly as defined by geography, the example I use when I'm speaking or teaching is something that people saw as a huge puzzle or contradiction in the 1960s; you had the passage and the signing of the Civil Rights Act of 1965. And then two days later you had the Watts riots. I see those two as completely consistent, because the Civil Rights Act was going at social segregation, and Jim Crow segregation in the south. And at the same time, the problems of the North were not being healed. So you have that kind of interesting [occurrence], within two days an explosion of violence as the result of spatial racism and racial segregation that exists geographically in the west and the north, and remembering the next summer when (Dr. Martin Luther) King went to Cicero, Illinois (to protest housing discrimination) and the complete violence of the protests. . . . We've really dropped the ball. We haven't addressed those problems that were ripe in the late 1960s and you can draw a direct line. And I think we're remembering that now on the remembrance of the 1967 Rebellion is on the horizon, that those problems still exist.

STRUCTURAL RACISM, WHAT DOES THAT MEAN?

The inter-institutional dynamics of how the police system works with the education system, with the transportation system, with the jobs system, with the health system to produce and reproduce racially disparate outcomes over time.

You're born in this zip code and you're not born in that zip code and that makes a difference for 25 years of your life. So what produces and what reproduces that difference? Look at wealth disparities. So that the average European American has 10-12 times greater wealth than the average African-American household. What produces and what reproduces that over time? That is structural racism.

When I say that structural racism is this generation's civil rights challenge, what I'm saying is we've got to stare in the face of the existence of tremendous data-driven racial inequities and get to the notion of how those are produced by these complex interrelations between education and housing and health and opportunity, and today, if we're really gonna have equal justice under law, we really ought to have equal opportunity for everybody no matter what zip code they're born into.

HOW ARE YOU SEEING THAT PLAYING OUT IN DETROIT?

We're at ground zero of structural racism and spatial racism in Southeast Michigan. And sometimes I say that we're the new Selma, and if we don't recognize that and if we don't rally to that, and call things by their true names? So what's incredibly disturbing to me is people are talking about this renaissance of Detroit, the restructuring, the resurrection of Detroit.

You look at the major documents underlying that, going back to Detroit Future City, looking at the blight removal task force report, looking at the bankruptcy plan of adjustment, those are completely acontextual. They're looking at the issues and challenges of Detroit economically in complete isolation from our history. If you're not addressing the root causes, there's no chance of having a success. And then people kind of throw up their hands in surprise that there's a tale of two cities emerging. That in 7.2 miles [Detroit's downtown and Midtown business core] where there's tremendous investment going on, largely public subsidized, we're actually increasing the economic divides. … All of these things are coalescing in Detroit in ways that are probably more serious than anywhere else in the country. And yet we're celebrating the fact that we have an M-1 light-rail that resolves the contradictions of the PeopleMover that went around in a circle and now just goes back and forth along a straight line for almost the exact same distance.

IS THERE A SENSE OF DENIAL AMONG THE POWERS THAT BE RELATED TO WHERE WE REALLY ARE VS. WHERE THEY'D LIKE TO THINK WE ARE?

One of the things that really bothers me is this sort of complete Balkanization of the region. So people can now structure their lives. There's actually probably less social interaction along racial lines today than there was 50 years ago or 60 years ago. Because we've been able to structure our lives. I can go in my little circle here, and never have to come to Detroit. And when I do come to Detroit I know what I'm doing; I'm going to a football game, I'm going to a baseball game, I'm going to the DIA. I'm listening to the opera. I come in on an expressway and I park in a secured parking garage and then I go out on an expressway without any interac-

tion with other people. Things have a façade of getting better, but the deep roots of where the problems are are not being addressed.

HOW DOES IMPLICIT BIAS PLAY OUT IN DETROIT WITH MORE BLACK POLICE OFFICERS AND WHAT COLEMAN YOUNG DID?

The police culture matters more than the police color. Changing the blue culture, regardless of the color of the person having the uniform – that is the real challenge.

[For example], you're telling me now that I have a black police chief, and in many respects that's laudable. That's significant. But it's not enough. Because they're coming from the same society. They're subject to the same kind of pressures that create these unconscious categories. And furthermore, within the police mentality, they're likely to be reinforcement heightened. So unless you're consciously trying to interrupt on the way in which police are trained, the incentive structure of how they operate, how they're rewarded and what they're rewarded for, then changing the color doesn't change enough. And you still have the root causes again that are not being addressed simply by diversifying a police force.

WHAT'S THE RELATIONSHIP BETWEEN POVERTY AND JUSTICE?

Poverty is violence. If people are living in poverty, it's really the absence of opportunity. And there's another dynamic that happens every day in Detroit and Southeast Michigan; and this is coming straight out of a graphic from Detroit Future City, as I recall the graphic, it says that 70 percent of the jobs in Detroit are held by people from the suburbs. And those are the better jobs. So everyday people wake up in their homes in the suburbs, get in their cars, and come into Detroit, park in a secured parking lot, go into the high rise buildings, and make a good living in Detroit.

Sixty percent of the people who have jobs in Detroit are working outside of Detroit. Which means that they wake up in Detroit – we know that a huge percentage of people don't even have access to a car. So they have to go to a completely dysfunctional system of public transportation to try to get connection to connection to get to their job on time. And they'll be punished if they don't. Not because they didn't wake up early enough but because the regional transportation system can't get them to the job they need. And those jobs are not the same high-quality jobs that the white suburbanites are taking.

You can't have a just, healthy society that's predicated on that level of inequality. §

Former Michigan Rep. Joe Haveman, R-Holland, has been in a leader in the prison reform movement in the state.

Three prison reform ideas drawing bipartisan support

By Bill McGraw | Bridge Magazine

The prison reform movement in Michigan — and across much of the nation — is one of the rare issues in this contentious era that attracts support from individuals, public officials and organizations with a wide variety of agendas and political views.

Among the voices calling for changes to laws and practices that have made Michigan a leader in locking up its own citizens — at the cost of some $2 billion a year — are Gov. Rick Snyder; the Detroit-based American Civil Liberties Union of Michigan; the free-market think tank Mackinac Center, as well as Joe Haveman, a former member of the state House from Holland, one of the most conservative areas of Michigan.

Until he left office in 2015, Haveman, a Republican, led the prison-reform effort in the Republican-controlled state legislature, and he continues to advocate for change as the director of government relations for the Hope Network, a nonprofit organization that deals with behavioral health care and neuro-rehabilitation.

"Michigan is behind a lot of states in corrections' reform," Haveman said. "There's so much to work on. One question is, 'Do you have the courage to produce real reform?' Recognizing we led the country in a lot of respects in toughening our corrections stance for the last 30 years."

Michael Reitz of the Mackinac Center noted the odd bedfellow nature of the prison reform coalition.

"The Mackinac Center and ACLU, for example, don't often agree on policy recommendations," he has written, "but we have proudly partnered on" programs to end civil asset forfeiture and criminal intent legislation, which says the severity of punishment for a crime should be related to the defendant's intent.

In a special message to the legislature last year on criminal justice reform, Snyder, a Republican, called for, among other things, addressing the root societal causes of criminal behavior, a theme often associated with liberal Democrats in the past

Here are three areas of criminal justice that have received widespread bipartisan support:

PRISONER RE-ENTRY: Easing life for former prisoners who have served their time can take many forms, such as "banning the box," which eliminates from job applications questions about an applicant's criminal past. That's the law in some states and major cities. Detroit, for instance, bans city contractors from asking about prior convictions.

SENTENCING: Michigan several years ago moderated its infamous "650 grams lifer law" that sentenced defendants to life without parole for possessing 650 grams (1.4 pounds) of such drugs as cocaine and heroin. There are many calls now to adjust sentences, especially for non-violent crimes and petty offenses such as writing bad checks, breaking into parking meters or parole violations. Seeking alternatives to prison for substance abuse and mental health problems is also gaining support.

The Mackinac Center notes Michigan has 3,100 crimes on the books, some of which, it says, are used to regulate the behavior of well-intentioned people and impose severe consequences on actions that most people don't consider wrong. The ACLU supports the Michigan Legislative Council's Criminal Justice Policy Commission, created by the Legislature in 2014, which is analyzing information on state and local sentencing and proposed release policies.

ELDERLY PRISONERS: It costs Michigan much more to keep people over 65 in prison than it does younger inmates, and there is wide agreement that most senior prisoners no longer present a threat to society. "We could save millions of dollars" by removing older prisoners from the Department of Corrections, Haveman said.

Heather Ann Thompson, the University of Michigan history professor and national expert on mass incarceration, said the nation is in the beginning stages of rethinking its prison policies.

"One of the most interesting things that has happened since I've been working on this is the bipartisan discussion for the need for criminal justice reform. And I am all for it. But I will say I'm also cautious about it and also feel the need to continually state that part one is agreeing that we need to stop this and end the crisis.

"Part two, though, is to decide what we do instead. What do we do to make sure that people don't end up in these positions where they are having to sell drugs, or where they are no longer educated. We're going to have to invest in our cities, were going to have to invest in our infrastructure, and sadly, that's where a lot of the bipartisan support seems to fall away. You know, we don't have as much support for taxation that would be needed to pay for schools, to pay for job training. And so I'm optimistic, but I'm also deeply cautious about how far the bipartisan moment will go." §

We're going to have to invest in our cities, were going to have to invest in our infrastructure, and sadly, that's where a lot of the bipartisan support seems to fall away.

Sirena and Ricky visit their father (middle) in prison

When parents go to prison

By Laura Herberg | WDET

Sirena, a 13-year-old from a Detroit suburb, has one word for what it's like having a father in prison: "Hard."

"When friends come over and they talk about their dads, it's hard," she says.

If someone asks about her father, she says he lives in Lansing. Sirena doesn't say that he's in a prison in Jackson serving a life sentence for homicide.

"It's hard. It's hard having one parent in the house," she says.

According to a federal Bureau of Justice Statistics report in 2000, more than half of the prisoners in state systems were parents, and 55 percent had at least one child 18 years or younger.

No current, reliable data show how many children in southeast Michigan have incarcerated parents. But according to Child Trends' analysis of the 2011–12 National Survey of Children's Health, in Michigan, 1 in 10 children have at some point had at least one incarcerated parent.

The U.S. Bureau of Justice Statistics report found that in 1999, African-American children were roughly nine times more likely to have an incarcerated parent than whites, which means that with Detroit's African-American population over 80 percent in the last U.S. Census, the number of children who've experienced an incarcerated parent in the area is likely higher than 1 in 10.

Scot Spencer helped author, "A Shared Sentence: the devastating toll of parental incarceration on kids, families and communities," a report from the Annie E. Casey Foundation that was released this year. He says children are often overlooked in the conversation about the punishment for crimes.

"It is not top of mind that there is a family that is behind an incarcerated person," says Spencer. "Simply by not knowing, or not having the consciousness, you don't think that there is some collateral impact on very vulnerable and impressionable people."

Sirena has a 15-year-old brother named Richard, who goes by Ricky. He loves his dad. But he says his dad missed a lot while they were growing up. And now it feels pretty normal with him away.

"It's just something that I grew up with so I grew around it," Ricky said. "Some of the stuff that I feel more comfortable talking to my dad about I've had to talk to my mom."

"Having an incarcerated parent is akin to the impact of divorce on the child," said Spencer. Children may experience separation anxiety or suffer from traumatic stress. They are likely to struggle academically.

With a potential provider out of the mix, their families are more likely to become and stay impoverished, which in turn can have an impact on the communities they come from.

Indeed, in the book "Blood in the Water: The Attica Prison Uprising of 1971 and its Legacy," author Heather Ann Thompson argues that the aggressive policing of black men in Detroit that started in the mid-1960s contributed to the decades-long decline of the city, alongside the departure of industries and whites.

June Walker (right), director of Prison Ministry at Hope Community Church, checks in with former prisoner Rosalynn Martin Davidson

....

169

Ricky (left), Sirena and their father in a Soul Train-style line at a One Day with God event.
....

In terms of whether or not children with incarcerated parents will end up incarcerated themselves, a review of the current research shows there is insufficient data to draw conclusions.

"There's no one-to-one link for having an incarcerated parent and facing criminal charges," Spencer said.

Children with parents in prison tend to be exposed to a lot of risk factors even before their parents become incarcerated. If the children themselves become incarcerated later in life, current research is not able to determine the causal factor. Did they end up in prison because their parent was incarcerated? Or was it because they witnessed domestic violence, their parent had a substance-abuse issue, or they received an inadequate education? At this point, the answer isn't clear.

June Walker, director of Prison Ministry at Hope Community Church on Detroit's eastside, said, "If you want a person who you've locked in a cage for 20-30 years to come out and be human, then you need to keep them connected to their family."

In addition to providing services for prisoners and returning citizens (as former prisoners are called by their advocates), the program serves loved ones of people who are incarcerated. Prison Ministry offers support groups, provides Christmas gifts for children with parents in prison, and assists with visitations.

Walker says she thinks too many inmates from Wayne County are sent across the Mackinac Bridge.

The five-hour-minimum drive from Detroit to Michigan's Upper Peninsula is an impossible trip for many of the people she works with. So, at least once a year, she takes a group up to see their incarcerated loved ones in the UP. Walker would like to see more prisoners located near their families.

Chris Gautz, a spokesperson for the Michigan Department of Corrections, said in an email that officials are "cognizant of the travel times" for family members. But, he says, the department can't always keep prisoners tied to a particular geographic region.

"Their location in prison is determined by their security level and their programming needs. Sometimes they need to take a specific program and it may only be offered at certain prisons," he wrote.

For example, if the prisoner needs to be in a drug rehabilitation program.

"Once they are close to paroling, we generally move them to prisons close to the county they are paroling to," he says, "so they can more easily make those family connections, as well as connect with possible employers and others to make the transition to the community easier.

Sirena and her brother have to travel a little longer than an hour to visit their dad in G. Robert Cotton Correctional Facility in Jackson. Because they are minors, they have to be accompanied by an immediate family member.

After passing through security — including taking their shoes and socks completely off and putting them back on — the children meet with their father in a group visitor room, alongside other prisoners and their families. When they first arrive and then later when they leave, if they'd like, the teens can kiss and hug their father. But during the visit, only hand-holding and putting hands on shoulders is allowed.

According to Sirena, when she and her brother visit her dad they usually "just sit and play tic-tac-toe and board games." If they get hungry, they can order a sandwich from a vending machine.

Ricky says he sees his dad once every couple of months. He feels like that's not as often as he should be visiting but, he says, "I have a lot going on in my life with sports and school… and I'm always tired." He is a teenager, after all.

Programmers behind an event called "One Day with God" are working to better connect children like Ricky and Sirena to their incarcerated parents by hosting a day of festivities tailored to encourage bonding. Activities range from relay races, to decorating photo frames, to daddy-daughter dances. The events take place inside prison.

Unlike normal visits, children, surrounded by volunteers, do not have to be accompanied by an immediate family member. They are also allowed to be as affectionate with their parents as they'd like.

At a recent "One Day with God" event held inside an auditorium at the Cotton Correctional Facility, 46 children came to spend time with some 25 fathers.

Sirena and Ricky were among the kids in attendance. On top of the high-energy activities, the fathers were given multiple opportunities to open up to their children.

Towards the end of the day, one of the leaders passed a microphone around. Sirena and Ricky's father was one of the men to take the mic.

In front of all the children, in front of over 100 volunteers, in front of a handful of prison guards and his fellow inmates, Sirena and Ricky's father said, "I just want to thank my children for saving my life. I've been through some real lows in here… and there's been many times I've wanted to give up. But their faces is what's kept me going. Hope is more important than the air is to breath, to a prisoner.

"So I want my children to know, Ricky and Sirena, I love you. And thank you for saving my life and I will do better."

By staying in contact with their father while he is in prison, these two siblings get to hear that their father loves them.

While their father serves out a life sentence, his children give him something to live for. §

According to Child Trends' analysis of the 2011–12 National Survey of Children's Health, in Michigan, 1 in 10 children have at some point had at least one incarcerated parent.

Photo by Joseph Sohm

CHAPTER 7

HOUSING

Photo by Dorian C. Shy

"What white Americans have never fully understood but what the Negro can never forget — is that white society is deeply implicated in the ghetto. White institutions created it, white institutions maintain it, and white society condones it." – Kerner Commission

Black flight to suburbs masks lingering segregation in metro Detroit

By *Mike Wilkinson | Bridge Magazine*

Nearly a half century ago, as Detroit licked its wounds following the violent uprisings of 1967, the Kerner Commission bemoaned the sad state of segregation in America's central cities and the housing woes endured by African Americans and the urban poor.

And few regions suffered worse from the separation of races than Detroit.

Forced by federal housing policy and local practices into slums and nearly all-black neighborhoods, African-Americans lived apart from the city's white population, which limited their ability to enroll in better schools in white neighborhoods or seize job opportunities across the city or suburbs.

A year after the fires of that summer, the commission, appointed by President Lyndon B. Johnson to examine the causes of riots across dozens of U.S. cities, recommended several policy changes to lessen segregation in low-income housing. They included:

- Making affordable housing available across metro regions

- Improving the quality of housing stock

- Making homeownership more attainable, and

- Creating policies that break down segregated neighborhoods and allow African Americans the freedom to live where they choose and closer to higher-paying jobs, what Michigan State University Prof. Joe T. Darden calls "the geography of opportunity."

Nearly 50 years later, experts say not much has changed in metro Detroit, even as many black Detroiters have spread into communities across the region. The Detroit metro area remains by some measures the most segregated in the nation and housing advocates say many communities remain unfriendly to people of color.

While U.S. Census data show metro-Detroit made modest gains in easing segregation between 2000 and 2010, it hardly feels like progress to those who monitor the housing industry.

"It hasn't changed at all," said Margaret Brown, executive director of the Fair Housing Center of Metropolitan Detroit, a nonprofit that investigates discrimination claims in Wayne, Oakland and Macomb counties. She said her group still receives hundreds of complaints annually from would-be tenants and homebuyers and that the number one complaint remains racial discrimination.

Segregated communities, as Bridge Magazine's reporting has shown, extract a disproportionate cost on people of color by limiting access to employment, to transportation that will get them to jobs, to clean water and air and to education, while making it far more difficult for African-American families to accumulate wealth.

Together but apart

Detroit is now 82 percent African-American, roughly double its presence in 1967. And blacks can now be found in almost every city and town in the larger region of Oakland, Wayne and Macomb counties. And yet, even as African Americans continue to follow whites to live and work in the suburbs, metro Detroit remains largely segregated, with whites in largely white neighborhoods and blacks living among blacks, even within the same town.

In fact, the average African-American resident in the region lives in a census tract that is at least 81 percent black, according to Brown University researchers. While most whites live in areas where they are far and away the majority.

Even in cities that appear integrated, like Ecorse, where African Americans comprise 42 percent of the population, the numbers deceive: West of the city's railroad tracks, blacks are 97 percent of the population. East of the tracks, they comprise just 11 percent.

It's not just where they live, but how: Recent housing statistics show that blacks still are far more likely than whites to live in rental apartments and homes of poorer quality and that consume a higher portion of their income.

And those African-American residents living outside Detroit are far less likely to live in middle-to-upper income suburbs like

Sterling Heights, Wyandotte or Birmingham, and more likely in older, inner-ring cities in flux, like Eastpointe, Warren and Oak Park, where property values are stagnant or falling.

"We really have made very little progress," said Peter Hammer, a Wayne State law professor and director of the Damon J. Keith Center for Civil Rights, which promotes the rights of vulnerable populations in urban areas.

Some may look at the paths taken, from African-Americans choosing Southfield, now majority black, or whites moving to Rochester and Romeo, and see them as personal choices. They may wonder if the segregation that now exists, years after the official abolition of mortgage redlining — when blacks were unable to get loans because of their race — is the result of preference, not discrimination.

But those who closely document Detroit-area housing patterns see less benign forces at work, even today.

"The whole notion of freedom of choice can't begin to explain the depths of the segregation in the metropolitan Detroit area," said Thomas Sugrue, an historian at New York University and author of the seminal "The Origins of the Urban Crisis: Race and Inequality in Postwar Detroit," a book that, among other things, examined Detroit's troubled racial history to explain segregation in the United States.

A native of Detroit, Sugrue shows in "Origins" that, long before 1967, blacks faced enormous housing discrimination, some of it legalized in real estate documents — such as restrictive covenants that banned homeowners from selling their homes to blacks — in federal lending, or in local housing practices. It led to the near universal separation of the races.

"There has never been a free market for housing in (metro) Detroit and in most American cities for African-Americans," Sugrue said.

Nearly 50 years later, segregation patterns may be fraying, but remain the worst of all metro regions in the country.

When a road become a moat

Historically, 8 Mile Road, the northern border of Detroit, was a racial demarcation line; blacks typically did not live north of it. For the 1950s, '60s and '70s, moving across that line — and into the western and southern suburbs — defined the white flight that helped depopulate the city.

Yet in recent decades tens of thousands of blacks moved north of 8 Mile. Yet many whites also moved — even farther north. What was the pattern in Detroit through the 1950s and 1960s, when the "black line" inched farther east and west within the city, is now happening well beyond Detroit.

177

KEY EVENTS IN DETROIT'S HISTORY OF SEGREGATION

For much of the past century, Detroit has struggled, sometimes violently, over integration. Segregated housing was legally protected for much of last century, but that gave way to more nuanced, illegal strategies to keep black families from white neighborhoods. A few key milestones:

OSSIAN SWEET: In 1925, the family of Dr. Sweet, an African-American, bought a bungalow on Detroit's East Side. Angry whites surrounded his home. After the crowd pelted the home with rocks, Sweet's younger brother fired two shots, killing one man and wounding another. He was later acquitted, with the help of ace defense attorney Clarence Darrow.

1943 RACE RIOT: Detroit endured three days of riots amid conflict over housing and jobs in a city attracting thousands of Southern blacks for wartime factory work. The riot left 34 dead (25 of them black) and 433 injured (75 percent were black).

RESTRICTIVE DEEDS: White Detroiters used "restrictive covenants" in housing deeds to bar sales to blacks. A Detroit family, the McGhees, challenged the practice. The U.S. Supreme Court, in 1948, banned such deeds.

COBO HATE: Detroit Mayor Albert Cobo, elected in 1949 on a pledge to keep white neighborhoods white, upholds vow to halt construction of public housing for low-income blacks in predominantly white sections of the city.

RAZING BLACK BOTTOM: After World War II and as the nation was building interstate highways, political leaders approved a plan that erased vibrant black districts where I-375 now sits just east of downtown. Paradise Valley and Black Bottom were the cultural and business centers of black life before being razed in the 1960s and 1970s, forcing blacks to oother areas of the city.

WHITE NEIGHBORHOOD ASSOCIATIONS: As the black population grew and sought housing beyond the confines of the central city, whites in many neighborhoods openly opposed integration in the 1950s and 1960s with vandalism and direct confrontation, protecting what were called "defended neighborhoods."

"So the old 8 Mile becomes 12 Mile and you have this notion of ripples of white flight which you still see today," Wayne State's Hammer said.

Consider the city of Warren, a traditionally white enclave in Macomb County, just northeast of Detroit, epicenter of the socially conservative, blue-collar demographic of so-called "Reagan Democrats." In 1970, Warren had just 132 blacks among it 179,000 residents. Today, there are more than 20,000 African-Americans living in the city, a full 15 percent of population.

An integration success story? On the surface, perhaps.

But most blacks in Warren now live in older neighborhoods, in smaller homes that they're renting in the southern tier of the community closest to Detroit. In neighborhoods just a few miles north, Warren still has nearly all-white census tracts where blacks account for less than 2 percent of the population.

"So the pattern," Hammer said, "is reproducing itself and we're showing cyclical patterns and we're not making any meaningful progress and actually dealing with the core problem."

At the time of the 1967 riots, nearly 90 percent of the region's blacks lived in the city of Detroit (actually, in one half of Detroit; many city neighborhoods remained all-white). Another 10 percent lived in just six other communities: Pontiac, Highland Park, Inkster, Ecorse, River Rouge and Royal Oak Township, according to the 1970 Census.

Today, blacks and whites in metro Detroit are both far more likely to see each other in their communities on any given day, yet only 5 percent of whites and blacks live in a census tract that's even close to the overall region's black-white mix (25 percent black).

Metro Detroit is not alone in its segregation: the Cleveland, Chicago, Milwaukee and New York City metro areas all struggle with segregation nearly on the scale of Detroit. In fact, there are few examples nationwide where communities have successfully avoided racial polarization.

Shaker Heights, outside Cleveland, and Oak Park, just outside Chicago, are two suburban communities that consciously promote racial integration through housing policy. But, as Sugrue points out, "These places are few and far between," and not close in scale to cities like Detroit.

Still, there are hints of progress to go along with concrete examples of continuing problems.

A survey on racial attitudes this past summer, sponsored by the Detroit Journalism Cooperative of which Bridge is a member, shows that blacks and whites in the region view the impact that race may have on housing patterns a bit differently.

While 12 percent of whites said the racial composition of a neighborhood played a role in their decision to live there, nearly 20 percent of blacks said it did. Sixty-percent of both groups said they lived in an area where most people looked like them.

However, one-quarter of whites said they'd be unwilling to live where they'd be in the minority, compared to 16 percent of blacks.

Those attitudes are reflected in the current demography of the region: Only a couple of metro Detroit communities — New Haven in northern Macomb County, Sumpter Township in southwestern Wayne County, West Bloomfield in Oakland County — have seen their black populations remain sizeable and stable over recent years.

Even then, the diversity in the community is not always reflected in the local schools. A Bridge investigation this year found that parents across Michigan often use the state's generous "Schools of Choice" program to move their children to less diverse schools.

For much of the 20th Century, blacks living in Detroit were blocked from some public housing, could not get homes loans and were not welcome in many white-dominated neighborhoods, problems well chronicled by advocates who fought to overcome the obstacles.

"What white Americans have never fully understood," the Kerner Commission wrote, "but what the Negro can never forget, is that white society is deeply implicated in the ghetto. White institutions created it, white institutions maintain it and white society condones it."

Even after President Lyndon B. Johnson signed the Fair Housing Act in 1968, which sought to eliminate housing discrimination, hurdles remained. Restrictive covenants and U.S.-backed redlining were gone, but some real estate agents still illegally steered black and white buyers to less diverse neighborhoods, a practice that housing advocates say continues today.

Every week black and white "testers" — who play the role of people looking for a home or apartment then report back to how they are treated — fan out across Wayne, Oakland and Macomb counties. The Fair Housing Center's Brown said she'd run out of money before the center would run out of trouble spots to investigate.

Recent housing statistics show that blacks still are far more likely than whites to live in rental apartments and homes of poorer quality and that consume a higher portion of their income.

What the testers find is disheartening, she said: landlords telling whites the rent is one price but blacks a higher one; blacks being told an apartment is no longer available when it is, or that a rental needs a co-signer while not asking the same of whites — all, if proven, blatant violations of housing law.

"When we send testers out, they (black testers) are told things that aren't true," Brown said.

Since 1977, the center said it has won over $11 million in settlements for tenants and homeowners. It recently challenged Oakland County over its use of federal housing money, alleging it was not using it to help low-income families as required and perpetuating segregation. The complaint is still under review by the U.S. Department of Housing and Urban Development, Brown said.

Segregation has often narrowed the paths of blacks leaving Detroit to neighborhoods where they could afford homes and felt they were considered welcome. Studies have shown African Americans are usually willing to move into racially mixed areas but less willing to become "pioneers" in all-white areas.

"The patterns of African-American movement into the suburbs outside of Detroit aren't random," Sugrue said.

Victimized again

Ironically, after decades of seeking equal access to home loans, blacks were given wider access to loans in the 2000s. But at a fearsome cost: The predatory lending that flooded into Detroit that decade — an estimated three-quarters of all loans from 2004 to 2006 carried higher interest rates — saddled tens of thousands of residents with high-interest loans they could not afford.

Then, when owners couldn't pay, banks foreclosed on 100,000 properties in Detroit, more than a quarter of all housing units in the city. That depressed the city's housing market further and contributed mightily to the problems that led the city to file for bankruptcy.

"You could say the next wave of housing market discrimination, one that provided access to loans and mortgages to African Americans, was a different form of exploitation," Sugrue said. "It was predatory."

In many cases, that led to foreclosures, first from lenders and later from the government. When owners could not pay their tax bills — Detroit has some of the highest property tax rates in the state — many lost their homes to auctions held by the Wayne County Treasurer. The ACLU of Michigan and the NAACP this year sued the treasurer's office, claiming assessments were not lowered to match lowering property values and that foreclosure was carried out in a discriminatory manner.

Photo by James R. Martin

Beyond that, Hammer said: "The other irony is housing is made available to African-Americans and other minorities oftentimes in markets that are in decline."

When opportunity finally struck, many bought homes in Detroit, their tiny piece of the American dream. But now, a city that now owns tens of thousands of vacant properties and is hoping to demolish many of them, many of those home sales are not looking like a sound investment, exacerbating the region's black-white wealth gap.

"What's the value of that home now?" Hammer said.

Not the first time

In the wake of the Kerner Commission findings, lawmakers made changes to alleviate housing discrimination, with mixed results.

In the 1970s, after the Federal Housing Agency began backing loans for the poor, speculators combined with shady appraisers to inflate home prices. They helped thousands of poor families get loans to buy their first homes in Detroit.

But the deals were often for unsound homes that never matched the value of their loans, with bribes to government officials greasing the wheels for costly mortgages. The new owners, most long-time renters, paid as little as $200 in down payments before moving in. When problems arose in the homes — some were slated for demolition before unscrupulous real estate agents made minor repairs and sold them — the owners just walked away.

The resulting scandal left the U.S. Department of Housing and Urban Development owning more than 25,000 derelict properties in Detroit, a foreshadowing of the subprime crisis 40 years later.

Around the same time, wealthier, whiter communities across Metro Detroit, including Warren, Livonia and Birmingham — which combined, in 1970, counted 191 blacks among their 315,000 residents — found themselves under scrutiny for not using federal money, as required, on low-income housing, or blocking the development of such units.

Ultimately, Birmingham, one of the wealthiest communities in the state, allowed the construction of low-income apartments and Warren is now home to the fourth largest black population in the region. Livonia, where fewer than 1 percent of residents were black as recently as 1990, now has more than 2,900 African Americans, roughly 3 percent of total population.

So there has been progress. Will it continue? Will the region find more racial balance in where people live and work, and create broader opportunities for success?

Margaret Brown, the housing official, was just a young girl in 1967, growing up in Northwest Detroit when the city erupted in violence that summer.

She remembers the civil rights struggles, the calls for fair housing and opportunity so that someday blacks could reach the "promised land" that Dr. Martin Luther King, Jr., prophesized the night before his death.

But today, the path to secure a good, safe place to live is still blocked by prejudice, still hampered by inequality, Brown said. Complaints of discrimination remain "constant, persistent, not changing.

"I would have thought the things we were fighting…would have disappeared by now," she said. "And here we are in 2016, and where is that land we were talking about?"

How to end housing segregation

For decades, some U.S. cities and towns have looked to break down racial segregation in housing, with mixed success. Here are some strategies:

Scattered site housing: In 1966 a black woman sued the Chicago Housing Authority claiming it had engaged in racial discrimination by only offering family public housing "within the areas known as the Negro ghetto." The U.S. Supreme Court agreed in an 8-0 vote. That sparked a settlement that began a great experiment: More than 4,000 Chicago public housing residents, many black, were given housing vouchers and moved into predominantly white neighborhoods all across the suburbs, always in small enough numbers that their arrival didn't spark white flight. A 2006 study concluded that black families that moved as part of this program had better health (including mental health), education and income outcomes than those who stayed in high-poverty areas of Chicago.

Fair housing ordinances: In the 1970s, residents of Oak Park, Illinois, west of Chicago, feared the waves of blacks leaving Chicago would move into the city and turn it into an all-black community. They created a housing center and worked with real estate agents and prospective tenants to ensure that black and white families, renters and prospective owners, where shown apartments and homes in all parts of the city. It sought to avoid having a "black" part of town and a "white" one. In 1970, the city was nearly all-white; the fear of it becoming all-black did not materialize: Today, it is remains a wealthy community where 68 percent of residents are white and 22 percent are African American, roughly the same as it was a decade earlier.

Enforcement and education: Margaret Brown of the Fair Housing Center of Metropolitan Detroit said civil rights and anti-discrimination laws are necessary — but so is continued enforcement to keep people honest. Her group, funded 70 percent by the U.S. Department of Housing and Urban Development, uses paid "testers" to investigate bias. She said some landlords and homeowners still flout discrimination laws and the cudgel of enforcement would lessen those problems.

Housing assistance: In Shaker Heights, just outside Cleveland, community leaders have long promoted integration. That belief guided school decisions on new buildings and busing and it was the reason it began, through a nonprofit, to offer down payment assistant to minorities looking to move into the city and into predominantly white areas. The city is now 55 percent white and 37 percent black, slightly more minority than it was in 2000.

Regional solutions: In 1976, Minnesota passed a law requiring all communities to build affordable housing for low-income families and much of it was built in the suburbs of Minneapolis. The region actually saw its segregation decline from 1970 to 1980. But despite those initial successes the region has become increasingly segregated in the years since as housing policies encouraged more people to move into high-poverty areas while the suburbs used land once designated for affordable housing for market-rate residential developments because there was no longer a market for low-income housing.

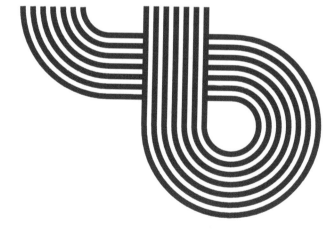

Tax Foreclosures Hurting Detroit's Recovery

By Lester Graham | Michigan Radio

Photo by Joseph Sohm

At one time, Detroit's black families had one of the highest home owner-ship rates in the nation. Now that rate is among the lowest. Every year in Detroit, thousands of people lose their homes to tax foreclosures. In many cases, it is unnecessary. The city is accused of illegal taxes and denying tax exemptions homeowners deserved.

When I got to Darryl and Alisa Beavers house, I was greeted by Jack-son, their small dog. They've been living in a three-bedroom, two-bath, 1600-square-foot home in Detroit's East side. There are a lot of nice houses in this neighborhood.

The Beavers have been renting with the idea of eventually buying the home from their landlord, a friend. But, Alisa says a few months back they didn't see or hear from the landlord for a while.

"And so we went over to his house and that's when we found out the land-lord passed away. And then we found out it was like maybe four years' worth of back taxes owed," Alisa said, her husband Darryl adding, "So, we got a foreclosure letter."

This is more than an inconvenience for the Beavers. It's more than just having to move. They've been working and spending their own money on this house.

"We fixed the house up to move into it, to live in it. We painted every-thing, we fixed everything in the house. The floors, we did everything. And the kitchen as well," Darryl explained. The couple also invested in a furnace and a hot water heater. They were invested in making the house comfortable with the expectation they'd one day buy it.

The house was put up for auction for back taxes. The Beavers saved some money and worked with the United Community Housing Coalition to put in a bid for the home. They didn't get the house. It sold for $4,400. It's worth around $40,000.

They'll soon meet with the new landlord to determine what their rent will cost, or make arrangements to purchase the house –presumably at market price, or learn when they have to be out. They've already received an eviction notice.

The Housing Coalition will help them find new place to live if it can.

Ted Phillips is the executive director of the non-profit advocacy group. The Coalition helps thousands of people facing tax foreclosure in Detroit to stay in their homes.

"(We) make sure that if there are ways to get out of foreclosure, there are various kinds of payment plans and what have you, we work with them to do that. We try to work with them so they're not throwing money away.

And what I mean by that is if somebody owes seven, eight, nine thousand dollars' worth of taxes, they have no business paying two or three thousand (dollars) and losing the house anyway. So, we try common sense kind of stuff," Phillips explained.

Phillips says the city has worked to reassess properties that were over-valued and over-taxed. But the job is not finished. Some people are paying a rate five times what they should.

In many cases, the homeowner should not be paying taxes at all. Their income falls below the federal poverty guideline and they should be getting an exemption.

"Very often the common scenario that we see is that somebody comes in for tax foreclosure, they should have been getting it (poverty exemption) forever, for that matter, you know, they're 70 years old, their income hasn't changed in years, but they didn't know about it and they first time they hear about it is when they're in foreclosure and about to lose their house," Phillips said.

Some homeowners are getting hit with both barrels. They're eligible for the poverty exemption, but not getting it. And they're charged taxes at an unreal rate.

Walter Hicks says the assessment of his house on Detroit's west side is ridiculous.

"Because what they had the house worth was, I think, 30 to 40,000 (dollars) and I got the house appraised, it was appraised for nine thousand," Hicks said.

On top of that, Hicks has been eligible for the poverty exemption in the past. His income has not changed, but he was denied the exemption a couple of years ago. The city said he owned another house in the city. The city said that made him ineligible for the exemption. It turns out that it's someone else's house. The man has the same first and last name.

The clerk at city hall told him nothing can be done that. It's too late. Hicks still has to pay the taxes. Hicks has repeatedly explained the situation to the city. His story has been reported in the news media. Still, he's heard nothing from the city.

"Not a thing. To rectify the problem—I know they done heard me, I know they know the issue. You know all I want them to do is to correct the error that they made," Hicks said.

Now, Walter Hicks is plaintiff in a lawsuit filed by the American Civil Liberties Union and the NAACP.

"The bottom line is people are losing their homes with an inability to pay taxes that they should never have had to pay in the first place," said Michael Steinberg with the ACLU.

The lawsuit originally charged the Wayne County Treasurer's Office and the City of Detroit with violating the Fair Housing Act. That's because black people in the county face tax foreclosure at a much higher rate than white people. A judge dismissed the case against the county, but the city is still in court. The ACLU also says the city is breaking state law for failing to assess property values properly.

"It's tragic. You know, the fact that the city is starting to come in line with state law helps people going forward, but it really doesn't help people who —and there's tens of thousands of them—who have lost their homes over the past five years," Steinberg said.

In emails responding to our questions, the Detroit Mayor's office showed progress on re-assessments of property. They noted a dramatic drop in foreclosures this year, about half of what they were last year. Many people were put on payment plans. Many people are getting poverty exemptions.

The City calls the ACLU lawsuit "recklessly irresponsible" and says it would "threaten basic city services to all Detroiters."

The city's future is threatened regardless. Here's why: without stable home ownership in a city, nothing is stable.

"One of the most important ways in which people acquire wealth, have that wealth increase and transfer that wealth from one generation to the other is the house," said Peter Hammer, a professor of law at Wayne State University.

That increase in wealth happened for the white middle class. New Deal programs during the Great Depression helped white people get ahead and buy homes. It did not help black people.

Many African-Americans who did by a home, bought it in inner-cities. Values in those locations often have plummeted. Instead of increasing wealth, many black families lost it.

"You look at the household and then you look at the city which really an aggregation of all the households. And the same things that are preventing the average household from aggregating wealth and being prosperous is also undermining the ability of the whole entire city of aggregating wealth and being prosperous," Hammer said.

In an effort to keep the City of Detroit afloat, it's already taxing at a higher rate than many other cities in the state. It's residents are among the poorest in the state. If the City is ever to see prosperity, it has to find a tax rate its citizens can afford or it will continue to force thousands of its residents out of their homes each year. §

Mike Wilkinson with Bridge Magazine contributed to the reporting of this story.

185

Walter P. Reuther Library, Wayne State University

Detroit's "Wailing Wall"

By Robin Schwartz | Detroit Jewish News

You don't have to travel far or look too hard to find a stark reminder of racial segregation in Detroit. Just a short distance from Royal Oak, Oak Park and Southfield, near Eight Mile and Wyoming, there is a park and playground bordered by a mural-filled wall.

The artwork is colorful, whimsical and uplifting with sketches of houses, people and symbols of peace.

But there is more to this scene than meets the eye. The 6-foot concrete wall that traverses the Alfonso Wells Memorial playground along Birwood Street has an ugly backstory.

"This is governmentally sanctioned apartheid," said Jeff Horner, a senior lecturer with Wayne State University's Department of Urban Studies and Planning. "The government actually saw fit to put in a physical barrier to separate the races."

Detroit's "Wailing Wall," also known as the "Eight Mile Wall" or "Birwood Wall," dates back to 1941. It was built to satisfy the Federal Housing Authority, which would not guarantee housing loans in "undesirable" neighborhoods. At the time, that meant communities with mostly African-American or Jewish families. So, a developer proposed building the half-mile wall as a clear dividing line meant to keep black families out. The FHA approved the loans and construction began.

"At least in some parts of history there's a narrative of the federal government as an agent of progress and there are examples of that," said Ben Falik, manager of Detroit service initiatives for the Jewish social action group Repair the World. "Then, there are also very concrete examples of when the federal government required and sanctioned segregation, and not just in the South; this is right here in Detroit."

Falik often brings groups of student volunteers to the wall for a firsthand look at the city's history. Parts are not covered with art and look exactly as it did 75 years ago. Teresa Moon grew up with the wall. Her family moved to Birwood in 1959, when she was just 6 years old. She still lives on the street today.

"We didn't know what it was. We had no idea it was a segregation wall," Moon said. "My parents never talked about it and neither did my grandmother. It wasn't something we discussed openly."

Teresa was about 15 when she finally learned why the wall was really there. She said it serves as a painful reminder at a time when our country is still very much divided.

"Wailing Wall"
....

Ben Falik
....

Jeff Horner
....

All photos by Robin Schwartz

187

"I can't take away what it is," she said. "I can't not tell the kids who are growing up over here what it is and why they built it and how anybody would have the audacity to build anything so minimal. It's only 6 feet tall; it's 12 inches wide; I can get on my tip-toes and look over it."

While not much is known about the Jewish community's response or reaction at the time the wall was built, history professor Lila Corwin Berman recounts one instance where a Jewish builder tried to extend the wall for his own benefit. In her book, "Metropolitan Jews: Politics, Race and Religion in Postwar Detroit," Berman wrote that Harry Slatkin tried to convince city leaders to go along with the plan.

"Slatkin had hoped he might snake the wall around the property he owned to protect his investment from black settlement," she writes. "The city rejected his 1953 effort to elongate the wall."

"STUFF STILL HAPPENS"

Moon says while it may be subtler today, "stuff still happens" to keep people apart.

"There are some places in this surrounding community I won't go because I know I'm not going to be treated fairly, and that's like a few miles from here," she said. "Is it ever going to change? Are we ever going to be where the color of my skin is not going to matter? I'm 63 years old and I can't see that will happen in my lifetime, and that's sad. It brings tears to my eyes."

She remains hopeful things will improve, especially for the younger generation. Moon recalls being a junior high school student in 1967, when she met and spoke to white students for the first time.

"That's when they started busing kids," Moon recalled. "That was my first experience going to school with white kids — and they were white Jewish kids. It was an experience because neither one of us knew anything about the other one. I hadn't been close to a white person ever in my life."

Detroit's Wailing Wall runs through a community that remains predominantly African American. Horner says, unfortunately, the lingering lesson of the wall is still relevant and timely today, more than seven decades later.

"The lesson is let people live wherever they want to live," he said. "Eliminate racial prejudice and hatred — and I think everything will be fine." §

Teresa Moon has lived around the Detroit's "Wailing Wall" since age 6. She learned its true meaning — to separate houses owned by blacks from new white subdivisions — when she was 15.

....

Photo by Robin Schwartz

Latinos and African-Americans in Detroit connected by wall, segregation

By Sergio Martínez-Beltrán | Latino Press

When Carmen Muñoz was faced with the Detroit Wall for the first time, she was not intimidated. Muñoz's mother used to tell her that "if someone tells you you can't, you will find a way."

And so she crossed the wall.

The Detroit Wall — a wall that starts in the Alfonso Wells Memorial Playground off 8 Mile and stretches for about half a mile — was built in 1941 and it is a standing symbol of segregation in Detroit. This wall served, essentially, as a border separating blacks from whites — reminiscent, in part, to the wall proposed by President-elect Donald Trump along the Mexican border.

Michigan State University environment, geography and spatial sciences professor Joe Darden said the wall came to be as part of a plan, proposed by a white developer and approved by the Federal Housing Administration, to segregate a white community from a black neighborhood.

"Segregation was supported by everybody at that time who was white essentially — the federal government, the city of Detroit, and the real estate brokers and the apartment managers," Darden said. "That wall came about because the federal government would only give these whites assistance if they could build housing in a place that they could guarantee will remain all white."

These practices, prior to the 1968 Fair Housing Act, gave power to white homeowners and, in Detroit, on the other side of 8 Mile, a community just for them.

"Before 1969, blacks could not get across that wall and after 1969, blacks were allowed to cross it and they did so," Darden said.

But this wall was only one of the many obstacles that minorities in Detroit faced before the 1968 Fair Housing Act and before segregation was opposed.

For Latinos in the city, renting or owning a house was a big problem and sometimes an impossible goal to achieve. There was discrimination against Latinos and, in some communities, they were not welcome.

Mexican immigrants started arriving in Mexicantown around the same time when the Detroit Wall was built — 1941.

Darden said Mexicans came to Michigan as agricultural workers but later transitioned to the better paid manufacturing industry.

"For a very long time, there was already a small cluster of Mexicans in the southwest section of Detroit, and, for protective reasons, they would cluster in that same particular part of Detroit," Darden said. "They were isolated."

Muñoz said she experienced that type of isolation and discrimination in her community.

"Across the street from our house there was a little girl my age but her mother wouldn't let her play with me because 'all Mexican girls carried knives in their stockings,'" Muñoz said.

She said the girl who told her this was white and the storyline that all Mexican girls carried a weapon with them was an excuse to not integrate with other neighbors, in this case, the Mexican family.

Muñoz, now 80 years old, attended St. Vincent School—now an apartment complex— with her 15 siblings. Her dad was a "rebel" and made an arrangement with the school principal to have all of his 16 children in the school. Muñoz's father's form of pay: all of his 16 children would clean the school every day.

"We were for a while the only Latinos and then we had two other families, a Sánchez and another Muñoz," Muñoz said.

Her father also helped, in part, Mexicans integrate into different communities. He would buy houses and have Mexican immigrants fix them — after the fixing, he would allow them to stay in the house as long as they paid rent.

In a place where Latinos were discriminated against and no one wanted to give housing to them, Muñoz's father helped his own community.

"My dad felt good about it because there weren't a lot of houses for them… because they were Mexicans," Muñoz said.

LATINOS IN THE CITY AND THE SUBURBS

U.S. Census data shows that there are more Latinos in the suburbs and the city of Detroit than in the past. However, to say that the suburbs and the city are integrated might be considered a stretch — the Latino population hasn't dramatically increased or decreased since at least 2000.

"In general the Latino community has been stable in that, despite the economic crisis and the mortgage crisis, we didn't experience a major loss of the Latino community per se," said Detroit councilwoman Raquel Castañeda-López.

And the suburbs follow the same stable trend.

In 2000, 1.4 percent of the population of Beverly Hills was Latino/Hispanic and, in 2010, 1.7 percent of the population identified as Latino/Hispanic; Plymouth's 2000 census had 1.3 percent of its population as Latino/Hispanic, in comparison to 2010 1.8 percent. That same trend can be found in many other Detroit suburbs.

And for the first time, Detroiters have a council member that identifies as Latina, representing Detroit's 6th District.

In 2013, Castañeda-López, the first Latina elected for city council, took office. One of the first things she did was to establish the Detroit Immigration Task Force.

She also worked with Mayor Mike Duggan to create the Department of Immigrant Affairs.

These programs help with the integration of immigrants and refugees into the participating cities — one of Castañeda-Lopez's many missions as a councilwoman.

"Detroit welcomes you," Castañeda-López said to those who may fear for their safety or rights after the presidential election. "We invite people to move to the city of Detroit where there is a little more diversity and people will find it a little bit easier to blend in despite the challenges of housing, crime and education." §

Top: The Detroit Wall and policies of segregation in the housing system have impacted blacks in the city since the 1940s.
....

Bottom: The 1942 riot at the Sojourner Truth homes, a new U.S. federal housing project, was caused by white neighbors' attempt to prevent Negro tenants from moving in. The sign was posted directly opposite the housing project
....

A Revitalized Detroit Attracts Young Jewish Residents

By Shari S. Cohen | Detroit Jewish News

While many Jewish Detroiters left the city between 1950 and 1970, a growing number of young Jews have chosen Detroit as their home during the past five to 10 years.

Jewish singles and couples, mainly in their 20s and 30s, have moved to a range of neighborhoods, including Sherwood Forest in northwest Detroit, Midtown and Lafayette Park as well as the North Side and West Village. Most work or attend school in Detroit and share an affinity for urban living. Some are employed by educational organizations or other nonprofit organizations dedicated to improving Detroit.

Rachel Klegon, 31, executive director of Green Living Science, a nonprofit environmental education organization, grew up in Farmington Hills. After graduating from Michigan State University in 2007, she took jobs with two Detroit-based nonprofits — Woodbridge Neighborhood Development Corporation and Summer in the City.

"I like urban areas and wanted to be in the city," she explains. "I always considered Detroit to be my city, and I felt very connected to it."

Since then, she has lived in Detroit's West Village, Woodbridge and North End neighborhoods. In the North End, which she describes as located between New Center and Hamtramck, she rents a home built in 2007.

"My street is very safe, and I have great neighbors," Klegon says. "It's right off I-75 so it's convenient — nothing is more than 20 minutes away."

She is friendly with people she met while living in Detroit's Repair the World Moishe House and Detroiters she knew from Temple Kol Ami, which she attended while growing up.

Andrew Stein, 35, is executive director of City Year Detroit, a nonprofit that trains and places AmeriCorps members in Detroit Public Schools for a year of service.

"I grew up in the suburbs with a certain perception of Detroit and other cities in general as a place where you went to the theater and sporting events — not where you live," he says.

However, while living in Washington, D.C., for 11 years, Stein says, "that narrative was flipped on its head."

In 2015, after accepting the City Year Detroit position, Stein wanted to live and invest in Detroit. "It opens up ways to be part of a community that you can't do when you're living outside," he explains, adding that his Detroit residency isn't a political statement or job requirement and that he doesn't consider himself a pioneer.

While their acquaintances here recommended Pleasant Ridge, Huntington Woods and Berkley, Stein's wife, Beth, wanted to consider Detroit. They looked at many Detroit neighborhoods with a Realtor specializing in Detroit and bought a house in Sherwood Forest in northwest Detroit last year. It was built for a Jewish doctor in 1955 and still had the original mezuzahs.

192

"The house was loved and cared for, and we found that this has always been a strong neighborhood," Stein says.

The Steins wanted to raise their children in a diverse neighborhood and have found their experience "overall, very positive."

"We have met friends who are young and others who have lived in the neighborhood for 30 or 40 years. We always feel safe in our neighborhood," he says.

They investigated many school options and chose a public charter school, Detroit Achievement Academy, for their daughter, Mia, 6. The Steins participate with a group of Detroit Jewish families who plan family events in the city, using Jtot Detroit to connect online.

Stein notes Sherwood Forest residents are very supportive of ongoing improvements on nearby Livernois, once known as the Avenue of Fashion. "Anytime something opens, everyone supports it," he says.

Detroit has had Jewish residents since 1762. The first Jewish neighborhood, Hastings Street, developed near downtown Detroit in the 1880s. By 1910, Jews began moving to newer neighborhoods to the north and later northwest, as African Americans moved into predominantly Jewish neighborhoods — a pattern that continued into the 1970s. In recent years, there has been a modest reversal of that trend with some new Jewish residents inspired by Detroit's revitalization.

According to historian Sydney Bolkosky's book, "Harmony & Dissonance: Voices in Jewish Identity in Detroit 1914-1967," some Jews left Hastings Street for better business opportunities, but others "wanted to escape escalating crime — which frequently served as a euphemism for their flight from the mounting black population."

Black Detroiters were crowded into a small section of the city and, with continued migration from the South, they faced a critical need for more housing. However, racial prejudice and discriminatory legal restrictions hampered their ability to rent and buy homes outside their existing neighborhoods.

Some powerful all-white, non-Jewish neighborhood organizations posted threatening signs, vandalized African-Americans' homes and threatened violence when blacks attempted to rent or buy homes in white neighborhoods. Black Detroiters faced less resistance when moving to Jewish neighborhoods.

"Jews didn't demonstrate or burn crosses; they simply moved out," recalls U.S. District Court Judge Avern Cohn, then a lawyer active with the Jewish Community Council, precursor of the Jewish Community Relations Council.

Cohn views the initial outward migration as mostly driven by upward mobility. "The initial movement from the Twelfth Street area was not racial," he says. "Families were living in two-family and four-family duplexes and apartment buildings. They were not fleeing; they were improving their housing stock."

After World War II, returning veterans sought to start families, and real estate developers created suburban-like developments in northwest Detroit — mostly brick, two-story, single-family homes with small front and backyards, and detached garages. Many young Jewish families bought houses in northwest Detroit around Bagley, Hampton and Vernor elementary schools. Synagogues, temples and stores followed them.

But, by 1958, Jews were on the move again — this time initially to Oak Park, Huntington Woods and Southfield, often moving to subdivisions developed by Jewish builders. By 1958, according to a study by Albert Mayer for the Jewish Welfare Federation, cited in Lila Corwin Berman's book, "Metropolitan Jews: Politics, Race and Religion in Postwar Detroit," 20 percent of Detroit's Jewish population lived in Oak Park and Huntington Woods. The Oak Park branch of the Jewish Community Center opened in 1959.

Why did Jewish Detroiters leave the city? There were multiple reasons — racial, economic, religious and sociological and, of course, many white residents who were not Jewish also moved to the suburbs. (Years later, many African Americans left Detroit for Oak Park and Southfield, too.)

According to Judge Cohn, as soon as a neighborhood became 30 percent black, whites started to leave. "Jews are white people, and they weren't used to integration," he says.

A key incentive for many families was the desire for newer, better housing that was readily available in the suburbs by the late 1950s. Government mortgage programs eased the financing for new homes that offered more space and privacy than some city neighborhoods. (Many northwest Detroit houses, while still fairly new because they were built in the late 1940s through the 1950s, were relatively small.)

Another reason for suburban migration was the lack of available land for expansion within the city. Detroit was designed as a city of single family homes and small apartment buildings, rather than higher-density vertical development. As Arco Construction CEO Walter Cohen, a longtime residential real estate developer and builder, notes, "You run out of land quick with single-family homes."

Plus, the city was bounded by the Detroit River to the south, the Grosse Pointes (with a discriminatory point system for prospective home buyers) to the east, and Eight Mile, a state-designated county boundary, to the north. Suburbs to the west of Detroit, such as Dearborn and Livonia, attracted very few Jews. The Jewish residential movement was north/northwest, facilitated by federally funded highways, new suburban sewer and water systems, and relatively inexpensive buildable land.

And there was a financial component as well. "A house is the most important investment any family has, and white homeowners felt threatened by integration," says Judge Cohn.

In addition, "Jews left because they were offered a good price," says builder Cohen.

Other factors were concerns about integrated public schools, crime and the desire for predominantly Jewish neighborhoods. But for many white people leaving Detroit, an underlying issue was a fear or dislike of African Americans.

CHANGING NEIGHBORHOODS

Harriet Berg, 92, a lifelong resident of Detroit and a dance company director, remembers the changeover of her northwest Detroit neighborhood during the 1960s and 70s. As a child, she lived in the Calvert-Wildemere area and later Glynn Court. After her marriage, she and her husband bought a house on Snowden near Schaefer in northwest Detroit.

"People moved out quietly in the summer and at night," she recalls. "Real estate agents had a lot to do with cleaning people out. They distributed fliers that said, 'Sell while you can.'"

Ira Harris, 78, a retired lawyer and Huntington Woods resident, grew up on Birchcrest and attended Hampton and Mumford High School. He lived in Detroit until the 1980s.

"It doesn't take much to stir people to white flight; they feared black people," Harris says. He, too, remembers scare tactics by real estate agents, some Jewish, who warned homeowners: "You better sell now before it [the housing price] goes through the cellar."

Ruth Kahn, 89, who has lived in Detroit's Green Acres neighborhood since 1957, says, "I never talked about it with anyone. They had a little more money so they moved to the suburbs."

By 1965, half of all Detroit Jews lived in the suburbs, according to Berman in Metropolitan Jews, and some Detroit-based synagogues and temples had moved as well. Congregation Shaarey Zedek built a sanctuary and school in Southfield in 1962, a move

that was quite controversial, according to Judge Cohn, and which was reportedly not approved by Shaarey Zedek's Rabbi Morris Adler.

Kathleen Straus, a Downtown Detroit resident, recalls Temple Beth El's membership vote to purchase land for a new suburban location. "I was one of only 14 members who voted against the move," she says. The temple completed a new building in Bloomfield Hills in 1973.

DEDICATED TO OPEN HOUSING

While many Jewish Detroiters were leaving for the suburbs, Jewish organizations and religious leaders had actively supported efforts to provide equal housing opportunities for all Detroiters. They were mindful that discriminatory housing covenants and deed restrictions had been used against Jews not many years before and were still in effect in some suburbs.

Mel Ravitz, initially an employee of the Detroit City Planning Commission, was elected to the City Council in 1961 — the first Jewish member since 1920. He was dedicated to open housing, stating that "only in a liberal community can there be real freedom and security for Jews."

The Jewish Community Council supported the Brickley ordinance, which prohibited discriminatory real estate practices and passed in 1962. During the 1960s, the Jewish Community Council met with real estate agents, some of whom were Jewish, especially those who were "sowing seeds of housing panic."

For example, Metropolitan Jews tells of the Benjamin Rich real estate agency (with the slogan "Get Rich Quick") that distributed postcards to neighbors after selling a house to African Americans. The postcard stated: "You have a new neighbor. If you want to sell your house, see us for quick action and top price."

While aggressive sales tactics were criticized by city agencies and religious organizations, one prominent Realtor denied that agents were the problem. He said that homeowners should "look into their own hearts."

U.S. Sen. Carl Levin, recently retired, was then general counsel for the new Michigan Civil Rights Commission and Michigan's assistant attorney general. In 1968, he took on a fair housing case involving Pulte, a suburban developer, who refused to sell land or houses to blacks, claiming there was no legal guarantee of non-discrimination in housing.

Levin won the case on behalf of Freeman Moore, an African American who sought to buy a Pulte home in a new subdivision near 13 Mile Road and Lahser. The ADL, Jewish Community Relations Council, Michigan Council of Churches and other organizations supported Moore's case. The Michigan Supreme Court ruled there was a guaranteed right of non-discrimination in housing. After that, Levin said, developers couldn't openly discriminate. Many Jews joined the Greater Detroit Commission for Fair Housing Practices. However, some members differentiated between discrimination in public and private housing, and Jewish leaders did not necessarily advocate that Jews should remain in integrated neighborhoods.

Miriam Kalichman, M.D., a retired pediatrician who grew up in Detroit's University District, recalls when her mother, Bettie Kalichman, testified at City Council on behalf of an open housing ordinance. "She appeared on television and subsequently received some hate mail," Kalichman says.

The proposed Detroit fair housing ordinance did not pass, but state and federal legislation was approved soon after. Detroit's 1967 riot was undoubtedly a more significant factor than open housing laws in the white exodus from the city. However, some city neighborhoods have maintained a racial mix.

Gene Turner, an African American Chrysler retiree, moved to Green Acres in 1971 when it was "very mixed."

"We didn't have any problems," he says. "[Yet] I wouldn't say I got invited to all of the neighborhood parties." Some years later, they moved to the University District. "We sort of upgraded," Turner says. Once a year, the neighborhood holds a reunion, and former residents who return are surprised at how nice the area is, he says. There is an influx of younger residents and housing prices have increased.

Reginald Stuart, now a retired journalist, moved with his family to Green Acres in 1975. He found the neighborhood to be diverse and without any problems for African Americans.

His friend and neighbor, Ruth Kahn, who has lived on Renfrew in Green Acres for 59 years, says, "I'm very comfortable here. My neighbors are lovely people."

Another Jewish Green Acres homeowner says the neighborhood was 60 to 70 percent white when she moved in about 30 years ago. "It became a friendlier neighborhood as it became more integrated. There are more young people now," she notes.

Harriet Berg and her husband, Irv, sold their house on Snowden in 1983, when he no longer wanted to handle home maintenance and stairs.

"We planned to buy a smaller house in Huntington Woods," she says. "We rented an apartment for a year in the Park Shelton [in Midtown near the Detroit Institute of Arts] and liked it so much we stayed and bought a condominium here.

"People would say that Detroit is coming back, and I said, 'not in my lifetime,' but I was wrong," Berg says.

"Every week a new restaurant opens and there is a Chabad House nearby." §

Andrew Stein and his daughter, Mia, 6, in front of their Sherwood Forest home

Rachel Klegon at Green Living Science, where she is executive director

HALL
SUPER MARKET
TANDARD
WILLIAM
DRUG
PRESCRIPTI
LIQUO
AS YOU
TRAVEL
ASK US
LIQUOR
ICE
69
TRY

CHAPTER 8
THE BLIND PIG

The blind pig, also known as the United Community League for Civic Action, was on the second floor of Economy Printing at 9125 12th Street. A police raid on this illegal bar and gambling joint sparked the 1967 Detroit uprisings.
....

Photo courtesy of the Bentley Historical Library

Bill Scott threw the first bottle at police, an act that encouraged violent uprisings by black Detroiters in 1967. His son grew up thinking his race didn't matter. Until one night, suddenly, it did.

He started the Detroit Riots. His son wrestles with the carnage.

By Bill McGraw

As much of the city slept, 19-year-old William Walter Scott III stood at the corner of 12th Street and Clairmount, watching as police escorted scores of black patrons out of a blind pig on Detroit's west side.

It was about 3:45 a.m. July 23, 1967, and William Scott, known as Bill, was among a crowd of mostly young African Americans gathering to watch the police hustle club patrons into waiting paddy wagons. He had a particular interest in two of the people being led away.

His father, William Walter Scott II, was the principal owner of the club, an illegal after-hours drinking and gambling joint. His older sister, Wilma, was a cook and waitress. The night was hot and sticky, and the crowd's initial teasing of the arrestees devolved into raucous goading of police as they became more aggressive, pushing and twisting the arms of the women.

"You don't have to treat them that way," Bill Scott yelled. "They can walk. Let them walk, you white sons of bitches."

By the time the wagons were full, the crowd had swelled, the taunts had grown more hostile and, though police manpower was thin early Sunday, several scout cars responded to the scene. Cops stood at the ready in the middle of 12th Street, billy clubs in hand, forcing the throng back on the sidewalk.

Scott, tall and lean, mounted a car and began to preach to a crowd long accustomed to the harsh tactics of the overwhelmingly white Detroit police in black neighborhoods: "Are we going to let these peckerwood motherf------ come down here any time they want and mess us around?"

"Hell, no!" people yelled back.

Scott walked into an alley and grabbed a bottle, seeking "the pleasure of hitting one in the head, maybe killing him," he remembers thinking. Making his way into the middle of the crowd for cover, he threw the bottle at a sergeant standing in front of the door.

CHAPTER 8

THE BLIND PIG

Bill Scott
....
Courtesy photo

The missile missed, shattering on the sidewalk. A phalanx of police moved toward the crowd, then backed off. As the paddy wagons drove away, bottles, bricks and sticks flew through the air, smashing the windows of departing police cars. Bill Scott said he felt ... liberated.

"For the first time in our lives we felt free. Most important, we were right in what we did to the law."

The rebellion was underway.

A personal history

Bill Scott's thrown bottle was a catalyst for one the most destructive civil disorders in U.S. history — five days of looting, arson and violence in Detroit that killed 43 people and resulted in thousands of injuries and arrests in a summer jolted by violence across dozens of U.S. cities.

But Scott, a bright but troubled product of the 12th Street neighborhood, left a legacy more enduring than broken glass. It's a legacy that carries echoes as the 50th anniversary of 1967 draws near and Detroit reevaluates whether the despair and tensions of erupted that summer continue today.

Three years after the looting and burning, Scott, by then 22 and a student at the University of Michigan, self-published a memoir titled "Hurt, Baby, Hurt" that describes his experiences growing up as a young black man in majority-white Detroit, working in his father's blind pig and living along 12th Street, the west-side thoroughfare that was Detroit's crowded and rowdy sin strip.

He writes of growing anger at what he felt was the city's racial oppression, where Detroit's notoriously aggressive, nearly all-white police were not shy about knocking heads on corners where black men lingered. Bill Scott's account of his role in the violence comes from the memoir.

In 1969, an early version of his book won a prestigious Hopwood Award, the U-M literary prize whose student winners over the years included future heavyweights Arthur Miller, Lawrence Kasdan and Marge Piercy.

Largely forgotten, Scott's memoir reads today like a newly discovered time capsule, but one with contemporary significance amid the divide between police and African-American communities across the nation. Perhaps no other account delves in such a deeply personal way into the rage and despair that drove so many black Detroiters into the streets that summer.

Scott, who spent a childhood steeped in self loathing, embarrassed by the radical black politics of his father and secretly imagining he was white, describes his political transformation through the racial animus he said he witnessed routinely in Detroit.

But the story of Bill Scott did not begin with a thrown bottle on that July night nearly 50 years ago. Nor would it end with his downward spiral, marked by drug addiction, mental illness and homelessness.

For Bill Scott would have a son, Mandela. And that son would have his own dramatic journey — from a privileged upbringing that led him to the Ivy League, to his own racial awakening, when he realized that no matter how carefully his life was constructed, his skin color would always set him apart from the white world he had so confidently navigated.

The saga of Bill Scott must be told without Scott himself. Now 68, he has disappeared somewhere in coastal Florida. The political fire and promise of his youth would be derailed by substance abuse and mental illness, those close to him say.

"I'd never met anyone remotely like him. It was terrifying and exhilarating," said Auburn Sheaffer Sandstrom, who first encountered Scott in a U-M graduate class and married him four years later.

Percy Bates, a professor of education at U-M, knew Scott briefly when Scott was a child and became closer to him in Ann Arbor, when Scott showed glimmers of his potential.

"Anybody who knew him knew that he was very bright, but he

Largely forgotten, Scott's memoir reads today like a newly discovered time capsule, but one with contemporary significance amid the divide between police and African-American communities across the nation.

201

William Scott, director of United Community League for Civic Action, owner of the blind pig, father of Bill and Wilma Scott.

....

Detroit Free Press photo

was just unable to use that brightness to any positive end," Bates said. "I think later he probably would not have been able to produce the book or anything like that that required persistent attention."

The father

The origins of the Scott family's story is a familiar one in Detroit.

William Walter Scott II, the owner of the blind pig and Bill Scott's father, was born in Georgia and came to Detroit as child, just as the "Great Migration" of African Americans from the South to a fresh start in northern cities began before World War I. The influx would boost Detroit's black population seven-fold within a decade as the auto industry transformed the city into an industrial metropolis starving for workers.

When Bill Scott, his sister Wilma and their siblings — Tyrone, Reginald and Charlotte — were young, their father made a good living at Dodge Main and other factories. But between 1947 and 1963 the city's manufacturing economy hemorrhaged 134,000 jobs, triggering the start of Detroit's long decline. William Scott lost his factory job, and subsequently the family lost its house.

Unable to find work, William Scott II turned to "the numbers," the illegal, lottery-like gambling game ubiquitous in black neighborhoods, even as his political activism grew.

He eventually became involved in organizing black political power by training volunteers for local campaigns. His second-floor suite of rooms on 12th Street was officially known as the United Community League for Civic Action. On the night of the 1967 raid, one room contained a wall chart of local precinct delegates. William Scott's wife, Hazel, worked in the Detroit office of G. Mennen (Soapy) Williams, Michigan's Democratic governor from 1949 to 1961 who was extremely popular in the black community.

But the elder Scott's disgust with Detroit's white political system grew. Years later, he would tell a sociologist studying the riot aftermath that political leaders pass legislation "just to control and contain the Negro."

Mr. Scott did not hide his militancy, or his anger. He fumed at being called "boy" by police and roughly frisked for no apparent reason. In 1973, when Coleman Young was elected Detroit's first black mayor on a police-reform platform, he told his daughter Wilma, "I can finally get off my knees."

"All the people have had their revolutions, and we're the last. It's something that's got to come, you can't stop it. When people get sick and oppressed, they're gonna riot," William Scott told the sociologist.

"My father was a survivor," said Wilma Scott, now 70, who spent more than 40 years as an office worker at Detroit's Henry Ford Hospital. "And he was a survivor without being a criminal. Except for the numbers, which he did not feel was a crime, okay?

"To this day, I understand his logic. He was a black man that was determined just to be free. It's as simple as that. To say he had to depend on a white man for his living — he did not like that. Especially after being in the factory and being laid off."

The son

Bill Scott was born two years after Wilma, in 1948. In his memoir, he describes a bleak childhood of constant moves, being bullied at school and spending lonely days wandering through alleys, looking for useable junk.

He was close to his mother, but she was often hospitalized with heart problems and died when Bill was 14. He said he feared his father, writing that he beat him, though Wilma Scott says she did not see such violence.

Bill Scott did not see his own early promise. He had trouble learning in school, and thought himself "ugly," "dull," "strange," "useless," even "mentally retarded." By age 10, he was unruly and suffering emotional problems. He was sent to the Hawthorn Center, about a state-run facility for emotionally-troubled children in Northville, and later to a similar institution, the Boys Republic in Farmington Hills. In his own mind, he wrote, he pretended to be white because, he felt, being black was bad, but white children were considered good.

It was in the early 1960s that Bates, the U-M professor, first met Bill Scott at a camp in Pinkney. The boy, he said, "didn't trust anybody, he couldn't get close to anybody. He was constantly acting out, calling people names, throwing stuff, hitting people. It was just clear that he had some serious issues."

But Bill Scott received counseling at the two youth homes and met adults who mentored him. He writes glowingly of both places, and they seemed to help him stabilize.

As he moved into middle school, the unruly boy began to

> "All the people have had their revolutions, and we're the last. It's something that's got to come, you can't stop it. When people get sick and oppressed, they're gonna riot."
>
> — William Scott

blossom. Scott writes of becoming intellectually curious and aware of the importance of good values: respecting women and elders; obeying the law; refraining from stealing or premarital sex. He began attending church. "I liked the sound of this heaven place," he wrote.

After a brief, tumultuous stay in a foster home, Scott returned to his father's three-room apartment near Detroit's 12th Street.

It was in this rapidly changing neighborhood that Bill Scott said he bumped into the reality of being a black man in Detroit. After years in white-run institutions and attending church, his values were "almost in exact opposition to the way my people lived" back on 12th Street.

Because of his polite bearing, he was mocked by neighborhood toughs, who called him "Proper" and "Whitey." He said he stood out because he was a "decent" person. "I didn't have processed hair, a rag hanging from my head or dirty clothes," he writes, "and, most of all, I had the 'proper thoughts.'"

At Northern High, Scott noted that virtually all the students were black and most of the faculty was white, a recipe for failure, he believed. He called Northern "a nigger factory" that churned out unschooled students who wanted to learn but were at the mercy of teachers who either didn't want to teach black students, or didn't know how.

Test scores showed 9th graders at Northern reading at a sixth-grade level. But Scott was smart and ambitious and determined to attend college, even as his white counselor tried to steer him to vocational courses. At one point, he tried to transfer to a more competitive majority-white city school, but was refused. So he made the best of it, playing drums in the band, lettering in football, learning to pole vault and, in 1966, graduating.

Three months later, some 2,300 Northern students attracted national attention by staging a walkout and boycott to protest their poor-quality education in a school that lacked the top-notch facilities and wider opportunities enjoyed by students at mostly white city schools, such as Redford High. The protests, a sign of growing militancy among young African Americans, were an unprecedented challenge to authority, and the principal and at least two other officials lost their jobs.

As he moved through his teens, Scott began to face another fact of life for many young black men in the 1960s: an overwhelmingly white Detroit police force.

Scott wrote that he tried to live like a "civilized Negro," staying active in a middle-class black church. But as he left a church meeting one day when he was 17, cops stopped him for jaywalking across 12th Street. When Scott asked what he had done, he said one of the officers threw him against the scout car and called him "boy."

204

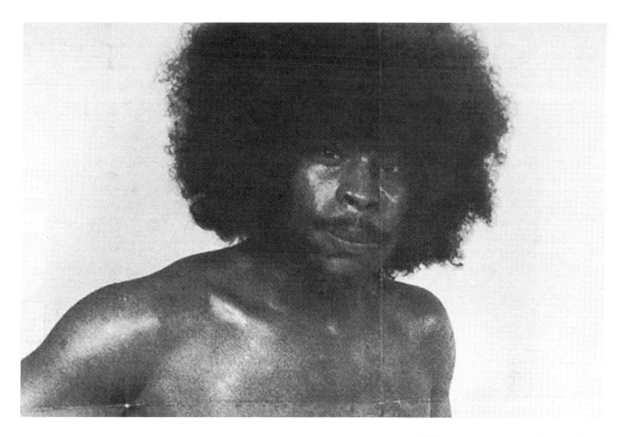

Bill Scott from a promotional poster for his book, "Hurt, Baby, Hurt."

They gave him a $10 ticket. Scott wrote that he ripped it up in front of them and threw in a trash can next to their car.

Next was a run-in with the department's notorious Big Four — three plainclothes cops with a uniformed driver in a big car — a unit that cruised precincts and routinely harassed blacks. Walking out of a store, Scott and brothers Tyrone and Reggie were stopped and frisked for no reason, Scott writes. The confrontation ended with Scott shouting, "You can kiss my black ass." He said police backed off when an angry crowd began to form.

Scott's racial consciousness continued to grow during a months-long job search in the spring and early summer of 1967 when, despite an uptick in the city's economy, 25 to 30 percent of black youths between 18 and 24 remained unemployed. Failing to find work, he was forced to drop out of Michigan Lutheran College, a Detroit school he attended before U-M.

The frustrations piled up, along with a growing perception that his fellow church members attended services to "wallow in their own self-hatred" and ask God's forgiveness "for being black." He felt like he was pulling himself up by his bootstraps — as society demanded — but getting nowhere.

It was these accumulated grievances, hardly unique to Bill Scott or to blacks in Detroit, that reached a boiling point in the summer

"Twelfth Street was like a jungle or an unsolvable maze," Scott writes, a "Hollywood strip" filled with "shady-looking characters" hanging out on corners.

"It was hard to predict what was going to happen next — I mean one night somebody might get shot or cut up and next night everybody on the street could be happy and cool; plain drunk."

of 1967, when dozens of U.S. cities exploded in violence. At age 19, the Bill Scott who threw the first bottle at police was a young man determined to break with his past. "I decided to reject anything that was white," he writes.

It also softened how he viewed his father.

"I began to look at the cat and see that he was farther ahead than anyone I'd met in my entire life and he was the only person I wouldn't listen to," Scott writes. "I guess he was the most courageous and bold man I ever saw in my life.

"I could now understand why my father had given up in the white conventional world. I was black and being black meant I had to live black…no more hating myself because I was black."

He went to work at his father's club.

The blind pig

There is not a street in Detroit today that resembles the 12th Street of 1967 in the stretch near the blind pig.

Fifty years ago, the mile-and-a-half section of 12th Street north of West Grand Boulevard was a densely packed commercial strip of markets, pharmacies, party stores, bakeries, shoe stores, beauty parlors and photo studios. With two and three-story buildings along both sides, and a cognstant flow of people and traffic, 12th looked like a typical Detroit shopping district when the city had 1.5 million or more residents.

Many blacks living on the side streets off 12th were upwardly mobile and already middle class. But the stretch of 12th north of Virginia Park had developed into a frenetic strip of legal and illegal adult entertainment: bars, prostitutes, pimps, pawn shops, gambling, drugs, after-hours drinking, crime and cops.

The neighborhood personified the city's rapidly changing geography after World War II. Up through the 1940s, the area had been largely Jewish, but as Jews began moving northwest, and African Americans took their place on side streets dense with apartment buildings and solid multi-family homes.

Urban renewal projects destroyed the downtown black ghetto in the 1950s and new laws cut into housing segregation, prompting even more African Americans to flood into the 12th Street neighborhood, though store owners remained mostly white.

"Twelfth Street was like a jungle or an unsolvable maze," Scott writes, a "Hollywood strip" filled with "shady-looking characters" hanging out on corners.

"It was hard to predict what was going to happen next — I mean one night somebody might get shot or cut up and next night everybody on the street could be happy and cool; plain drunk."

For much of the summer of 1967, Scott earned $25 a night as

doorman at his dad's club, letting people in and trying to keep police out. The club was dark and smoky, with a bar, pool table, gambling room, kitchen and a dance floor with loud music from a juke box. "Everyone was dancing, laughing, having a nitty-gritty-funky good time," Scott recalled.

Blind pigs like the one William Scott operated were long an institution in Detroit's black neighborhoods. They served blacks when African Americans were barred from downtown restaurants and bars before World War II. After the color line was broken in mainstream establishments, blind pigs continued to play a major cultural role in black Detroit, historian Sidney Fine wrote, and raids by white cops were often seen as having "racial and symbolic significance."

Police raided William Scott's club twice in 1966 and again in June 1967, when the vice squad arrested 28 people on misdemeanors. The DPD tried to stage other busts but couldn't get an undercover cop past the door. Once, they burst through the doors only to find a children's Halloween party in progress.

As summer unfolded in 1967, police confrontations with black residents added to racial tension in Detroit. Rumors of impending unrest raged across the city amid scattered disorders in African-American neighborhoods across the country, including a small, two-day disturbance on Kercheval Avenue on Detroit's east

Auburn Sheaffer Sandstrom, a doctoral candidate at Cleveland State University, meets with the African Wisdom Circle, an informal weekly coffee-house group in University Heights, Ohio, that includes James E. Page, left, and John Omar. The group discusses issues of race, gender and the meaning of being human.

Photo by Peggy Turbett

207

Bill Scott's sister, Wilma Scott, in her Detroit home in November.

Photo by Brian Widdis

side in 1966. By late July 1967, violence had torn through 33 American cities, most notably Newark, where six days of violence left 26 people dead.

Detroit was still on edge from the fatal shooting in June of a black Vietnam veteran. The man had dared to take his pregnant wife to Rouge Park, then surrounded by an all-white neighborhood. Whites taunted the couple with racial slurs, pelted them with bottles and suggested they might rape the woman. Someone shot the veteran; his wife was not assaulted but would suffer a miscarriage, according to the Michigan Chronicle.

Then, on July 1, a black prostitute was fatally shot at 12th and Hazelwood. Police variously said the assailant was a pimp or a prospective customer, but rumors circulated in the black community that an off-duty white officer had killed her after she allegedly slashed him with a knife.

Bill Scott said he was at the blind pig during the police raid in June and an officer hit him in the head. He wrote that he chose to "Uncle Tom my way out" that night and play nice with police, but he fumed. The next time, he vowed, he would fight back, "hopefully to kill him if need be."

208

On the early morning of July 23, 1967, Scott wasn't working the door; his job search had finally borne fruit, and he had found a good position in an auto factory. But he writes that he drove up to the club in time "to see this honky cop swing a sledgehammer into the plate glass door."

After Scott whipped up the crowd, thrown the bottle and watched the last paddy wagon drive away, he said he entered the club to find the interior in shambles. The jukebox and wine bottles were broken; even the typewriter he used for his writing had been smashed.

He said he returned to the street and threw a litter basket through the window of a drug store, triggering an alarm and jacking up the adrenalized atmosphere on 12th Street. "I had to destroy something," he writes.

People slowly entered the drugstore. "I wasn't even thinking about looting at the time it all started," Scott writes. "My interest was to strike out at something that was more powerful and more legitimate than me; at the time this was the white store owners."

He joined others in breaking windows, and mounted a box to play traffic cop, directing drivers along the increasingly unruly street. There were no real police in sight. At one point, a "young diddy-bopper" stopped him on the street and said, "I am so glad you started this thing."

Scott says he was staggered by the comment, as his actions began to sink in. He felt sick to his stomach, but soon recovered, believing that whatever the motivation of the looters, they shared a lack of respect for the law, "the law that had abused them and their right to live," he writes.

"Yes, I started a riot, although it was going to happen some other time. Nevertheless, I had made it possible for cats to get those material things they desired when there was a larger human fight on hand."

Official city reports and studies by historians and other experts generally support the chronology of the riot's beginning that Scott outlines. While he is the only person to claim he started the disorder, no official or researcher ever confirmed he was the instigator.

In "Violence in the Motor City," Fine, the U-M professor, took note of Bill Scott's account and also wrote that police identified another young man, dubbed "Greensleeves" for his green shirt and pants, who screamed at police and urged bystanders to fight back. Fine wrote that Greensleeves, Scott "and, no doubt, others, helped to communicate" their outrage to the crowd, "which probably saw the blind pig raid in the context of long-standing grievances."

By 9 o'clock that Sunday morning, police reappeared on 12th Street. And Bill Scott went home to sleep.

"Yes, I started a riot, although it was going to happen some other time. Nevertheless, I had made it possible for cats to get those material things they desired when there was a larger human fight on hand."

— Bill Scott

Arrest, and regrets

Scott awoke Sunday afternoon to find smoke in the house, which was on a nearby residential section of 12th Street. A neighboring home was on fire, and his father figured the flames would spread before the fire department could arrive. Firefighters showed up, though, and extinguished the blaze, but it rekindled, destroying their house and most of their block.

12th Street was a chaotic scene, with sirens, fires and stunned people running back and forth, fearing for their lives. Scott went to stay with a friend.

The next morning, with widespread confusion across the city, Scott looked for a newspaper. He walked more than a mile, to the usually busy corner of Grand River and West Grand Boulevard, but the streets were deserted, with buildings burned and looted. He watched as two young men climbed through the broken window of a drugstore when suddenly a line of squad cars drove up. Scott told the police he was only watching, but they cuffed him and took him downtown.

Charged with illegally entering the store, Scott spent the next 15 days in a gulag of crowded, sweltering, stinking lockups, from the oily confines of precinct garages to stifling buses with shut windows in the July sun to the Belle Isle bath house, as Detroit Police sought innovative ways to store thousands of arrestees, before being released.

Taking the bus back to 12th Street, Scott got off at Seward and walked past the hollowed-out neighborhood of loose bricks, broken glass and boarded-up buildings.

Days of looting, arson and sniping had left 43 people dead; 1,189 injured; more than 7,000 arrested; 2,509 businesses and homes looted or burned; and metro Detroiters rattled to their cores.

"The further I walked down Twelfth, the more I became aware of the destruction around me, which made me feel less of a man for being part of it," he writes.

"A man doesn't destroy his home; he protects it at all cost. This I hadn't done; I let another man come and force me to destroy my own. This put me at his mercy. I became a boy once more. He could control me completely."

Bill Scott spoke to his father, who was laying low, fearing retaliation from police for what had happened outside his club. He returned to the factory where he had found work, but was fired for missing two weeks with no

People on 12th Street on Sunday, July 23, 1967, several hours after the raid on the blind pig, which was located in the building in the left background, with the "Economy Printing" sign.

Detroit Free Press photo

211

explanation. His car had been towed, and he couldn't afford to get it back. He was filled with hatred, he wrote. The thought of killing police constantly crossed his mind.

A month later, Bill Scott paid the $1.80 Greyhound bus fare and moved to Ann Arbor, "never to return," he wrote, "until?"

That is how his book ends. But not his journey.

Ann Arbor

Bill Scott never did move back to Detroit. For the Ann Arbor of that era was a cauldron of activism, music, drugs and experimental ways of living and thinking, with John Sinclair and the White Panthers, SDS, feminist scholars, the Black Action Movement, Iggy and the Stooges and $5 tickets for small amounts of marijuana. A CIA recruiting office on Main Street was bombed in 1968.

Scott was admitted to the University of Michigan and earned a degree in education in 1970 and a master's degree in journalism in 1972. He won a second Hopwood Award in 1972 for a short story titled "The Black Astronaut on the Moon," a novel with racial themes.

He worked as a drug counselor, dressed well and had a steady stream of girlfriends. He also traveled, spending time in the Pacific Northwest. At at one point he suffered a debilitating back injury in an automobile accident, for which he began taking pain medication, and various street drugs.

He returned to U-M in 1987 to the school of education to work on his second master's degree. That's when he met Auburn Sheaffer.

The daughter of a dentist, Sheaffer was a white girl raised in comfort in nearly all-white Findlay, Ohio, 100 miles south of Detroit. She had become fascinated with the black experience. She had studied the Underground Railroad in grade school, written a paper on racism in eighth grade and discovered novelist Toni Morrison as a teenager. The immersion in black culture had a powerful effect.

She first encountered Scott in an advanced English class titled "Class, Gender and Race in U.S. Literature." Sheaffer first noticed Scott sitting by the window as the class discussed slave-era writing. He was tall, and wore a fedora, dark glasses, clogs and a tweed jacket. Sheaffer recalls a lot of debate coming from the feminists in the class when suddenly the black guy in the big hat spoke up.

"When I hear upper-class white women talking about black men with venom in their voices I worry about my penis getting cut off," he said.

The other students were horrified.

"Stricken!" she recalled. "Just stricken! I mean, silence! Horror! It landed like a lead balloon."

Despite the outburst, there was chemistry between Sheaffer and Scott, despite the difference in their backgrounds and ages. He was 39; she was 24. He was raised on Detroit's streets. She took opera les-

Bill Scott with his sister Wilma and an unidentified friend

....

Courtesy photo

sons growing up, spent a college year in Paris and belonged to a sorority. "I was pedigreed," she recalled.

The attraction was immediate.

"Man, he was beautiful," she says. "Forty years old and a radical revolutionary, fine-ass poet from Detroit." She adds: "It was primordial with me. I wanted to make him my man."

They drank at Ashley's bar, discussed radicals and poets and attended anti-racism meetings. Scott shared his encyclopedic knowledge of history and politics. When Sheaffer won her own literary award, Scott sent her flowers and the soundtrack to "A Man and a Woman," a romantic French film from 1966.

Sheaffer, young and in love, failed to pick up on some danger signs. While it is unclear if he has ever received a diagnosis, his sister Wilma says she believes he suffers from paranoid schizophrenia, which worsened as he grew older.

213

Alan Wald, now retired, was the professor in the class where Sheaffer and Scott met.

"Bill was not prepared for any kind of graduate class," Wald said. "He didn't really have the power of concentration or the commitment to carefully read the books and engage in thoughtful dialogue. He wanted to get up and sort of pontificate his opinions.

"He gave me the impression of someone who was already mentally in trouble."

Percy Bates, the U-M education professor who had known Bill Scott since his youth, remembers well how Scott later would call him when he was in trouble – usually involving a problem with a young woman.

"Generally the crisis was pretty much the same," Bates said. "He was into what he was doing, but they were trying to rehabilitate him or trying to get him on the right track. I think in most cases, he succeeded in getting them on his track rather than them being able to get him off where he was."

Despite her concerns, Sheaffer stayed in the relationship, but one day their lives took an ominous turn. One of Scott's activist friends introduced the couple to crack cocaine in the late 1980s, when crack's surge in major cities was becoming an epidemic. It wasn't long before drugs consumed their lives, leaving Scott more paranoid and unpredictable.

In February 1991 Sheaffer gave birth to a son. They named him William Walter Mandela, after the South African anti-apartheid leader Nelson Mandela, who had visited Detroit the previous summer.

The baby's early life was not promising. Sheaffer recalls speeding down I-94 in a car filled with alcohol, drugs and young Mandela eating chocolate to keep him quiet while mom and dad looked for drugs and got high.

There were run-ins with police. Over the years, Bill Scott was arrested for larceny from a building, retail fraud and possession of marijuana, and did several short stints in the Washtenaw County Jail. Sheaffer was busted for similar petty crimes.

Marriage ends. Mandela's life begins

The liaison between Sheaffer and Scott did not end well. One night in 1992, Sheaffer found herself curled up in a fetal position, emaciated and covered in bruises from what she says was her husband's physical abuse.

She sat on the dirty carpet of a cluttered Ann Arbor apartment, going through crack withdrawal while her baby slept in the next room. Scott was out on the streets, trying to find more crack. She knew if he scored, he would not share.

"I'd never been in a more dark or desperate place. If I could, I would have jumped out of my own skin."

That is Sheaffer speaking last year on the stage of the popular Moth Radio Hour, the nationwide storytelling showcase in which ordinary people talk before live audiences, with their stories distributed via radio and podcast. Her talk is titled "A Phone Call."

Worried that her druggie lifestyle would cost her her baby, Sheaffer said she punched in a phone number for a Christian counselor recommended by her mother.

It was the middle of the night. The man she awakened immediately started listening in a way that reassured Sheaffer. She talked for several hours. He listened to Sheaffer discuss Scott's abuse and her drug problem. "This man didn't judge me," she told the audience. "He just sat with me, and was present and listened and had such a kindness, such a gentleness." He would say, "Tell me more."

As dawned neared, the conversation wound down and Sheaffer thanked the man repeatedly. Then she asked how long he had been a Christian counselor. He told her that he had been trying to avoid that subject but had to be honest now.

"That number you called? Wrong number."

He was not a counselor, but a random Good Samaritan who had listened and cared. She never learned the man's name and never talked to him again. Yet his hours of listening led her, gradually, to get her life together.

She divorced Scott in 1995, and eventually took Mandela — the "sticky, chocolate-covered baby boy," as she put it — back to lily white Findlay, where she raised him, surrounded by her parents and other relatives.

Sheaffer later remarried and settled in Akron, where she teaches college English composition and studies for a doctorate in urban education.

Bill Scott, made a different choice, heading south, eventually settling in Daytona Beach, Fla., according to relatives, where by all accounts he has struggled. He has spent much of his time homeless, been arrested more than 50 times, for misdemeanors like trespassing, sleeping in the park and having an open container of alcohol, and such felonies as stealing from stores, a weapons charge and drug possession.

In July, I spent three days in Daytona Beach with photographer Brian Kaufman in a failed effort to find Scott. Street people and the director of a local homeless-aid center said

"I'd never been in a more dark or desperate place. If I could, I would have jumped out of my own skin."

— Auburn Sheaffer

215

Scott hadn't been seen for months. His family has no idea where he was. Public records show he is not in jail and had not died in the county that includes Daytona Beach.

But this is not the end of Bill Scott's story. For closer to home, there is his son, a talented young man with a promising future, like his father before him.

Mandela

Now 25, Mandela Sheaffer remembers with fondness being raised as a biracial child surrounded by white people in Findlay, Ohio.

"It was a great place to grow up," he says.

Mandela Sheaffer is thoughtful and self-assured. He talks quietly and laughs easily, like his mother. He wears his hair in dreadlocks, pulled back and resting neatly on his shoulders. His glasses are the browline style popular in the 1950s and famously worn by Malcolm X.

He he said he didn't meet the black side of his family in Michigan until he was 21.

In Findlay, he recalls a few sideways glances from people while growing up because he looks black. Once, when he was 10, he said the manager of a market followed him down the aisles as if he might steal something. But by high school, Sheaffer was a football star, signing autographs for little white kids and feeling almost no discomfort.

"I was protected," he said. "Generally, it was pretty cool."

That does not mean young Mandela did not struggle with his blackness — and work to figure out the meaning of race in his life. He said he went through an identity crisis for years.

"I'm biracial. I grew up in a white community. I didn't even know what it meant to be black in America. I was in a protective bubble."

With good grades and his athleticism, colleges came calling. He narrowed his choices to Stanford and Princeton, and decided to go East. When he traveled to the Princeton campus in New Jersey for a football visit, the team paired him with a group of black players to show him around. It surprised him.

"I honestly didn't know almost any black people in Ohio," he said.

He said he began to realize that society was demanding he figure out if he was black or white. He said he tried to locate a middle ground.

"It's almost an internal pressure, I would say. It's almost like you have to perform for the black population and perform for the white population, not in a bad way. But I had to come to the conclusion that I was Mandela. I didn't want to identify either way. I just want to be me, right?"

"It was absolutely a struggle," he said.

Then Bowling Green happened.

Leaving the bubble

In March 2012, Sheaffer sat on the porch of a house in Bowling Green, Ohio — home of Bowling Green State University. The house was the home of his longtime girlfriend, who was white, as were her roommates. As he waited for the women to return, he said he bantered with the dozens of young people walking past. A pink flamingo on the porch added to the light-hearted mood.

It was a typical night in Bowling Green. He asked people how their night was going, and recalled: "At one point, someone said he was having a shitty night, so I went off the porch and gave him a hug. It was fun. The porch is right by the sidewalk. Everyone was within five yards of me."

Suddenly, a squad car screeched to a stop in front of the house. Sheaffer, saying he had no idea what was happening, did not want to get involved in a possible police matter so he stepped inside and closed the door. After a few minutes, as more police arrived, he learned the cops were after him.

They wanted to see his ID, so he opened the door. The officers grabbed him, dragged him out of the house, snapped on handcuffs and took him to jail.

Mandela Sheaffer near his home in Chicago's West Loop neighborhood.

....

Photo by Alyssa Schuka

At 6-foot-2 and 200 pounds, Sheaffer was bigger than most of the officers.

"They said, 'Don't resist, don't resist, we'll put you down.' I was like, 'I'm not doing anything.' You could tell they were freaked out, just by my presence. I said, 'Guys, you're making a huge, huge mistake. I don't even know why you're arresting me in the first place.' And they really couldn't tell me."

He spent 18 hours behind bars. Meanwhile, back at Princeton, student activists began a social media campaign on his behalf to publicize what some believed was racial profiling.

A month earlier, in Florida, George Zimmerman had shot and killed Trayvon Martin, the 17-year-old African American high school student, and protests were beginning to spread nationwide. The Black Lives Matter movement was born the next year, when a jury acquitted Zimmerman.

"Racism claimed in student arrest," read the headline in the Daily Princetonian student paper.

He was booked for disorderly conduct and obstructing official business. Police said he "recklessly" yelled at passersby "under circumstances in which the conduct is likely to provoke a violent response," according to the Daily Princetonian's reporting, citing police records. The police report said that when Sheaffer walked into the house he had delayed "the performance of a public officer."

But the police story gradually fell apart. The charges were dropped and he was released from jail. Sheaffer said the BGSU chief of police later called him to apologize.

University spokesman Dave Kielmeyer recently confirmed Sheaffer's version. After reviewing the incident, then-Police Chief Monica Moll "determined the officer could have made a better decision," Kielmeyer said.

Sheaffer said he later learned the initial police officer suspected he might be up to no good when he noticed an African-American man on the porch of a house the officer knew to be occupied by young white women.

Sheaffer said the incident left him distraught, and introspective.

"That's when I had the stark realization that I'm black in America — that night," he said. "Without a doubt, I'd been protected my whole life, in a white community. If I had been in Findlay it would have been fine. But 20 minutes away, it just blows up in your face."

The encounter with police, he said, "flipped a switch" inside him.

"I started to really identify being black in America at that point because it was cast on me. I really wanted to keep 'I'm Mandela, I'm myself.' But in America, I'm black. No matter what."

One way Sheaffer processed the incident was to pour his energy into his senior thesis, a major research paper that is a long tradition for Princeton students.

In some ways, he was following the path of his absent father, Bill Scott, who wrote about his evolving racial identity, racism and encounters with police four decades earlier. Mandela Sheaffer was thinking about race and the meaning of being black in the most personal terms. He called the exercise was cathartic.

"It was not until I was unlawfully and unjustly arrested at the age of 21 that my eyes were opened to the fact that I was, in fact, a 'black' adult male," he wrote in the thesis, "living in a white society where I could be harassed, detained and jailed, even though I had never had so much as an after-school detention in my entire life."

Sheaffer said he knows the "white privilege" of his family, friends and fellow students at an Ivy League school, and his ability to hire a lawyer, gave him an advantage many black suspects do not have, leaving them to linger in county jails for weeks.

And he's conscious of the privilege he continues to enjoy. Today, Mandela Sheaffer makes good money working with corporate clients in his job with Microsoft in Chicago. His 27th-floor apartment looks out on one of the city's magical landscapes of a curving river flanked by glittering skyscrapers. It's a status that young African Americans from his father's era could scarcely imagine.

But Sheaffer said he wonders if he should be doing more.

He notes the irony of his white mother being more politically militant than he is. A year ago at Thanksgiving, when she was visiting, Auburn Sheaffer joined Chicagoans on Michigan Avenue to protest the shooting death by police of an unarmed 17-year-old African American named Laquan McDonald. Mandela Sheaffer stayed home.

"Right now," he says, "it would be admirable for me to just throw everything away and start fighting, and doing whatever, but it's not logical. It wouldn't make sense right now where I am with my life."

William Walter Mandela Sheaffer is the grand-son of the militant hustler who owned the blind pig where Detroit's deadly 1967 insurrection began. He is the son of the man who tossed a bottle that helped to start the disorder and then wrote about it in a searing memoir.

Mandela, succeeding in Chicago, does not know either man.

He did not meet William III. And he does not remember his father, though he has a photo of his dad holding him. He said he has not read his father's book, though he believes he will check it out one day. But he's not without his father's writings. Mandela has note fragments written on cards and books that his father sent to him when he was little and living with his mom.

One note refers to a tiny koala bear, given to Mandela, that was originally part of a pair his parents had carried as tokens of their love.

"Dearest Mandela, you are now the keeper of the bear. Once there was two and now there is just one," the father wrote. "Now you keep him safe with love and hope."

THE INTERSECTION ON DETROIT PUBLIC TELEVISION

THE INTERSECTION: AN INTRODUCTION

http://dptv.org/intersection

As the 50th anniversary of Detroit 1967 rebellion approaches, the Detroit Journalism Cooperative begins a yearlong examination of the social and economic conditions that led to the uprising and whether these same issues persist in the city today.

DETROIT POLICE CHIEF ON COMMUNITY RELATIONS

http://dptv.org/chiefcraig

Detroit Police Chief James Craig speaks candidly on the topic of police-community relations and the steps that are needed to build trust and mutual respect.

EVERYDAY RACISM

http://dptv.org/everydayracism

Understanding what it's like to live as someone of a different race can be a challenge, but one Australian company has done just that by developing an app called Everyday Racism.

TRANSITIONS TO SUCCESS

http://dptv.org/transitionstosuccess

Transitions to Success is a nationwide multi-platform program that redefines the way we view poverty—by treating poverty as a medically- and environmentally-based condition.

CULTURAL COMPLIANCE TEACHING TEACHERS

http://dptv.org/culturalcompetence

Faced with increasingly diverse classrooms, Metro Detroit schools are introducing cultural competence training to help teachers better understand and relate to students of different races, ethnicities, sexual orientations, experiences and upbringings.

CRIME & PUNISHMENT IN MICHIGAN

http://dptv.org/crimeandpunishment

The U.S. imprisons more people than any other country, but in Michigan the "get tough on crime" era may be coming to an end.

CRIMINAL JUSTICE REFORM IN MICHIGAN

http://dptv.org/prisonreform

The state legislature debates proposed legislation that some people have labeled "presumptive parole," while others have hailed it as "safe and smart parole reform."

SCHOOL SUSPENSIONS AND THE "CRADLE-TO-PRISON PIPELINE"

http://dptv.org/cradletoprison

Studies show that Michigan schools suspend African-American students at a far higher rate than their white counterparts. This profile looks at one 14-year-old student who has been suspended multiple times since second grade and the potential impact of such punishment on his future.

HIGH SCHOOL CHOICE AND THE LONG COMMUTE

http://dptv.org/highschoolchoice

One African-American family living in a predominantly white suburb with a highly rated school system has decided the best option for their children means traveling nearly two hours a day to a school of choice with a more diverse student population.

THE BRIDGE COMES TO DELRAY

http://dptv.org/delray

For more than a decade, the people of Detroit's Delray have been waiting for a new bridge to Canada to be built in their neighborhood, which will mean the relocation of hundreds of families.

EXPLORE MORE STORIES FROM THE INTERSECTION AT WWW.DETROITJOURNALISM.ORG/INTERSECTION.

COMMUNITY TOWN HALLS ON DPTV

COMMUNITY ENGAGEMENT HELPED INFORM THE STORYTELLING FOR THE INTERSECTION. COMMUNITY VOICES ADDRESSED ONGOING ISSUES IN A SERIES OF SPECIAL BROADCASTS ON DETROIT PUBLIC TELEVISION.

May 5, 2016 - MiWeek Community Conversation: Detroit Neighborhoods || DPTV.org/townhalls

August 1, 2016 - American Black Journal Special: Racial Attitudes || DPTV.org/townhalls

August 1, 2016 - American Black Journal Special: Racial Attitudes || DPTV.org/townhalls

MORE BOOKS FROM MISSION POINT PRESS

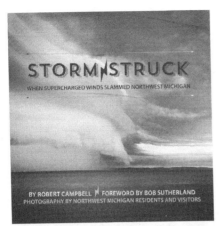

STORM STRUCK:
When Supercharged Winds Slammed North-west Michigan

By Robert Campbell; Foreword by Bob Sutherland
Photography by Northwest Michigan Residents
and Visitors

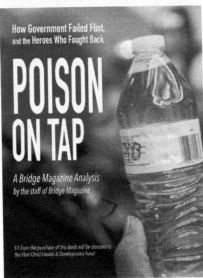

POISON ON TAP:
How Government Failed Flint and the Heroes Who Fought Back

A Bridge Magazine Analysis of the Flint water crisis.

Sometimes truth is stranger and scarier than fiction—such is the case with the Flint Water Crisis. Bridge Magazine staff painstakingly document one of the most significant cases of environmental injustice in U.S. history. —Marc Edwards, Virginia Tech professor whose work helped prove that the regulators were wrong

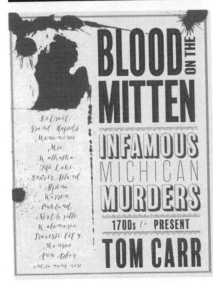

BLOOD ON THE MITTEN:
Infamous Michigan Murders
1700s to Present

By Tom Carr

In this hugely effective debut, Tom Carr sheds keen illumination upon a regional inventory of killers, kooks, cutthroats and the aggressively unhinged. The tales are horrific and humorous by turns — grisly, goofy, poignant dispatches expertly summated by a skilled veteran reporter who's no stranger to the back stairs habituated by a true sleuth. Story telling at its fully imagined best." — Ben Hamper, bestselling author of *Rivethead*

INSIDE UPNORTH:
The Complete Tour, Sport and Country Living Guide to Traverse City, Traverse City Area and Leelanau County

By Heather Shaw, Jodee Taylor, Tom Carr and many others

Super fun things to do in the Grand Traverse Area for eager tourists and locals a bit lazy about getting out.

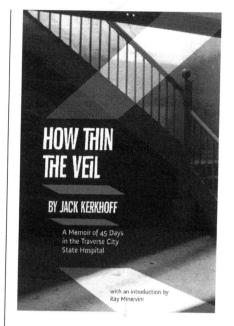

HOW THIN THE VEIL:
A Memoir of 45 Days in the Traverse City State Hospital

by Jack Kerkhoff

with an introduction by Ray Minervini

How Thin the Veil is a 45-day account of Kerkhoff's treatment, his conversations with the nurses and doctors (some of them with their real names), his interactions with the inmates, and his trips to downtown Traverse City watering holes. There's also romance in the form of Suzy, a pretty, lisping waif whose "bad spells" had kept her hospitalized for eight years.

First published in 1952, *How Thin the Veil* shines a "hard-boiled" light on the mid-century conditions of patients of mental illness.

Ray Minervini, who restored and developed Building 50 of the old Traverse City State Hospital, provides an insider introduction to this classic memoir of mental illness.

AN UNCROWDED PLACE:
A Life Up North and a Young Man's Search for Home

By Bob Butz

Originally published in *TRAVERSE: The magazine*, this collection of essays features the quiet musings and hilarious contretemps of a self- proclaimed mountain man. Butz takes readers hunting, trapping, bushwhacking, and fishing. He falls in love, rebuilds a house, and raises a boy. A charming and insightful account of living the dream of the Up North life.

MISSIONPOINTPRESS.COM

79248486R00148

Made in the USA
Columbia, SC
29 October 2017